The Visual Basic

Programmer's Guide to Java

For Windows 95 & Windows NT

The *Visual Basic*
Programmer's Guide to Java

For Windows 95 & Windows NT

YOUR PROFESSIONAL TOOLKIT
FOR OBJECT-ORIENTED PROGRAMMING

JAMES W. COOPER, Ph.D.

VENTANA

toExcel

San Jose   New York   Lincoln   Shanghai

This edition republished by arrangement with toExcel, a strategic unit of Kaleidoscope Software, Inc.

For information address:
toExcel
165 West 95th Street, Suite B-N
New York, NY 10025
www.toExcel.com

ISBN: 1-58348-217-2

Library of Congress Catalog Card Number: 99-61416

Printed in the United States of America
0 9 8 7 6 5 4 3 2 1

Technical Support no longer available for this title

About the Author

Dr. Cooper is a researcher in the Digital Libraries department at IBM's T. J. Watson Research Center. A prolific technical writer with 10 previous books and dozens of articles published in the field of computers and chemistry, Dr. Cooper has worked in a variety of research initiatives in the lab, including application development, laboratory automation, health care, and K-12 education applications. Prior to joining IBM in 1984, Dr. Cooper led the U.S. software group of Bruker Instruments, a manufacturer of analytical instruments used in chemistry and physics research. He is well versed in a number of computer languages, including in Visual Basic, Java, C, C++, Pascal, and various assembly languages. He is also widely known as an expert in software systems for competitive swimming, and he developed and supervised the utilization of the swimming software used at the 1995 Special Olympics World Games.

Acknowledgments

Thanks go to Alan Marwick for his support and to the rest of our research group for their interest and patience with me during this project. I'd especially like to thank Gennaro Cuomo for his helpful technical comments and Gunnars Ziedins for reading the manuscript and asking good questions as it developed. And thanks to Bob Johnson for suggesting the project in the first place.

I'd also like to thank the Ventana staff, notably Paul Cory, for their equanimity during the breakneck conclusion of this project.

And finally, I could never have gotten this all done without the unflagging support of my wife, Vicki.

James W. Cooper
Wilton, CT
Nantucket, MA
Winchester, England
November, 1996

Dedication

For Elliott.

Contents

Introduction

The tremendous attention that Java has been receiving since its official release in January 1996 means that programmers of all kinds have been examining the language to see whether they can use it in their work.

Visual Basic programmers have been in the forefront of user-interface construction for years. As a group, they have written most of today's Windows applications. While Java may, at first, seem to be a wildly different language than Visual Basic (VB), it's really quite easy to learn if you have some VB experience. Furthermore, it gives you a powerful way of moving from stand-alone Windows programming to GUI programming of Web pages and interactions of client and server processes across networks.

Many people who started programming in Visual Basic gravitated to it because of its seductive appeal: a GUI builder and a few lines of code could give you a nice-looking Windows program! Java has a similar seductiveness: it's a lot of fun to write elegant little programs that do so much so easily. And Java allows you to not onlybuild user interfaces, but also to enhance Web pages and communicate across networks.

Many of the programmers who have jumped into Java come from a C++ background, and this style of programming can seem a bit foreign to VB programmers at first. Actually, Java has been specifically designed to eliminate most of the confusing aspects of C++, and you will quickly find that, except for small syntactical differences, you'll have no trouble picking it up.

Although Java has so far been used primarily to improve the functionality of Web pages, it is a complete, powerful, object-oriented language. In this book, we'll see how to build powerful stand-alone applications as well as *applets*, programs that run on Web pages.

When you compile Java, it is converted into a machine-independent binary format called *byte codes*. These binary programs are then interpreted by a program called the Java Virtual Machine (JVM). This approach is, in fact, quite analogous to Visual Basic, where the compiled code is simply a series of byte codes calling Windows resources. Java, then, is quite similar in approach to Visual Basic, but has some significant advantages and disadvantages depending on what you want to accomplish. In fact, for the most part, the performance of Java and Visual Basic programs are quite similar.

But while the two languages are similar in performance, Java has a large number of important advantages over Visual Basic that make it more and more the language of choice for many applications:

◆ Java is fully object-oriented, making many types of common programming errors much harder to make.

◆ Java allows you to develop programs that can be compiled on any platform and will execute on any platform that provides a Java interpreter.

◆ Java allows you to write code that can be embedded securely in Web pages without the worry of applications doing mischief or damage to your machine.

◆ Java allows easy access to network functions at a high level of programming abstraction.

◆ And, Java allows multitasking within a program using *threads*.

What We Cover in This Book

In this book, we will cover Java from the basic concepts to actually compiling code. We're assuming that that you may know Visual Basic or a similar language system such as PowerBuilder, but not C or C++, and that you are not familiar with object-oriented programming. While all of the Java programs are completely portable to any platform, the development tools (as well as comparisons to Visual Basic) are targeted to the Windows 95 platform.

We have used code examples extensively throughout this book so that you can see exactly what Java code looks like, and, in some cases, directly compare it to equivalent Visual Basic code. We'll be building both applications and applets, with an emphasis on making useful Java programs with professional-looking user interfaces.

Even if Visual Basic is not your main area of expertise, you'll find this book a thorough introduction to Java. By the time you finish this book, you should be a pretty experienced Java programmer.

What's in This Book

We start you at the beginning, installing Java and writing simple one or two line programs in the first couple of chapters, and then go on to cover the syntax of Java in Chapter 3, comparing it with Visual Basic.

Then in Chapter 4, we explain exactly what object-oriented programming is, and what its advantages are. In Chapters 5 and 6 we build some Java objects and learn about the concept of inheritance.

In Chapters 7–11, we take up the Java visual controls, how to lay them out, and how graphics are handled in Java, culminating with a simple two-window program.

In Chapter 12, we explain how to read and write files and handle *exceptions* when input and output errors occur. Then we go on in Chapter 13 to discuss threads for multitasking your programs, and, in Chapter 14, we explain how to display images in both applications and applets.

In Chapter 15, we explain how to construct menus and dialogs and illustrate how the file dialog and our own Color dialog can be used. Then, in Chapter 16, we take up reading and writing binary files.

In Chapters 17 and 18 we complete our introduction to Java by discussing keyboard and mouse interactions.

Starting in Chapter 19, we take up more advanced topics, including how to build custom controls by extending or subclassing from existing visual controls. Then, in Chapter 20, we discuss how to package these useful classes up for distribution.

Chapter 21 gives you an introduction to constructing Web pages and using HTML, the Web page markup language. In Chapter 22, we discuss the details of embedding one or more applets in Web pages. Then, in chapter 23, we begin discussing making interactive Web pages using CGI scripting, and in Chapter 24 we outline the JavaScript language (which is totally distinct from Java) and show how it can make forms more interactive. Finally, we complete this section in Chapter 25 by building client-server communications using TCP/IP sockets.

We complete the book in chapter 26, by discussing the Java *Math* classes and show how to use them to build classes for manipulating matrices.

The book concludes with five appendices:

◈ Appendix A.   Detailed information about the contents of the book's Companion CD-ROM.

◈ Appendix B.   The references to books we have used in our study of Java and related issues. The numbers you find in brackets throughout this book refer to this reference list.

◈ Appendix C.   How printing can be carried out in Java now and in the future.

◈ Appendix D.   An outline of the NetRexx language as an alternative for learning Java.

◈ Appendix E.   A list of the features to be included in Java 1.1.

Contents of the Companion CD-ROM

First and foremost, the Companion CD-ROM contains the complete working code for every example program in this book—all the Java programs and a few Visual Basic programs for comparison. They are grouped into directories by chapter number: \chapter4, \chapter12, and so forth.

You will also find:

- ◈ The complete Java 1.02 JDK (Java Development Kit) for installation on your hard disk.
- ◈ A trial copy of WinZip for compressing and decompressing files with long filenames under Windows 95.
- ◈ A 30-day trial copy of Alibaba, a personal Web server for testing Web client and server development on a single PC.

Forging Ahead

Now lets start on the adventure: learning a powerful and exciting and new language. In just three or four short chapters, you'll be writing programs and beginning to see the seductive power of a language that helps you develop sophisticated programs so easily.

1

What Is Java?

In the past year, Java has become one of the most popular new languages of all time. Programmers, the technical press, and management at all levels suddenly need to understand this language and how it can be used to advance their objectives. In this book, we will explain what Java can and cannot do, and teach you how to use it from the beginning, without assuming knowledge of other similar languages.

The Genesis of Java

The Java language was designed at Sun Microsystems over a five-year period, culminating in its first release in January 1996. The developers, led by James Gosling, originally set out to build a language for controlling simple home devices with embedded microcomputers. Thus, they started with the object-oriented concepts of C++, simplified it, and removed some of the features, such as pointers, that lead to serious programming errors.

The team's working name for this evolving language was "Oak," but as it neared completion, they found that Oak was already registered as a trademark. As the story goes, they came up with the name "Java" while taking a break at a coffee shop.

While the team may have originally had in mind compiling this language for a specific microprocessor, they developed both the Java language and a hypothetical computer called the Java Virtual Machine or JVM instead. Then, they developed Java compilers that produced binary code designed to execute on the JVM rather than on a PC or Sun workstation.

Executing Java Programs on Real Computers

To actually execute Java programs, they developed Java *interpreters* that ran on various machines and under various operating systems. These interpreters load and read the binary "byte codes" of compiled programs and call functions to execute those instructions. Thus, Java became a language that would execute on a number of systems and now has implementations for virtually all common computers and operating systems.

Sometime during development, it suddenly became obvious that Java would be an ideal language for use on the Internet, whose popularity was growing at a phenomenal rate, because programs embedded in Web pages would execute on any computer system that had a Java-enabled Web browser. They added a window manager to allow easy development of user interfaces; they also added network communication methods such as Web page URLs and sockets.

Since Java could now run on nearly any kind of workstation, it became an ideal vehicle for adding powerful computational capabilities to Web pages. You could browse Web pages from any platform and see the same behavior in the embedded Java program.

Java Applets

A Java *applet* is a program designed to be embedded in a Web page. You can write applets to compute expense reports, plot data curves, parse search queries, and check for the validity of data the user enters before it is sent to a server. Applets can be quite complex; they are not limited to simple animations or single windows. They can access remote databases or other sources of information and compute and display complex information right on your Web browser page.

Java applets are designed to be quite *secure*, however. They can be safely downloaded over a network without causing concern that they might be able to do damage or mischief to your computer.

They cannot write any information onto your hard disk unless you specifically give them access to a directory. They cannot access any other resources on your network or any other hardware or peripherals on your computer. Likewise, they can't access any specific memory locations and can't modify or delete running programs or program files or data on your hard disk. Thus the concept of a "virus" written in Java is a contradiction: the only damage they could ever do is consume computer time, and you can easily terminate such a program at once.

Netscape Navigator versions 2.x and 3.x impose additional protection; they don't allow applets to write any files to your disk, even if you define a directory that applets can write to.

Java applets are also restricted from writing into memory outside of the Java address space. This is accomplished mainly because Java has no memory pointer type and thus a malicious programmer cannot point to memory he or she might want to attack. Java applets are also scrutinized class by class as they are loaded by the run-time environment in your browser, and checks are made to assure that the binary code has not been modified such that it might interact with or change any part of the memory of your system.

Further, applets cannot access resources on any other computer on your network or elsewhere on the Internet, with one exception: they can open TCP/IP connections back to the machine running the Web server from which they were downloaded.

To add even more protection and prevent programmers from spoofing users into giving them confidential information, all windows that you pop up from an applet have a banner along the bottom reading "Unsigned Java Applet" in Navigator and "Warning: Applet Window" in Explorer. The banner serves to prevent hackers from designing an exact copy of a familiar screen and luring users into typing confidential information into it.

Java Applications

In contrast to applets, Java applications are full-featured programs that run on your computer and have full access to its resources. They can read, write, create, and delete files and access any other computer on the network.

You will quickly appreciate that it is possible to develop full-fledged applications in Java: database viewers, word processors, spreadsheets, math packages, and file and network manipulation programs. In fact, one of Java's great strengths is that it makes accessing other computers on your network extremely easy.

Now you can write quite sophisticated programs in Visual Basic as well, so you might ask whether Java is really "ready" for all this attention. Can you write real, significant programs in Java? Figure 1-1 shows a simple data entry program for a search tool that allows you to enter terms as well as Boolean conditions from drop-down list boxes. Figure 1-2 shows the exact same program created in Java.

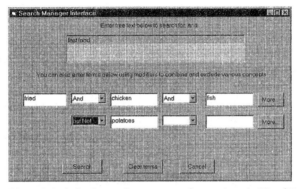

Figure 1-1: A simple search query entry form written in Visual Basic.

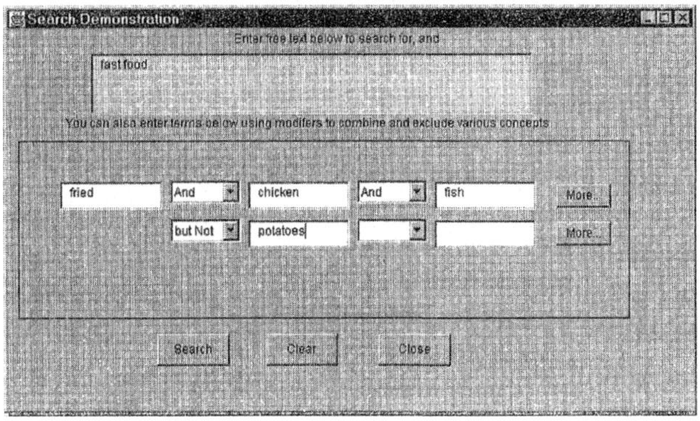

Figure 1-2: The same simple search query entry form written in Java.

The forms shown in Figures 1-1 and 1-2 are complete, working programs. If you want to see how they work, you'll find their sources and binaries on the Companion CD-ROM in the \Chapter1 folder.

But what about Java? How does it really stack up? Is it real or is it a toy? Let's take a moment and look at some of the advantages of each language.

Advantages of Visual Basic

Visual Basic has been an effective tool for creating programs:

◈ Visual Basic has an excellent environment for building a graphical user interface (GUI). The Form editor, which allows you to drag and drop any of a large number of visual controls onto a form and attach code to them, is as yet unsurpassed. However, by the time this book is published, any number of GUI builders that have roughly the same functionality as Visual Basic should be available for Java in mature second versions from companies like Symantec, Rogue Wave, Borland, and Microsoft.

◈ Visual Basic has more visual controls than Java. Since VB has been around much longer, there are more third party vendors supplying GUI controls for the development environment. However, this is already much less true than even three months ago; vendors have produced grid controls, toolbars, tree lists, and picture buttons for Java. And we'll soon see how easy it is to write your own controls in Java—something not for the faint of heart in VB.

◈ Visual Basic allows easy access to databases. Many, many programmers start working in VB because it provides easy access to databases. Java allows this too, and a complete database access specification called JDBC has been prepared and implemented.

Advantages of Java

As you can see, the advantages of Java outnumber those of Visual Basic for creating Web content:

◈ Java is object oriented. Java requires that you write 100 percent object-oriented code. As we will see, object-oriented (OO) programs are easier to write and easier to maintain than the spaghetti code that is often the result of VB programming.

◆ Java works on most platforms. While VB is exclusively a Windows product, Java binary byte code runs identically on most UNIX machines, Macintoshes, and PCs running Windows 95, Windows NT, OS/2, and Linux.

◆ Java is network enabled. It is trivially simple to write code in Java that works across networks. The use of URLs, TCP sockets, and remote classes is essentially built into the language.

◆ Java is multithreaded. You can write programs in which several sections run simultaneously in different execution threads.

◆ Java allows you to add major function to Web pages. If you are interested in building interactive World Wide Web pages that compute, collect, or display data, Java is the language of choice. There simply is not a better way to add interactive controls to Web pages that can then be viewed on any computer platform and operating system.

With all of these pluses, the only possible drawback is that you'll have to learn a new language. This is, of course, what this book is about, and we'll see some very significant advantages to Java as we begin to explore it.

Moving On

So far, we've looked at the reason Java was designed and compared it briefly to Visual Basic. Next we'll look at how to install Java and compile Java programs. Then, to become fluent in Java, you'll need to learn two things: Java's syntax and the rationale behind object-oriented programming. We'll take these up in the following chapters, and soon you, too, will be a Java expert.

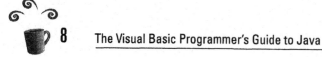

2

Installing & Using Java

In order for you to begin writing Java programs, you will need to download and install the Java compiler and libraries. In this chapter we'll cover where to get them and how to set up your computer to use them effectively.

Installing the Java Developers Kit

The Java Developers Kit (JDK) is provided free of charge from the JavaSoft division of Sun Microsystems (http://java.sun.com). You can download two files: the development kit library and executables and the documentation files. They are also provided on this book's Companion CD-ROM. For Windows 95, the files are called JDK-1_0_2-win32-x86.exe and JDK-1_0_2-apidocs.zip. You can download sources of some of the libraries from the Sun site as src.zip as well.

To install the JDK libraries, simply run the .exe file:

```
JDC-1_0_2-win32-x86
```

This will create a \java directory with a number of directories under it, notably \java\bin and \java\lib.

To install the documentation, you must unzip it using a zip program that preserves long filenames. WinZip from Nico-Mak Computing (http://www.winzip.com) is one such program. The 16-bit Windows or DOS versions of PKZIP will not preserve the needed long filenames and you shouldn't try to use them.

Using WinZip, unpack the apidocs file into the directory \java\api.

Modifying Autoexec.bat

You need to add the \java\bin directory to your path so that the command line programs java and javac are available to you. If you have installed the programs on your C drive, add the following statement to the bottom of your autoexec.bat file:

```
path=%path%;c:\java\bin;
```

In earlier versions of Java, you also needed to add the CLASSPATH environment variable to your system by inserting the following statement in your autoexec.bat file:

```
set CLASSPATH=c:\java\lib\classes.zip;
```

or if you were using Symantec Café, you would insert:

```
set CLASSPATH=c:\cafe\java\lib\classes.zip;
```

but this is no longer necessary in Java 1.0.2 and thereafter.

This library file, classes.zip, contains all of the compiled Java packages we will be discussing throughout the remainder of this book. However, if you are using additional library files, you do have to include their paths in the *CLASSPATH* statement:

```
set CLASSPATH=c:\myclass\myclasses.zip;
```

In any case, you should, in general, not unzip the Java classes in these files: they are not compressed and the zip file is just used as a convenient library format.

It does turn out, however, if you do unzip these files into the directories specified in the classes.zip file, your programs will compile and execute a bit faster.

Java Program Files

All Java source files have the .java extension. For example the simulated search window program we showed in Chapter 1 is called Srchapp.java. Note that since this is a four-character extension, it qualifies as a long filename under Windows 95; all of the tools you use for handling Java programs must be able to deal with long filenames. (This does not apply to a Windows 3.1 version of Java that has recently been released.) You can download the Windows 3.1 version from the site

`http://www.alphaworks.ibm.com`

When you compile a Java program, it produces one or more files having the .class extension which you then can operate on either directly with the Java interpreter or with the appletviewer program.

Writing Java Programs

You can write Java programs using the EDIT program provided with Windows 95. This is just a simple DOS Window-based character editor, but it allows you to read and write files having long filenames. You can also use the WordPad editor for this purpose.

Further, there are any number of integrated development environments that feature automatic indenting and syntax highlighting. These include Symantec Café and Visual Café, Sun Java Workshop, and Borland Open JBuilder, among others. Note, however, that whatever editing system you use, source code files for Java programs always have the .java extension.

Compiling Java Programs

After you've written your first Java program, you compile it by running the javac compiler. Several of the integrated development environments do this for you under the covers. Symantec's Café system actually uses a native x86 compiler called "sj" under the covers to perform this compilation considerably faster than Sun's javac compiler.

For example, let's compile the simple simulated search application we referred to in the last chapter. This program is in the \chapter1 directory of the Companion CD-ROM and is called Srchapp.java. Before you can compile it, you must copy it to a directory on your disk where the compiler can read and write files. Then, to compile it, type:

```
javac Srchapp.java
```

If you have Symantec Café loaded, you can use its much faster native Intel compiler and simply type:

```
sj Srchapp.java
```

Note that you must specify the program filename using the exact case of the long filename and that you must include the .java filename extension as part of the command line.

The Javacompiler will produce one or more output files having the .class extension. In this case, it generates the file:

```
Srchapp.class
```

To execute this program, run the Java interpreter, specifying the main file of the program:

```
java Srchapp
```

Note that here, the exact case of the filename is again required, but that the filename extension (.class) is *not* required. In fact, if you include the class extension, it is an error. The Java interpreter runs the main program and searches for the other required class files in the path specified by the CLASSPATH environment variable. In this case, the interpreter looks first in the current directory, where the Srchapp.class program is located, and finds the MainPanel1.class file as well. Then it looks in the classes.zip file in the c:\java\lib directory for any needed Java support files.

Applets vs. Applications

The Srchapp program we worked on in the previous section is a Java *application,* a stand-alone program that runs without respect to a Web browser or Web page. By contrast, *applets* are programs that are embedded in Web pages and can only be run by your browser or by a test program called appletviewer.

As we noted in the previous chapter, an applet is restricted in the access it has to your computer. It cannot read or write local files or environment variables and it cannot gain access to your network or to other computers, except the computer providing the Web server. To embed an applet in a Web page, you need to include an <applet> tag in the HTML text of your Web page. A Web page that simply displays an applet is contained in the file Srchapp.html, which has the contents:

```
<html>
<body>
<applet code="Srchapp.class"
       width = 400 height =300>
</applet>
</body>
</html>
```

The Srchapp program we have been discussing has been written so that it can run either as an application or as an applet; so it will, in fact, work when embedded in a Web page.

If you want to view it as an applet, you can simply load the Web page into your browser, or you can run the appletviewer program from your command line:

```
appletviewer Srchapp.html
```

Note, in particular, that the target file for the appletviewer program is an HTML file, not a .class file. You can look at the same sort of search application front end embedded in a Web page by typing the above command.

Figure 2-1 shows the search application running in the appletviewer and Figure 2-2 shows the applet running on a Web page in the Netscape Navigator browser.

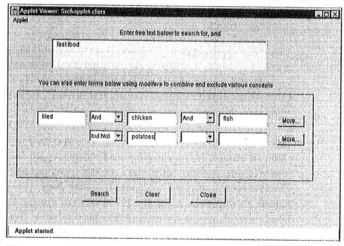

Figure 2-1: The simulated search application running using the appletviewer program.

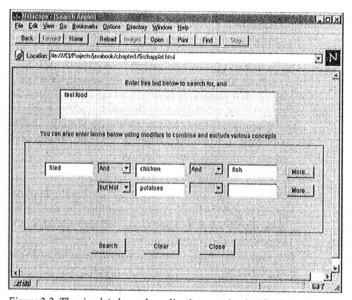

Figure 2-2: The simulated search application running inside Navigator.

Performance & Just In Time Compilers

Since Java is an interpreted language, some have indicated their concern that its performance will be unacceptable. There are two points that address this concern: first, the Java byte-code interpreter for the most part just makes direct calls to the operating system for all graphical operations, making it roughly equivalent to Visual Basic.

Second, for more computationally bound operations, Just In Time (JIT) compilers have now become available. These JIT compilers interpret the byte codes as usual, but also translate them into local machine language so that if the code is executed more than once in a loop, all further executions will be executed as native machine instructions. Performance of first generation JIT compilers so far has provided a 5x- to 10x-speed increase, and greater improvements are on the horizon.

Moving On

Now that we have a grasp of how Java is installed and how to compile simple programs, let's look at the language itself and see how it compares with Visual Basic and other related languages.

3

Syntax of the Java Language

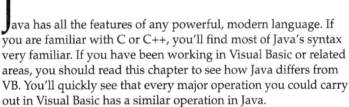

Java has all the features of any powerful, modern language. If you are familiar with C or C++, you'll find most of Java's syntax very familiar. If you have been working in Visual Basic or related areas, you should read this chapter to see how Java differs from VB. You'll quickly see that every major operation you could carry out in Visual Basic has a similar operation in Java.

The two major differences between Java and Visual Basic are that Java is *case sensitive* (most of its syntax is written in *lowercase)* and that every statement in Java is terminated with a semicolon (;). Thus Java statements are not constrained to a single line and there is no line continuation character.

In Visual Basic, we could write:

```
y = m * x + b              'compute y for given x
```

or we could write:

```
Y = M * X + b              'compute y for given x
```

and both would be treated as the same. The variables Y, M, and X are the same whether written in uppercase or lowercase.

In Java, however, case is significant, and if we write:

```
y = m * x + b;              //all lowercase
```

or:

```
Y = m * x + b;              //Y differs from y
```

we mean two different variables: *Y* and *y*. While this may seem awkward at first, having the ability to use case to make distinctions is sometimes very useful. For example, programmers often capitalize symbols referring to constants:

```
Const PI = 3.1416          ' in VB
final float PI = 3.1416;    ' in Java
```

Note the *final* modifier in Java means that the named value is a constant and cannot be modified.

Programmers also sometimes define data types using mixed case and variables of that data type in lowercase:

```
class Temperature          //begin definition of
                           //new data type
Temperature temp;          //temp is of this new type
```

We'll cover classes in much more detail in the chapters that follow.

Data Types

The major data types in Java mirror those in Visual Basic, as shown in Table 3-1.

Java	Representation	Visual Basic
boolean	true or false	Boolean
byte	signed 8-bit value	Byte
short	16-bit integer	Integer in VB16
int	32-bit integer	Long
long	64-bit integer	
float	32-bit floating point	Single
double	64-bit floating point	Double
char	16-bit character	
String	16-bit characters	String

Table 3-1: Data types in Java compared with Visual Basic.

Note that the lengths of these basic types are irrespective of the computer type or operating system. For example, in Visual Basic 3.0, an integer was 16-bit and a Long 32-bit, while in 32-bit Visual Basic 4.0, both Integers and Longs are 32-bit.

Characters and Strings in Java are always 16 bits wide to allow for representation of characters in non-Latin languages. The 32-bit version of Visual Basic 4.0 also represents characters in Strings as 16-bit entities. Both use a character coding system called Unicode, in which thousands of characters for most major written languages have been defined.

You can convert between variable types in the usual simple ways:

❦ Any wider data type can have a lower data type having fewer bytes assigned directly to it, and the promotion to the new type will occur automatically. If y is of type float and j is of type int, then you can write:

```
float y;     //y is of type float
int j;       //j is of type int
y = j;       //convert int to float
```

to promote an integer to a float.

❦ You can reduce a wider type(more bytes) to a narrower type by *casting* it. You do this by putting the data type name in parentheses and putting it in front of the value you wish to convert:

```
j = (int)y;    //convert float to integer
```

Boolean variables can only take on the values represented by the reserved words *true* and *false*. Boolean variables also commonly receive values as a result of comparisons and other logical operations:

```
int k;
boolean gtnum;

gtnum = (k >6);        //true if k is greater than 6
```

Unlike C or Visual Basic 3, you cannot assign numeric values to a boolean variable and you cannot convert between boolean and any other type.

Declaring Multiple Variables

You should note that in Java, you can declare a number of variables of the same type in a single statement:

```
int i, j;
float x, y, z;
```

This is unlike Visual Basic, where you must specify the type of each variable as you declare it:

```
Dim i As Integer, j As Integer
Dim x As Single, y As Single, z As Single
```

Numeric Constants

Any number you type into your program is automatically of type *int* if it has no fractional part or type *double* if it does. If you want to indicate that it is a different type, you can use various suffix and prefix characters:

```
float loan = 1.23f; //float
long pig  = 45L;          //long
long color = 0x12345;     //hexadecimal
int register = 03744;     //octal: leading zero
```

Java also has three reserved word constants: *true, false,* and *null,* where *null* means an object variable that does not yet refer to any object. We'll learn more about objects in the next chapters.

Character Constants

You can represent individual characters by enclosing them in single quotes:

```
char c = 'q';
```

Java follows the C convention that the *white space characters* (non-printing characters that cause the printing position to change) can be represented by preceding special characters with a backslash, as shown in Table 3-2. Since the backslash itself is thus a special character, it can be represented by using a double backslash.

Character	Meaning
'\n'	newline (line feed)
'\r'	carriage return
'\t'	tab character
'\b'	backspace
'\f'	form feed
'\0'	null character
'\"'	double quote
'\''	single quote
'\\'	backslash

Table 3-2: Representations of nonprinting characters.

Variables

Variable names in Java can be of any length and can be of any combination of uppercase and lowercase letters and numbers, but like VB, the first character must be a letter. Further, since Java uses Unicode representations throughout, you can intermingle characters from other language fonts if you wish, but this is usually more confusing than it is useful:

```
π = 3.1416;
```

Note that since case is significant in Java, the following variable names all refer to different variables:

```
temperature
Temperature
TEMPERATURE
```

You must declare all Java variables that you use in a program before you use them:

```
int j;
float temperature;
boolean quit;
```

This is analogous to the usual practice in VB of declaring:

```
Option Explicit
```

which then requires that you declare every variable in advance:

```
Dim j As Integer
Dim temperature As Single
Dim quit As Boolean              'in VB4 only
```

Declaring Variables as You Use Them

Java also allows you to declare variables just as you need them rather than requiring that they be declared at the top of a procedure:

```
int k = 5;
float x = k + 3 * y;
```

This is very common in the object-oriented programming style, where we might declare a variable inside a loop that has no existence or *scope* outside that local spot in the program.

Multiple Equals Signs for Initialization

Java, like C, allows you to initialize a series of variables to the same value in a single statement:

```
i = j = k = 0;
```

This can be confusing, so don't overuse this feature. The compiler will generate the same code for:

```
i = 0; j = 0; k = 0;
```

whether the statements are on the same or successive lines.

A Simple Java Program

Now let's look at a very simple Java program for adding two numbers together. This program is a stand-alone program, or application. We'll see later that Java applets have a similar style in many ways, but do not require the *main* function we show below.

```
import java.awt.*;
import java.io.*;

class add2
{
 public static void main(String arg[])
  {
  double a, b, c;   //declare variables
  a = 1.75;         //assign values
  b = 3.46;
  c = a + b;        //add together
//print out sum
  System.out.println("sum = " + c);
  }
}
```

This is a complete program as it stands, and if you compile it with the javac compiler and run it with the Java interpreter, it will print out the result:

```
sum = 5.21
```

Let's see what observations we can make about this simple program:

◈ You must use the import statement to define libraries of Java code that you want to use in your program. This is similar to defining calls to system functions in VB using the Declare statement, and similar to the C and C++ #include directive.

◈ The program starts from a function called *main* and it must have *exactly* the form shown here:

```
public static void main(String arg[])
```

◈ Every program module must contain one or more classes.

◈ The class and each function within the class is surrounded by *braces* { }.

◈ Every variable must be declared by type before or by the time it is used. You could just as well have written:

```
double a = 1.75;
double b = 3.46;
double c = a + b;
```

◈ Every statement must terminate with a semicolon. They can go on for several lines but must terminate with the semicolon.

◈ Comments start with // and terminate at the end of the line.

◈ Like VB and most other languages (except Pascal), the equals sign is used to represent assignment of data.

◈ Like VB, you can use the + sign to combine two Strings. The String "sum =" is concatenated with the String automatically converted from the double precision variable c.

◈ The println function, which is a member of the *OutputStream* class *out* in the *System* class, can be used to print values on the screen.

Compiling & Running This Program

This simple program is called add2.java in the \chapter3 directory on your example disk. You can compile and execute it by copying it to any convenient directory and typing:

```
javac add2.java
```

and you can execute it by typing:

```
java add2
```

Arithmetic Operators

The fundamental operators in Java are much the same as they are in Visual Basic and most other modern languages. Table 3-3 lists the fundamental operators in both Java and Visual Basic.

Java	VB	Operation
+	+	addition
-	-	subtraction, unary minus
*	*	multiplication
/	/	division
%	Mod	modulo (remainder after integer division)

Table 3-3: Comparison of Java and VB operators.

The bitwise and logical operators are derived from C rather than from VB (see Table 3-4).

Java	VB	Operation
&	And	bitwise And
		Or	bitwise Or
^	Xor	bitwise exclusive Or
~	Not	one's complement
>> n		right shift n places
<< n		left shift n places

Table 3-4: Logical operators in Java and VB.

Increment & Decrement Operators

Like C/C++ and completely unlike other languages, Java allows you to express incrementing and decrementing of integer variables using the ++ and -- operators. You can apply these to the variable before or after you use it:

```
i = 5;
j = 10;
x = i++;  //x = 5, then i = 6
y = --j;  //y = 9 and j = 9
z = ++i;  //z = 7 and i = 7
```

Combined Arithmetic & Assignment Statements

Java allows you to combine addition, subtraction, multiplication, and division with the assignment of the result to a new variable:

```
x = x + 3;        //can also be written as:
x += 3;           //add 3 to x; store result in x

//also with the other basic operations:
temp *= 1.80;     //mult temp by 1.80
z -= 7;           //subtract 7 from z
y /= 1.3;             //divide y by 1.3
```

This is used primarily to save typing; it is unlikely to generate any different code. Of course, these compound operators (as well as the ++ and -- operators) cannot have spaces between them.

Making Decisions in Java

The familiar if-then-else of Visual Basic, Pascal, and Fortran has its analog in Java. Note that in Java, however, we do not use the then keyword:

```
if ( y > 0 )
  z = x / y;
```

Parentheses around the condition are *required* in Java. This format can be somewhat deceptive; as written, only the single statement following the if is operated on by the if statement. If you want to have several statements as part of the condition, you must enclose them in braces:

```
if ( y > 0 )
  {
  z = x / y;
  System.out.println("z = " + z);
  }
```

By contrast, if you write:

```
if ( y > 0 )
  z = x / y;
  System.out.println("z = " + z);
```

the Java program will always print out z= and some number, because the if clause only operates on the single statement that follows. As you can see, indenting does not affect the program; it does what you say, not what you mean.

If you want to carry out either one set of statements or another depending on a single condition, you should use the else clause along with the if statement:

```
if ( y > 0 )
  z = x / y;
else
  z = 0;
```

and if the else clause contains multiple statements, they must be enclosed in braces, as in the code above.

There are two or more accepted indentation styles for braces in Java programs: that shown above will be familiar to VB and Pascal programmers. The other style, popular among C programmers, places the brace at the end of the if statement and the ending brace directly under the if:

```
if ( y > 0 ) {
  z = x / y;
  System.out.println("z=" + z);
}
```

You will see both styles widely used, and, of course, they compile to produce the same result.

Comparison Operators

Above, we used the > operator to mean "greater than." Most of these operators are the same in Java as they are in VB and other languages. In Table 3-5, note particularly that "is equal to" requires *two* equal signs and that "not equal" is different than VB.

VB	Java	Meaning
>	>	greater than
<	<	less than
=	==	is equal to
<>	!=	is not equal to
>=	>=	greater than or equal to
<=	<=	less than or equal to

Table 3-5: Comparison operators in Java and VB.

Combining Conditions

When you need to combine two or more conditions in a single if or other logical statement, you use the symbols for the logical and, or, and not operators (see Table 3-6). These are totally different than any other languages except C/C++ and are confusingly like the bitwise operators shown in Table 3-4.

Java	Meaning	VB
&&	logical And	And
||	logical Or	Or
~	logical Not	Not

Table 3-6: Boolean operators in Java and VB.

So, while in VB we would write:

```
If ( 0 < x) And (x <= 24) Then
  Msgbox "Time is up"
```

in Java we would write:

```
if ( (0 < x) && ( x <= 24) )
  System.out.println ("Time is up");
```

The Most Common Mistake

Since the "is equal to" operator is == and the assignment operator is = they can easily be misused. If you write:

```
if (x = 0)
  System.out.println("x is zero");
```

instead of:

```
if (x == 0)
  System.out.println("x is zero");
```

you will get the confusing compilation error, "Cannot convert double to boolean," because the result of the fragment:

```
(x = 0)
```

is the double precision number 0, rather than a boolean true or false. Of course, the result of the fragment:

```
(x == 0)
```

is indeed a boolean quantity, and the compiler does not print any error message.

The switch Statement

The *switch* statement is somewhat analogous to the VB Select Case statement; you provide a list of possible values for a variable and code to execute if each is true:

```
Select Case j                    'in VB
  Case 12:
      Msgbox "Noon"
  Case 13:
      Msgbox "1 PM"
  Case Else
    Msgbox "Some other time…"
End Select
```

In Java, however, the variable you compare in a *switch* statement must be either an integer or a character type and must be enclosed in parentheses:

```
switch ( j )
{
 case 12:
  System.out.println("Noon");
  break;
 case 13:
  System.out.println("1 PM");      "
  break;
 default:
  System.out.println("some other time...");
}
```

Note particularly the break statement following each case in the *switch* statement. This is very important in Java, as it says "go to the end of the switch statement." If you leave out the break statement, the code in the next case statement is executed as well.

Java Comments

As you have already seen, comments in Java start with a double forward slash and continue to the end of the current line. Java also recognizes C-style comments that begin with /* and continue through any number of lines until the */ symbols are found.

```
//Java single-line comment
/*other Java comment style*/
/* also can go on
for any number of lines*/
```

You can't nest Java comments; once a comment begins in one style it continues until that style concludes.

Your initial reaction as you are learning a new language may be to ignore comments, but they are just as important at the outset as they are later. A program never gets commented at all unless you do it as you write it, and if you ever want to use that code again, you'll find it very helpful to have some comments to help you in deciphering what you meant for it to do. For this reason, many programming instructors refuse to accept programs that are not thoroughly commented.

The Ornery Ternary Operator

Java has unfortunately inherited one of C/C++'s most opaque constructions, the ternary operator. The statement:

```
if ( a > b )
  z = a;
else
  z = b;
```

can be written extremely compactly as:

```
z = (a > b) ? a : b;
```

The reason for the original introduction of this statement into the C language was, like the post-increment operators, to give hints to the compiler to allow it to produce more efficient code. Today, modern compilers produce identical code for both forms given above, and the necessity for this turgidity is long gone. Some C programmers coming to Java find this an "elegant" abbreviation, but we don't agree and will not be using it in this book.

Looping Statements in Java

Java has only three looping statements: while, do-while, and for. Each of them provides ways for you to specify that a group of statements should be executed until some condition is satisfied.

The while Loop

The *while* is quite analogous to VB's. In VB, we write:

```
i= 0
while ( i < 100 )
  x = x + i
  i = i + 1
wend
```

while in Java we write:

```
i = 0;
while ( i < 100)
  {
    x = x + i++;
  }
```

The loop is executed as long as the condition in parentheses is true. It is possible that such a loop may never be executed at all, and of course, if you are not careful, that a *while* loop will never be completed.

The do-while Statement

The Java *do-while* statement is quite analogous, except that in this case the loop must always be executed at least once, since the test is at the bottom of the loop:

```
i = 0;
do
 (
   x += i++;
 }
while (i < 100);
```

This is entirely analogous to the *do-loop* statement in VB:

```
i = 0
Do
 x = x + i
 i = i + 1
Loop While i < 100
```

The for Loop

The *for* loop is the most structured. It has three parts: an initializer, a condition, and an operation that takes place each time through the loop. These sections are separated by semicolons:

```
for (i = 0; i< 100; i++)
 {
   x += i;
 }
```

Let's take this statement apart:

```
for (i = 0;        //initialize i to 0
   i < 100 ;       //continue as long as i < 100
   i++)            //increment i after every pass
```

In the loop above, *i* starts the first pass through the loop set to zero. A test is made to make sure that *i* is less than 100 and then the loop is executed. After the execution of the loop, the program returns to the top, increments *i*, and again tests to see if it is less than 100. If it is, the loop is again executed.

Note that this *for* loop carries out exactly the same operations as the while loop illustrated above. It may never be executed and it is possible to write a *for* loop that never exits.

Declaring Variables as Needed in for Loops

One very common place to declare variables on the spot is when you need an iterator variable for a *for* loop. You can simply declare that variable right in the for statement, as follows:

```
for (int i = 0; i < 100; i++)
```

Such a loop variable exists or has *scope* only within the loop. It vanishes once the loop is complete. This is important because any attempt to reference such a variable once the loop is complete will lead to a compiler error message. The following code is incorrect:

```
for (int i =0; i< 5; i++)
   x[i] = i;
//the following statement is in error
//because i is now out of scope
System.out.println("i=" + i);
```

Commas in for Loop Statements

You can initialize more than one variable in the initializer section of the Java for statement, and you can carry out more than one operation in the operation section of the statement. You separate these statements with commas:

```
for (x=0, y= 0, i =0; i < 100; i++, y +=2)
   {
   x = i + y;
   }
```

It has no effect on the loop's efficiency, and it is far clearer to write:

```
x = 0;
y = 0;
for ( i = 0; i < 100; i++)
  {
    x = i + y;
    y += 2;
  }
```

It is possible to write entire programs inside an overstuffed for statement using these comma operators, but this is only a way of obfuscating the intent of your program.

How Java Differs From C

If you have been exposed to C, or if you are an experienced C programmer, you might be interested in the main differences between Java and C:

- Java does not have pointers. There is no way to use, increment, or decrement a variable as if it were an actual memory pointer.

- You can declare variables anywhere inside a method you want to; they don't have to be at the beginning of the method.

- You don't have to declare an object before you use it; you can define it later.

- Java does not have the C struct or union types. You can carry out most of these features using classes. It also does not support typdef, which is commonly used with structs.

- Java does not have enumerated types, which allow a series of named values, such as colors or day names, to be assigned sequential numbers.

- Java does not have bitfields: variables that take up less than a byte of storage.

- Java does not allow variable length argument lists. You have to define a method for each number and type of argument.

Moving On

In this brief chapter, we have seen the fundamental syntax elements of the Java language. Now that we understand the tools, we need to see how to use them. In the chapters that follow, we'll take up objects and show how to use them and how powerful they can be.

4

Object-Oriented Programming

There are two kinds of people: those who divide everything into two categories and those who don't. Likewise, there are two kinds of programming: procedural and object-oriented. In this chapter we'll begin to understand what objects are and why they make programming easier and less prone to errors.

A *procedural* program is written in the style you are probably most familiar with; one in which there are arithmetic and logical statements, variables, functions, and subroutines. Data are declared somewhere at the top of a module or a procedure and more data are passed in and out of various functions and procedures using argument lists.

This style of programming has been successfully utilized for a very long time, but it does have some drawbacks. For example, the data must be passed correctly between procedures, making sure that it is of the correct size and type, and the procedures and their calling arguments may often need to be revised as new function is added to the program during development.

Object-oriented programming differs in that a group of procedures are grouped around a set of related data to construct an *object*. An object is thus a collection of data and the subroutines or *methods* that operate on it. Objects are usually designed to mimic actual physical entities that the program deals with: customers, orders, accounts, graphical widgets, and so on.

More to the point, most of *how* the data are manipulated inside an object is invisible to the user and only of concern inside the object. You may be able to put data inside an object and you may be able to ask it to perform computations, but how it performs them (and on exactly what internal data representation) is invisible to you as you create and use that object. Once someone creates a complete, working object, it is less likely that programmers will modify it. Instead, they will simply derive new objects based on it. We'll be taking up the concept of deriving new objects in Chapter 6.

Objects are really a lot like C structures or Visual Basic Types except that they hold both functions and data. Objects, however, are just the structures. In order to use them in programs, we have to create variables of that object type. We call these variables *instances* of the object.

A Visual Basic Procedural Program

Let's take a very simple example. Suppose we want to draw a rectangle on our screen. We need to design code for drawing a rectangle and specifying what size it is (as well as its position on the screen). Now, our first thought might have been to simply write a little subroutine to draw the rectangle and then draw each rectangle we want by calling this subroutine:

```
Call DrawRect (10, 10, 200, 150)
Call DrawRect (40, 40, 150, 100)
```

A complete Visual Basic program to draw two rectangles when the Draw button is clicked is:

```
Option Explicit

Private Sub Draw_Click()
 Call DrawRect(10, 10, 200, 100)
 Call DrawRect(40, 40, 150, 75)
End Sub
'-------------------------------------------------------
```

```
Sub DrawRect(ByVal x As Integer, ByVal y As Integer, _
    ByVal width As Integer, ByVal height As Integer)
'convert from pixels to twips
Dim Tpp As Integer

 Tpp = Screen.TwipsPerPixelX
 x = x * Tpp
 y = y * Tpp
 width = width * Tpp
 height = height * Tpp
 Line (x, y)-(x + width, y + height), vbBlue, B
End Sub
```

The window this program displays is shown in Figure 4-1. The code for this program is on the Companion CD-ROM as rect1.vbp in the \chapter4 directory.

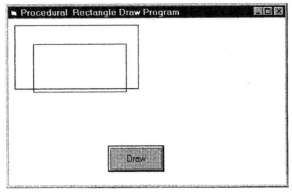

Figure 4-1: Window displayed by procedural Visual Basic rectangle drawing program.

The problem with this program is that the drawing routine has to know a lot about the display characteristics. We call the routine using pixel coordinates, but we must convert the coordinates to VB's unusual coordinate system of *twips*. This DrawRect routine is publicly available for modification throughout the program, and if we need more arguments, such as color or line thickness, we would just have to add them to an ever-growing list of subroutine arguments. Further, if we wanted to draw some other shapes, we'd have to go through the same pixel-to-twip conversion for that routine as well, in addition to adding arguments to it if we decided we need to specify color or line thickness.

A Visual Basic Object-Oriented Program

If we were to rewrite this program using object-oriented style, we would design a rectangle object that could *draw itself*. We wouldn't have to know how it did the drawing or whether the algorithm or calling parameters changed from time to time.

In VB version 4.0, we would do this by creating a Rectangle class with a draw method inside it:

```
'A rectangle class
'remembers its position and shape
'and knows how to draw itself on a form
Private x As Integer, y As Integer
Private width As Integer, height As Integer
Private Tpp As Integer
Private frm As Form
Private color As Long
'--------------------------------------------------
Public Sub setColor(c As Long)
 color = c
End Sub
'--------------------------------------------------
Public Sub draw()
 frm.Line (x, y)-(x + width, y + height), color, B
End Sub
'--------------------------------------------------
Private Sub Class_Initialize()
 Tpp = Screen.TwipsPerPixelX
 color = vbBlue    'set default color
End Sub
'--------------------------------------------------
```

```
Public Sub setForm(f As Form)
 Set frm = f      'remember form to draw on
End Sub
'_____
Public Sub reshape(xpos%, ypos%, w%, h%)
 x = xpos% * Tpp
 y = ypos% * Tpp
 width = w% * Tpp
 height = h% * Tpp
End Sub
```

Note that this VB Rectangle class contains both private data and subroutines for manipulating it.

Note that we added a *setColor* function or *method* to allow us to change the color of the object if we want to. Then our main calling program simply creates two different rectangle objects and draws them when the button is clicked. Each *instance* of the rectangle object remembers its position and size and draws itself on the form on command:

```
'Main Rectangle Drawing Program
Dim rect1 As New Rectangle 'create 2 rectangles
Dim rect2 As New Rectangle
'_____
Private Sub Form_Load()
 rect1.setForm Form1       'tell them where to draw
 rect2.setForm Form1

End Sub
'_____
Private Sub draw_Click()

 'specify sizes and positions
 rect1.Reshape 10, 10, 200, 100
 rect2.Reshape 40, 40, 150, 75

 rect1.draw                'and draw them
 rect2.draw
End Sub
```

In this program we create two *instances* of the *Rectangle* class, named rect1 and rect2. Using the *setForm* method, we tell them where they are to draw. Next, we set their size and position properties using the Reshape method and then tell them to draw themselves using the *Draw* method. This program is called rect2.vbp on the Companion CD-ROM. The display generated by this program is illustrated in Figure 4-2.

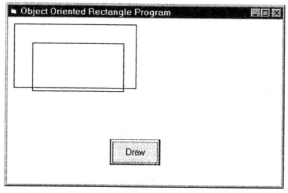

Figure 4-2: Rectangle drawing using an object-oriented Visual Basic program.

Now at first this might seem like more work, but it pays off well. The rectangle object *encapsulates* all of the rectangle knowledge, and you as the user of that object only have to know to set its shape and to draw it. Thus, the overall effort to maintain your program is greatly reduced! Further, each copy, or instance, of the Rectangle class contains its own size, location, and color data so it can always draw itself. This simplification of our overall programming effort becomes even more obvious as our objects become more complex.

Building Java Objects

Let's look at how we would do the same thing in Java. The procedure is quite analogous:

- We create a rectangle class.
- We create instances of that class, each with different sizes.
- We ask each instance to draw itself.

A Java object is also called a class. Remember that in our very first simple program in Chapter 3, "Syntax of the Java Language," we used the key word "class" in creating the outer wrapper of our example program. Each Java class is an object that can have as many instances as you like.

When you write a Java program, the entire program is one or more classes. The main class represents the running program itself, and it must have the same name as the program file. In the rectangle example, the program is called Rect1.java and the main class is called Rect1.

Classes in Java contain data and functions, which are called *methods*. Both the data and the methods can have either a *public* or a *private* modifier, which determines whether program code outside the class can access them. Usually we make all data values private and write public methods to store data and retrieve it from the class. This keeps programs from changing internal data value accidentally by referring to them directly.

If we want users of the class to be able to use a method, we, of course, must make it public. If, on the other hand, we have functions that are only used inside the class, we would make them private.

While a Java program can be made up of any number of .java files, each file can contain only one public class, and it must have the same name as the file itself. There can be any number of additional classes within the file that are not declared as public. These would normally be used only by the public class in that file. You do not declare classes as private; they either have a public modifier or none at all.

Creating Instances of Objects

We use the *new* operator in Java to create an instance of a class. For example, to create an instance of the Button control class, we could write:

```
Button Draw; //a Button object

//create button with "Draw" label
Draw = new Button("Draw");
```

Remembering that we can also declare a variable just as we need it, we could also write somewhat more compactly:

```
Button Draw = new Button("Draw");
```

Don't be confused by the fact that the variable name and the label of the button are the same; they are unrelated, but convenient in many programs.

Remember, while we can create new variables of the primitive types (such as int, float, etc.), we must use the *new* operator to create instances of objects. The reason for this distinction is that objects take up some block of memory. In order to reserve that memory, we have to create an instance of the object using the *new* operator which allocates a memory block to be used by the object.

Constructors

When we create an instance of a class we write ourselves, we usually need to write code that initializes variables inside the object. This code is put in the class's *constructor* routine. A constructor routine has the same name as the class, is always public, and has no return type (not even void):

```
class Rectangl
{
private int xpos, ypos;
private int width, height;
private Graphics g; //where to draw
```

```
public Rectangl(Graphics gr)      //constructor
{
g = gr;                           //copy where to draw
}
```

In the above example, our Rectangl class has the handle to the current window's graphics object passed to it, and it saves that handle in a private variable *g*. We might also set the rectangle position, size, and color to default values in the constructor to make sure that they never contain irrational values:

```
class Rectangl
{
private int xpos, ypos;
private int width, height;
private Graphics g; //where to draw
private Color c;

  public Rectangl(Graphics gr)
  {
  g = gr;             //copy where to draw
  c = Color.blue;     //default color
  width = 200;        //default size
  height = 100;
  x = 0;
  y = 0;              //default position;
  }
```

A Java Rectangle Drawing Program

In the following example, we see a complete Rectangl class, including its draw routine:

```
import java.awt.*;
//Simple Rectangle drawing example

public class Rect1 extends Frame
```

```
{
  private Button Draw;              //Button on window
  private Rectangl rect1;           //two rectangles
  private Rectangl rect2;
//----------------------------------------------
public Rect1()                      //window class constructor
  {
  super("Rect1 window");            //create window with title
  addNotify();                      //connect to OS window system
  reshape(50, 50, 475, 225);        //size of window

  Draw = new Button("Draw");        //create button
  add(Draw);                        //add to window
  Draw.reshape( 178, 148, 82, 32);  //set button shape

  //Create rectangles and tell them where to draw
  rect1 = new Rectangl(getGraphics());
  rect2 = new Rectangl(getGraphics());

  //define their shapes
  rect1.reshape(10, 10, 200, 100);
  rect2.reshape(40, 40, 150, 75);
  show();                //display window
  }
//----------------------------------------------
//click event is received here
public boolean action(Event evt, Object obj)
  {
  clickedDraw();         //button clicked
  return true;
  }
//----------------------------------------------
public void clickedDraw()
//button clicked
  {
  rect1.draw();          //draw two rectangles
  rect2.draw();
  }
```

```
//-----------------------------------------------
public static void main(String args[])
//program starts here
  {
  new Rect1();  //create instance of Rect1 class
  }
} // end of Rect1 class
```

The Rectangl Class

The program Rect1 also contains the definition for the *Rectangl* class. We spell it without the *e* because Java already has a class named *Rectangle:*

```
class Rectangl
{
private int xpos, ypos;
private int width, height;
private Graphics g;

  public Rectangl(Graphics gr)
  {
  g = gr;        //where to draw
  }
//-----------------------------------------------
  public void reshape(int x, int y, int w, int h)
    {
    xpos = x;    //remember size and posn
    ypos = y;
    width = w;
    height = h;
    }
//-----------------------------------------------
  public void draw()
  //draws rectangle at current position
  {
   g.setColor(Color.blue);
   g.drawRect(xpos, ypos, width,height);
  }
} //end of Rectangl class
```

This is a complete working program as shown and is called Rect1.java in the \chapter4 directory on the Companion CD-ROM. Let's look at how it works. You can see its window display in Figure 4-3.

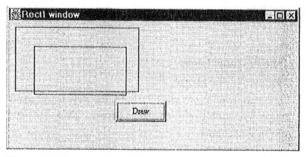

Figure 4-3: The Rect1.java program for drawing two rectangle objects.

First, the *main* routine is where the program actually starts. If you want to write a stand-alone application, one and only one of its classes must have a main routine, and its "signature" must be *exactly*:

```
public static void main(String arg[])
```

While that main routine appears to be part of a class, it is actually in a way grafted on (because of the *static* qualifier) and it is the entry point for the program. All this main routine does is create one instance of the program class *Rect1*:

```
new Rect1();
```

Constructors

When you create an instance of an object, the code in the *constructor* routine is executed automatically. This is the place where we will initialize the window variables and create instances of the rectangle object:

```
public Rect1()    //window class constructor
  {
```

The first three lines initialize the window itself, creating a title bar title, attaching it to the underlying windowing system, and setting the shape of the window:

```
super("Rect1 window"); //create window with title
addNotify();        //connect to OS window system
reshape(50, 50, 475, 225);   //size of window
```

Then we create an instance of the *Button* class for the Draw button.

```
Draw = new Button("Draw");     //create button
add(Draw);              //add to window
Draw.reshape( 178, 148, 82, 32);//set button shape
```

Finally, we create two instances of the *Rectangl* class and define their shapes:

```
//Create rectangle and tell them where to draw
rect1 = new Rectangl(getGraphics());
rect2 = new Rectangl(getGraphics());

//define their shapes
rect1.reshape(10, 10, 200, 100);
rect2.reshape(40, 40, 150, 75);
show();            //display window
  }
```

Now we have two rectangle objects we can draw whenever we need to by simply telling each one to "draw itself:"

```
rect1.draw();
rect2.draw();
```

Methods Inside Objects

As we noted above, functions inside a class are referred to as *methods*. These functions can be *public*, meaning that you can access them from outside the class; *private*, meaning that they can only be accessed from inside the class; and *protected*, meaning that the methods can be accessed only by other classes in the same file.

Syntax of Methods

A method inside an object is just a function or subroutine. If it returns a value, like a Visual Basic Function, you declare the type of the return:

```
int getSize()
{
}
```

If it returns no value, like a VB Subroutine, you declare that it is of type *void*:

```
void resize(int width, int height)
{
}
```

In either case you must declare the type of each of the arguments. It is usual to use descriptive names for each of these arguments so the casual reader can figure out what each method does.

Variables

In object-oriented programming, you usually make all of the variables in a class *private*, as we did above with *xside* and *yside*. Then you set the values of these variables either as part of the constructor or using additional *set* and *get* functions. This protects these variables against accidental access from outside the class and allows you to add data integrity checks in the *set* functions to make sure that the data are valid.

We could, of course, have made the *Rectangl's height* and *width* variables public and set them directly:

```
rect1.width = 300;
rect1.height = 200;
```

but this gives the class no protection from erroneous data such as:

```
rect1.width = -50;
```

So, instead, we use *accessor* functions such as resize to make sure that the data values we send the class are valid:

```
rect1.resize(300, 200);    //call resize method
```

and then within the class we write this accessor function with some error checking:

```
public void resize(int w, int h)
{
 if (w > 0 )
  width = w; //copy into width if legal
 if (h > 0)
  height = h;        //and into height if legal
}
```

Multiple Methods With the Same Name

Our *Rectangl* class had one constructor, containing a handle to the windowing system's graphics object:

```
public Rectangl(Graphics gr)
```

However, we can have more than one constructor and, in fact, more than one version of any method, as long as they have different argument lists or *signatures*. So we could declare our rectangle's shape at the same time we create it:

```
public Rectangl(Graphics gr, int width,
            int height)
{
 g = gr;
```

```
width = w;  //save width and height
height = h;
}
```

The Java compiler must be able to distinguish these various versions of the same method by either the number or the type of arguments. If two different methods have the same number and type of arguments, the compiler will issue an error message.

Passing Arguments by Value

All primitive types (int, long, float, boolean) are passed into methods by *value*. In other words, their values are *copied* into new locations that are then passed to the subroutine. So, if you change the value of some argument to a method, it will not be changed in the original calling program.

For example, suppose we need to swap the values of two integers several times in some program. We might be tempted to write a private *swap* method like this:

```
private void swap (int x, int y)
{
//this looks like it will swap integers,
//but it won't
int temp = x;
x = y;
y = temp;
}
```

and then call this method from the main class:

```
int a = 5;      //assign two values
int b = 10;
swap (a, b);       //integers passed by value
System.out.println("a=" + a + " b=" + b);
```

However, we find that *a* is still 5 and *b* is still 10. And, of course, the reason why this won't work is that the memory locations containing the arguments *x* and *y* are *copies* of the original calling parameters, and switching them will not switch the originals.

Reference Types

Objects, on the other hand, are called *reference types*, because they are passed into methods by reference rather than by value. While actual pointers to memory locations don't exist at the programmer level in Java, these references are, of course, pointers to the block of memory that constitutes an instance of an object.

Now, as we noted earlier, there are object versions of the primitive types, called Integer, Long, Float, and Boolean. We might at first imagine that we could write a method that would swap objects, since they are passed into the method by reference:

```
private void Swap(Integer x, Integer y)
 {
//swaps Integer objects, but to no avail
 Integer temp = new Integer(x.intValue());
 x = y;
 y = temp;
 }
```

However, if we write a program to use this method, we find, sadly, that this method still does not affect the calling parameters:

```
Integer A = new Integer(a);
Integer B = new Integer(b);
Swap (A, B);        //objects passed by reference
System.out.println("a=" + A + " b=" + B);
```

Why is this? What's going on here? Well, remember that the values passed into the *Integer* class's *Swap* method are pointers to the original objects A and B. Let's suppose that they have the address values 100 and 110. Then when we create the new Integer temp, let's suppose its address is 300. After the *Swap* method completes, *x* will have the value 110 and *y* will have the value 300. In other words, we changed the values of the pointers, but did not change the contents of the objects. In addition, these are just local copies of the pointers to these objects, so we haven't swapped the references in the calling program in any case. In fact, the Integer class does not have any methods to change its contents, only to create new Integers, which will not help us in this case.

So even though objects are passed into methods by reference, changing the values of the pointers we used does not change the contents of the objects themselves. If we want to make an effective swap, we would have to create an object whose *contents* we could change.

For example, we could create a Pair class with a *swap* method:

```
class Pair
{
Object a; //two objects we will swap
Object b;
//----------------------------------------
public Pair(Object x, Object y)
{
a = x;
b = y;
}
//----------------------------------------
public Pair(int x, int y)
{
a = new Integer(x);
b = new Integer(y);
}
//----------------------------------------
public void swap()
{
Object temp = a;   //swaps values of objects
a = b;
b = temp;
}
//----------------------------------------
Object geta()
{
return a;   //returns values of objects
}
//----------------------------------------
Object getb()
{
```

```
    return b;
  }
}      //end Pair class
```

and accessor methods geta and getb to obtain the values after swapping. Then we could call these methods as follows:

```
Pair p = new Pair(A, B);  //copy into object
p.swap();                 //swap values inside object
A =(Integer)p.geta();     //get values out
B =(Integer)p.getb();
System.out.println("a=" + A + " b=" + B);
```

And, if you think this is silly in this case, you are right. After all, swapping the values of two numbers or objects only requires three lines of code in any case. However, this does illustrate an important concept. If you want to change values, you have to do it inside the object, not by switching copies of the references to the objects.

Object-Oriented Jargon

Object-oriented programs are often said to have three major properties:

* **Encapsulation.** We hide much of what is going on inside methods in the object.

* **Polymorphism.** Many different objects might contain methods that have identical names, such as our *draw* method. While they may do the same thing, the way each is implemented can vary widely. In addition, there can be several methods within a single object with the same name, but different sets of arguments, as we illustrated above.

* **Inheritance.** Objects can inherit properties and methods from other objects, allowing you to build up complex programs from simple base objects. We'll see more of this in the chapters that follow.

Moving On

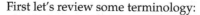

First let's review some terminology:

❧ Objects in Java are created using classes.

❧ Each class may have one or more constructors, none of which have a return type.

❧ Functions inside the class are called methods and may be public or private.

❧ Each variable whose type is declared to be of that class is called an instance of that class.

❧ Variables inside the class are usually private and are referred to as instance data since each instance of the class may have different values for these variables.

❧ One and only one class per program may have a public static method called main, where the program actually begins.

In this chapter, we wrote our own rectangle drawing class and explored most of the thicket of object-oriented jargon. In the next chapter, we'll look at some useful built-in classes that round out the Java language and then go on to the last important new concept: inheritance.

5

Using Classes in Java Programming

Now that we've seen how simple it is to create objects in Java, it won't surprise you to discover that *everything* in Java is accomplished using classes. There are no library functions or independent subroutines in Java; only objects of various types and their methods. While this may take a slight attitude readjustment, you'll quickly see that the consistency this approach brings to Java makes it a very easy language to learn and use.

The String Class

Like Visual Basic, Strings in Java are among the most commonly used objects and contain a fairly rich set of methods for manipulating character strings. Strings are not arrays in the sense that they are in C or VB, but you can manipulate groups of characters in an analogous manner. Remember that Strings contain 16-bit Unicode characters, so they can represent a wide variety of fonts and languages.

String Constructors

The fact that an object may have any number of constructors, each with different arguments, is another example of polymorphism. The most common string constructor is:

```
String s = new String("abc");
```

but you can also create a string from an array of characters from some file or network socket:

```
String(char[])                          //from array of char

//from specified part of array of char
String(char[], int offset, int count)

//from array, setting upper byte
String(char[], int hibyte, int offset, int count)
```

The third constructor above is used to assure that the upper byte of each 16-bit character is set to a known value, usually zero. This function is very important in Windows 95, where Java 1.0 otherwise sets this upper byte to an indeterminate value, making comparisons with other strings impossible.

String Methods

There are a wide variety of methods in the *String* class. Some of the most common are:

```
length()
equals(String)
startsWith(String)
endsWith(String)
toUpperCase()
toLowerCase()
indexOf(String)
subString(int begin)
subString(int begin, int end)
```

To reiterate, these are *methods* that operate on a String object, not functions to be called with a string as argument. Thus, to obtain the length of a string, you might perform the following steps:

```
//create an 8-character string
String abc = new String("alphabet");
int len = abc.length();          //len now contains 8
```

You can look over the plethora of other string methods in the String documentation provided with the SDK.

The String + Operator

The + sign in Java is said to be "overloaded" with respect to strings. In other words the + sign has a somewhat different meaning when used with strings than it does when used with numbers. Thus, you can combine strings much as you can in VB and Pascal:

```
String h = new String("Holiday");
String fs = new String("for Strings");
String title = h+ " " + fs;
//prints "Holiday for Strings"
System.out.println(title);
```

You can also use the + operator to combine basic numeric types with strings. They are automatically converted to strings:

```
int count = 24;
System.out.println("Found " + count + " blackbirds");
// prints out "Found 24 blackbirds"
```

Note that there are no leading or trailing spaces in numbers produced in this fashion, and you must be sure to include them in your code.

Conversion of Numbers to Strings & Vice Versa

You can convert any simple numeric type (int, float, double, etc.) to a string in one of two ways.

The simplest way is to convert using the *String* class's *valueOf()* method:

```
int length = 120;
String strLength = new String().valueOf(length);
//returns a string "120"
```

There is a version of this method for each of the basic types; in other words, this method shows polymorphism.

You can accomplish the same thing using the *toString()* methods of the *Integer*, *Float*, and *Double* classes, which are object classes wrapped around the base numeric types:

```
int length = 120;
String strLength = new Integer(length).toString();
```

To convert a String to a number, you can use the *intValue()*, *floatValue()*, and related versions of the *Integer* and *Float* classes:

```
String strLength = new String("120");
int length = new Integer(strLength).intValue();
```

These are relatively unforgiving methods, and throw exceptions if the string has even a single leading space in it. Thus, you should use the *String* class's *trim()* method to remove leading and trailing spaces before calling these methods.

The second way to convert a string to a number is using the *parse* methods of the *Integer* and *Float* classes. These methods are just as unforgiving in requiring that the string may only contain digits, but since the *parse* methods are *static* members of their classes, you don't need an instance of the class to use them:

```
int i = new Integer("120").intValue();
int j = Integer.parseInt("120");
float x = Float.parseFloat("123.45");
```

Changing String Contents

The String class is designed to be *immutable*: once you have created a string you cannot change its contents. The *StringBuffer* class is provided so you can change individual characters of a String and then put the changed result back into a string.

You can create an instance of the *StringBuffer* class from a string:

```
String alph = new String("abcde");
StringBuffer buf = new StringBuffer(alph);
```

Then you can examine or change any character using the following methods:

```
public char charAt(int n);               //get char at posn n
public void setCharAt(int n, char ch); //set char
public StringBuffer insert(int n, char c);
```

as well as with a host of other useful methods listed in the documentation. When you have changed the characters in the string buffer, you can regenerate the string with the *toString* method:

```
alph = buf.toString();
```

Comparing Strings

You can compare a String variable with a constant or another variable using the *equals* method or using the == operator:

```
String a = "abc";
String b = "abc";
if  (a == "abc") System.out.println("a=abc");
if  (a == b) System.out.println("a=b");
if  (a.equals("abc")) System.out.println("a=abc");
```

Each of these approaches produces a true result aand prints out the expected message. You can also check for equality irrespective of case:

```
String a = "abc";
String A = "ABC";
if  (a.equalsIgnoreCase(A)) System.out.println("a=A");
```

The Array Class

Arrays are a built-in class whose syntax is part of the language, much as Strings are. Arrays can be singly and multiply dimensioned and may consist of any base numeric type or of any object. You declare an array object by:

```
float x[] = new float[100];        //dimension array
```

and you can access it by enclosing the index in brackets. Note that array indices always begin at 0 and end at one less than the array dimension:

```
for (i=0; i<100; i++)
  x[i] = i;
```

You can determine the dimensioned length of any array from its length property, x.length in this case. Note that this is not a method which would be followed by parentheses, but a publicly accessible property.

When you declare a new array, its elements are initialized to 0 if it is numeric or to *null* if it is an array of objects. You can also declare specific contents for an array:

```
int a[] = new int[5];
a[] = {1, 3, 5, 7, 9};
```

You can also declare arrays of more than one dimension by including several dimensions in successive brackets:

```
float x[][] = new float[12][10];

int z[][][] = new int[3][2][3];
```

Because Java actually handles these multidimensional arrays as arrays of *objects*, each with their own dimensions, you do not have to specify all of the dimensions in the initial declaration. The leftmost dimensions must be specified, but dimensions to the right may be omitted and defined later:

```
float abc[][] = new float[100][];
```

Here, abc is actually a single-dimensional array of float[], where these dimensions are not yet defined.

Garbage Collection

Once we begin allocating large amounts of memory in any program, we are naturally concerned about how that memory can be released when we are done with it. In fact, some of the most annoying bugs in programs in other languages come from allocating but not releasing memory correctly.

In Java, this is never your concern, because the Java run-time system automatically detects when objects are no longer in use and deletes them. Thus, while we can use the *new* command prolifically to allocate memory as we need it, we never have to concern ourselves with the *management* of that memory and its subsequent release.

The finalize Method

All objects have a *finalize* method which will be called before the object is deleted and garbage collected. You do not need to release assigned memory but you may want to close open files or network connections in this method. You should end any finalize method by calling *super.finalize()* to assure that the system cleans up correctly.

Constants in Java

If you have been programming in VB, C++, or Pascal, you are probably familiar with named constants. These are used whenever you can improve program readability. Named constants do not change during a program's execution, but you may elect to change their values during the development of a program:

```
'In VB
Const PI = 3.1416

//In C or C++
const PI = 3.1416;
```

In Java, values which cannot be changed are said to be *final,* and as usual must be members of some class. If you make reference to such constants, you must refer to the class they are members of as well. For example, the *Math* class contains definitions for both *pi* and *e*:

```
float circumference = 2 * Math.PI * radius;
```

Similarly, most of the common colors are defined as RGB constants in the *Color* class:

```
setBackground(Color.blue);
```

You can declare constants by making them *final* and *public* if you want to access them from outside the classes:

```
Class House
{
public final int GARAGE_DOORS = 2;
...
```

Then, whether or not you have a current instance of the *House* class, you can always refer to this constant:

```
System.out.println("Doors =" + House.GARAGE_DOORS);
```

Note also that Java has three "built-in" constants: *true, false,* and *null.*

Moving On

In this chapter, we've learned about the built-in Java *String, StringBuffer,* and *Array* classes, and how to print out numbers as strings. We've also touched on Java's automatic garbage collection and on how to use named constants in classes. Now, we're ready to take up inheritance as the last major new topic before we complete our first tour around the Java language.

6

Inheritance

The greatest power of programming in object-oriented languages comes from *inheritance*: the ability to make new, customized, more versatile objects from already completed objects without changing the original objects. One of the reasons this approach is so powerful in actual code development is that it allows you to write new classes based on existing classes without changing the existing class in any way. Thus, if you have working code in one class, you don't risk "breaking" it by writing modifications. This is also one place where our analogy with Visual Basic breaks down. Visual Basic version 4 does not have the capability to create new classes that inherit methods and data from their parent classes.

To see how we can use inheritance in Java, let's consider a simple applet called Rect2, an applet analog of the Java application we wrote in Chapter 4, "Object-Oriented Programming." Remember that applets can run only on Web pages and have extremely limited access to your computer's resources. An applet does not have a *main* routine but starts directly in the constructor of the class you have declared *public*.

```java
import java.awt.*;
import java.applet.*;

//This applet draws a rectangle
public class Rect2 extends Applet
{
 Rectangl r1;                          //one instance of the
rectangle

 public Rect2()                        //constructor
 {
 r1 = new Rectangl(150, 100);          //create rectangle
 r1.move(10, 10);
 }
//---------------------------------
public void paint(Graphics g)
 {
 r1.draw(g);                           //draw rectangle
 }
 }
//=================================
class Rectangl
{
private int width, height;
private int xpos, ypos;
 public Rectangl(int w, int h)         //constructor
 {
 width = w;                            //save shape
 height = h;
 }
//---------------------------------
public void move(int x, int y)
{
 xpos = x;                             //save location
 ypos = y;
}
//---------------------------------
public void draw(Graphics g)
 {
 g.drawRect(xpos,ypos, width, height); //draw
 }
 }
```

This simple program consists of two classes, Rect2 and Rectangl. The Rect2 class is the public class and is the one launched by the applet. To run this applet, you compile it as usual by:

```
javac Rect2.java
```

and then execute it by embedding it in a simple Web page, rect2.html:

```
<html>
<Head><title>Draw Rectangle Applet</title></head>
<body>
<applet code="Rect2.class" height=200 width =300>
</applet>
</body>
</html>
```

You will note that the Rect2 class is related to the *Applet* class itself:

```
public class Rect2 extends Applet
```

The *extends* keyword indicates that the *Rect2* class is derived from or inherits from the *Applet* class. Thus, this new *Rect2* class is not just an *instance* of Applet but a class that has all the properties of Applet *in addition to* any properties you might change. For example, in this simple class, there are only two methods: the constructor and the paint method. In the constructor method, we create an object of type Rectangl of size 150 X 100. (As before, we avoid spelling *Rectangle* with an *e* because the Java system already has such a class.)

The *paint* method is called by the underlying window system of your computer operating system through the Java run-time system whenever some action occurs that requires that the window be repainted. In this case, we replace whatever the system might do during a paint method with a call to the *draw* method of the rectangle we just created in the constructor.

Our *Rectangl* class also consists of only two methods, a constructor, which saves the dimensions inside the object, and a *draw* method, which actually draws the rectangle on the screen. Fortunately, the Java graphics system has a *drawRect* method, so we don't have to draw it a line at a time. To view this class in action, we simply run the appletviewer program:

```
appletviewer Rect2.html
```

The displayed window is shown in Figure 6-1.

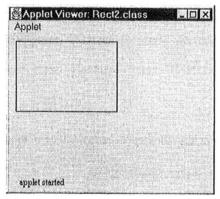

Figure 6-1: The Rect2 program displayed using the appletviewer.

Drawing a Square

Now a square is just a special case of a rectangle, so it is not surprising that we can derive a Square class from the Rectangl class. We will declare this class as follows:

```
class Square extends Rectangl
{
public Square(int side)
{
super(side,side); //pass the dimensions to the parent
}
}
```

The *super* method call in the Square constructor passes the arguments to the parent class—in this case the *Rectangl* class. In other words, it calls the Rectangl constructor with both sides equal. This super method must always be the *first* line of code in the constructor. It passes data up the inheritance chain where it initializes all the parent classes.

Now you might ask, where's the square? How do we draw it? Well, we don't. The *Square* class has no methods of its own. It *inherits* all the methods of the *Rectangl* class and thus, the draw method is contained automatically. We simply pass the height and width values into the *Rectangl* class and use all of its methods. The complete program shown below is identical to the Rect2 program except for the small, new *Square* class:

```
import java.awt.*;
import java.applet.*;

//This applet draws a square
public class Sqr extends Applet
{
  Square s1;                  //one instance of the square object

  public Sqr()                //constructor
  {
  s1 = new Square(100);       //create square
  s1.move(10, 10);
  }
//--------------------------------
public void paint(Graphics g)
  {
  s1.draw(g);
  }
}
//================================
class Square extends Rectangl
{
//This square class is derived from Rectangl
  public Square(int side)
  {
```

```java
  super(side, side); //sides are the same size
  }
}
//=================================
class Rectangl
{
private int width, height;
private int xpos, ypos;
 public Rectangl(int w, int h)  //constructor sets w & h
 {
 width = w;      //ssave shape
 height = h;
 }
//-----------------------------------
public void move(int x, int y)
{
xpos = x;     //save location
ypos = y;
}
//-----------------------------------
public void draw(Graphics g)
 {
 g.drawRect(xpos,ypos, width, height); //draw rectangle
 }
 }
```

Again, note that the Square object has no specific *draw* method, but that it *inherits* one from its parent *Rectangl* class. It also inherits any methods that the parent of the parent contains, as far back as the inheritance tree extends. The only requirement is that these methods be declared public in the base class, and if they are over-ridden in descendant classes, that these be declared public as well.

Figure 6-2 shows this Sqr application running, and the files Sqr.java and Sqr.html in the \chapter6 directory of the Companion CD-ROM contain the code.

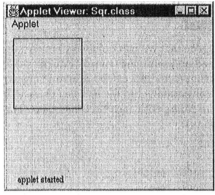

Figure 6-2: The Sqr program, showing the Square class derived from the Rectangl class.

Inheritance Terminology

Inheritance terminology includes a number of interchangeable terms. We can say that the *Square* class is *derived* from the *Rectangle* class, or that it is a *subclass* of the *Rectangle* class. We also can say that the *Square* class *extends* the *Rectangle* class. Finally, we might say that the *Square* class *inherits* from the *Rectangle super class*. If you write a method in the derived class that has the same name and calling arguments as one in the parent class, you have *overridden* the method in the parent class.

The instanceof Operator

Java provides the *instanceof* operator that you can use to discover whether an object is derived from a given class:

```
Square sql = new Square(50);
if (sql instanceof Rectangl)
  System.out.println("Is a rectangle or descendant");
```

Overriding Methods in Your Derived Class

Now let's suppose that we want to always make sure that squares are drawn in red and with lines twice as thick as the lines of the rectangle, but that rectangles can be drawn in any color. First, we'll add a color parameter to the *Rectangl* class and a *setColor* method to store colors with each *Rectangl* object. This new class looks like this:

```
class Rectangl
{
private int width, height;
private int xpos, ypos;
private Color color;

  public Rectangl(int w, int h)  //constructor
  {
  width = w;                      //save shape
  height = h;
  color = Color.blue;            //default color
  }
//-------------------------------------
public void move(int x, int y)
{
xpos = x;                        //save location
ypos = y;
}
//-------------------------------------
public void setColor(Color c)
{
color = c;
}
//-------------------------------------
public void draw(Graphics g)
  {
  g.setColor(color);             //set to current color
  g.drawRect(xpos,ypos, width, height);
  }
}
```

Note that in the constructor, we set the default color of the rectangle to blue:

```
color = Color.blue;  //default color
```

by saving this color in the private color variable. Now, all rectangles will be blue by default, although we could call the new *setColor* method to draw them in other colors.

Having added this method to the base *Rectangl* class, we now want to make a *Square* class that will always draw in red and with lines that are twice as thick as those of the rectangle. In order to do this, we must somewhere always make sure that the *setColor* method is called before drawing the square. The simplest way is simply to call this method in the square's constructor:

```
public Square(int side)
  {
  super(side, side);        //sides are the same size
  setColor(Color.red);      //all squares are red
  }
```

But how do we go about making thicker lines? It turns out that in version 1.0 of the Java *window manager* class, there is no line thickness method. So, the simplest way to draw a thicker square is to draw it, transpose it one pixel in both directions, and draw it again. The only way we can manage to do this is to override the rectangle's move method to keep a copy of the X- and Y-coordinates and then to override the rectangle's draw method to do this double-drawing. Our complete *Square* class is shown below:

```
class Square2 extends Rectangl
  {
  private int xpos, ypos;    //saved copies

//This square class is derived from Rectangl
  public Square2(int side)
  {
  super(side, side);        //sides are the same size
  setColor(Color.red);      //all squares are red
  }
//-----------------------------------
```

```
public void move(int x, int y)
{
//overrides base move method to
//save copies of coordinates
xpos = x;
ypos = y;
super.move(x, y);                //call parent procedure
}
//------------------------------------
public void draw(Graphics g)     //overrides Rectangle draw
 {
 super.draw(g);                  //draw in original position
 move(xpos+1, ypos+1);           //transpose one pixel
 super.draw(g);                  //draw it again
 move(xpos-1, ypos-1);           //move it back
 }
}
```

This program is called Sqr2.java in \chapter6 on the Companion CD-ROM. When you execute it, the rectangle and square display appears as shown in Figure 6-3.

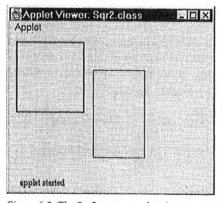

Figure 6-3: The Sqr2 program, showing a square drawn with double the line thickness of the rectangle.

You should think for a moment about how we derived and built the Square2 class. Was editing the Rectangl class the best way to do this or should we have derived a Rectangl2 class that had the color features we wanted?

Understanding public, private & protected

A *public* method or variable can be accessed by any code inside or outside the class. You can access a public method *foo()* by calling *a.foo()* and a public variable *bar* by referring to *a.bar*.

A *private* method or variable can only be accessed within the class. You can call them directly within the class, but cannot call them or refer to them outside the class.

There are also three other visibility levels for variables: *private protected*, *protected*, and default, if no keyword is specified. A *private protected* method or variable can only be accessed within that class and classes derived from it. A *protected* method or variable is visible not only in derived classes, but also in all other classes in the same package. Packages are convenient ways of grouping related classes and allowing the reuse of class names. The *import* statements that start all of our programs are importing the contents of packages.

Methods and variables that are not marked as public, protected, or private are not nearly as well hidden as private methods. These methods are visible within the package but not within derived classes. Thus, other classes in the same package can refer to them almost as if they were public. For this reason, it is always advisable to mark your methods and variables private unless you intend them to be public.

Inheriting Event Methods

In our simple example above, we used the *paint* method. In fact, we overrode the default paint method with one in our own program class to carry out some specific drawing. The paint method is one of the methods that you never call directly; instead it is called by the window manager whenever the window needs to be repainted. These methods are essentially the wrapping of events in the windowing system. If you include these events in your program, it is important that they have the exact signature (calling arguments) shown in the reference guide, since this is the only way the Java run-time system can know to call them over the equivalent system events.

The paint method, for example, always has the form:

```
public void paint(Graphics g)
```

where *g* represents the current Graphics object in use by the windowing system.

Other common methods include the *mouseDown* and *mouseUp* methods, which again, you never call, but are called by the system in response to user actions. These methods are really the encapsulation of mouse events and each has a default action. If you choose, you can derive a new method within your class for any of these event methods and they will be called first. Table 6-1 lists the common event methods.

Common Event Methods	
gotFocus	called when focus moves to control
keyDown	called when key is pressed
keyUp	called when key is released
mouseDown	called when any mouse button is pressed
mouseDrag	called when mouse moves with button down
mouseEnter	called when mouse moves over control
mouseLeave	called when mouse leaves control
mouseUp	called when any mouse button is raised
paint	called when control is to be redrawn

Table 6-1: Common Event Methods

We'll see examples of overriding many of these event methods after we have formally taken up the Abstract Windows Toolkit (awt).

Abstract Classes

As you begin to design larger projects, you may find that you'd like to define the behavior of a class without writing the code for a specific method. For example, all shapes have an area, but in the basic *Shape* class, it is pointless to define an *area()* method, since each kind of shape will require a different sort of calculation.

Instead, you might choose to define an *abstract Shape* class in order to define the methods you expect all shapes to be able to carry out:

```
abstract class Shape
 {
 public double area();
 public double circumference();
 }
```

Then we can create a *Rectangl* class that inherits from this basic *Shape* class:

```
public class Rectangl extends Shape
 {
 //etc.
 }
```

It is important to note, however, that if you say your class is derived from an abstract class, you *must* provide methods for every method defined in the abstract class. If you don't, your new class is also treated as abstract and you won't be able to create instances of that class.

In this example, the *Rectangl* class we create must have methods for computing the area and circumference:

```
public class Rectangl extends Shape
 {
 public double area()
 {
  return width * height;
 }
 public double circumference
 {
 return 2 * width + 2 * height;
 }
 }
```

Interfaces

Interfaces are another special kind of class definition: a class without any code associated with it. Since Java does not allow multiple inheritance, in which objects could inherit from two sets of parents, interfaces provide a way to create a set of classes that have rather different purposes but a few similar methods. If you say that a particular class *implements* an interface, it is a promise that you have included methods in your class corresponding to each of the methods in the definition of the interface. We'll see specific examples of interfaces when we discuss layout managers in Chapter 8, "Writing a Simple Visual Application in Java," and filename filters in Chapter 12, "Files & Exceptions."

For now, let's assume that we want to have a class *Squasher* that contains a method *squash*. We want to apply the method squash to our *Square* class, as well as to other *Shape* classes we might develop, like oval or circle. We don't even have to specify what this method does, only that it exists:

```
public interface Squasher
{
public void squash(float percent);
}
```

Note that this looks just like a class, except that the *squash* method contains no code, and the keyword *interface* replaces the keyword *class*.

Now, let's suppose we want to redefine our *Square* class to use this method. We could declare it as:

```
public class Sqr extends Rectangl implements Squasher
```

Now we are saying that we promise that we will include a method *squash* in this class and it will do whatever that method is supposed to do.

Moving On

In this chapter, we finally covered the last major piece of object-oriented programming: the use of inheritance to create new classes derived from existing classes. Once we derive a new class from an existing one, we can add more functions and override specific methods to give the new object more features.

We also looked briefly at the concepts of abstract classes and interfaces and how we can use them to give more common functionality to a group of unrelated classes.

In the next chapter, we'll look in detail at the visual controls available in the awt and compare and contrast them with those in Visual Basic.

7

Java Visual Controls

Most Java programs are visual programs, providing visual interfaces to file and network processes as well as ways of entering data into interactive Web pages. In this, Java is little different from Visual Basic, which is also an interpreted language for graphical user interfaces.

While Java really grew out of the UNIX world, it has become extremely popular for Windows 95 as well as most other common operating system platforms, including Solaris, OS/2, Macintosh System 7, AIX, and many other UNIXes. The visual controls are primarily those common to all of these platforms, although it is not difficult to write additional controls directly in Java.

The fundamental visual controls in Java are:

- TextField—a single-line text entry field.
- TextArea—a multiple-line text entry field.
- Checkbox—a combination of check box and Radio (Option) buttons.
- List—a list box.
- Button—a simple push button.
- Choice—a drop-down list control.

◈ Menu—a drop-down menu from the window's toolbar.

◈ Scrollbar—horizontal and vertical scroll bars.

◈ Panel—an area where you can group controls and paint images or graphics.

◈ Canvas—a base class for creating your own controls.

All of these controls are part of the java.awt class, where *awt* stands for one or more of the following:

◈ a window toolkit

◈ advanced window toolkit

◈ another window toolkit

◈ abstract window toolkit

◈ awful window toolkit (as it is called by critics)

As we noted, the toolkit is an intersection of the window functions found on all of the common windowing systems. Since the controls on each platform are actually implemented using the native platform functions, they look somewhat different on each platform but have the same logical properties on each.

The Visual Class Hierarchy

All visual controls are children of the *Component* class, which is in turn derived from the *Object* class. All objects in Java are derived directly or indirectly from this class. Therefore, all of the methods of the Object and Component classes are automatically available to any of the visual control classes. This is illustrated in Figure 7-1. Table 7-1 includes some of the common methods in the Object and Component classes.

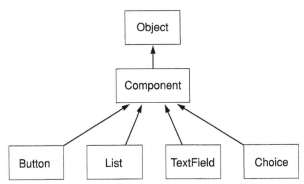

Figure 7-1: Some of the visual classes in the object inheritance tree.

Method	Description
paint	Called to redraw control.
reshape(x, y, w, h)	Changes control shape and location.
resize(w, h)	Changes control size.
handleEvent(Event, Object)	Called to receive most user interactions.
action(Event)	Called to receive mouse clicks.
enable	Sets control to active.
disable	Disables control's response to use.
getBackground	Gets background color.
setBackground(Color)	Sets background color.
hide	Hides control.
gotFocus	Called if control receives focus.
show	Shows control.
isEnabled	Returns boolean whether currently enabled.
isVisible	Returns boolean whether control is visible.
keyDown	Called if character key is pressed.
keyUp	Called if character key is released.

Method	Description
locate	Returns x and y location.
lostFocus	Called if control loses focus.
mouseDown	Called if mouse is pressed over control.
mouseUp	Called if mouse is released over control.
mouseEnter	Called if mouse enters area of control.
mouseExit	Called if mouse leaves control area.
move(x, y)	Moves the control to new location.
repaint	Causes control to be repainted.
requestFocus	Asks system to give focus to control.
resize(w, h)	Changes size of control.
setBackground(Color)	Sets background color.
setForeground(Color)	Sets foreground color.
setFont(String, int, int)	Sets font to named font, style, and size.
size	Returns current size of control.

Table 7-1: Common methods in the Component class.

These methods have default results built into the Java system. However, if you write your own version of these methods that have the exact same calling sequence as that of the standard methods, you are *overriding* or *subclassing* these methods and replacing them with your own. Often, you want to do some small thing and then have the system-defined default action take place as well. You do so by calling the same method in the parent class using *super* to represent that class:

```
//derived resize method
//saves a local copy of the width and height
int w, h;
public void resize(int width, int height)
{
```

```
w = width;                          //Save a local copy
h = height;
super.resize(width, height);        //call parent
}
```

Event-Driven Programming

Like Visual Basic, Java is an *event-driven* programming language. Since the programs exist in a windowing environment, the display is affected by events such as mouse movements and clicks, key presses, window resizing, and window rearrangement. For a program to behave as expected in such an environment, it must be receptive to all of these events and take appropriate action.

In Table 7-1, there are two kinds of methods: those you can call and those that are usually called by the Java run-time in response to events in the windowing system. The methods whose descriptions start with "called" are called by the windowing system. These are the mouse and keyboard events shown in Table 7-2. The remaining methods are ones you can call yourself.

Event	Description
paint	Called to redraw control.
handleEvent(Event, Object)	Called to receive most user actions.
action(Event)	Called to receive mouse clicks, Enter key, and list box double-click.
gotFocus	Called if control receives focus.
keyDown	Called if character key is pressed.
keyUp	Called if character key is released.
lostFocus	Called if control loses focus
mouseDown	Called if mouse is pressed over control.
mouseUp	Called if mouse is released over control.
mouseEnter	Called if mouse enters area of control.
mouseExit	Called if mouse leaves control area.

Table 7-2: Mouse and keyboard convenience methods.

Action Events

The *action* method and ACTION_EVENT event occur when a button, check box, radio button, or panel is clicked on. You can subclass the *action* method to discover which of these events actually caused the *action* method to be called. You will recall we used the *action* method in our first program (in Chapter 4) to take action when the Draw button was clicked:

```
public boolean action(Event evt, Object obj)
{
 if (evt.target == Draw)
  {
   clickedDraw(); //call draw button method
   return true;
  }
 else
   return false;
}
```

The arguments to the *action* method are an Event object and a general argument object. This argument object's type and value vary with the kind of event. You can always determine which control caused the ACTION_EVENT by simply comparing its target field with the names of the controls you expect to generate events. If you handle the action event, you should return *true*. If you don't recognize what caused it, return *false*.

The handleEvents Method

While the *action* method catches one specific event, named ACTION_EVENT, you can catch a large number of other events in the *handleEvents* method. Table 7-3 contains a complete list of events that can occur in Java.

Event	Description
ACTION_EVENT	An action event.
GOT_FOCUS	A component gained the focus.
KEY_ACTION	The key action keyboard event (Enter key).
KEY_ACTION_RELEASE	The key action keyboard event.
KEY_PRESS	The key press keyboard event.
KEY_RELEASE	The key release keyboard event.
LIST_DESELECT	List item unselected.
LIST_SELECT	List item selected.
LOAD_FILE	A file loading event.
LOST_FOCUS	A component lost the focus.
MOUSE_DOWN	The mouse down event.
MOUSE_DRAG	The mouse drag event.
MOUSE_ENTER	The mouse enter event.
MOUSE_EXIT	The mouse exit event.
MOUSE_MOVE	The mouse move event.
MOUSE_UP	The mouse up event.
SAVE_FILE	A file saving event.
SCROLL_ABSOLUTE	Scroll has been moved by more than one unit.
SCROLL_LINE_DOWN	The line down scroll event.
SCROLL_LINE_UP	The line up scroll event.
SCROLL_PAGE_DOWN	The page down scroll event.
SCROLL_PAGE_UP	The page up scroll event.
WINDOW_DEICONIFY	The deiconify window event.
WINDOW_DESTROY	The destroy window event.
WINDOW_EXPOSE	The expose window event.
WINDOW_ICONIFY	The iconify window event.
WINDOW_MOVED	The window move event.

Table 7-3: Java events.

All of the events described in Table 7-3 result in a call to the *handleEvents()* method. In addition, the mouse events, key events, and focus events may be called as individual routines, as shown in Table 7-2. All of the methods called by the windowing system have analogous event names and these events can be recognized in the *handleEvents()* method as well.

If you want to intercept any of these events in your program, you must subclass the *handleEvents* method and check to see which event has occurred. In the *handleEvents* method, you must check both for the type of event and the control that caused it. A typical routine to check for events is:

```
public boolean handleEvent(Event evt)
    {
    // all events are intercepted here
    // and vectored to private methods
 if (evt.id == Event.MOUSE_DOWN && evt.target == beanie)
   {
   mouseDownBeanie(event);
   return true;
   }
 else
 if (evt.id == Event.SCROLL_PAGE_UP &&
                  evt.target == scrollbar1)
    {
    scrollValue(event);
    return true;
    }
 else
 if (evt.id == Event.WINDOW_DESTROY)
 {
    hide();        // hide the Frame
    dispose();     // free resources
    System.exit(0); // exit
    return true;
  }
 else
   return super.handleEvent(event); //else pass to parent
 }
```

Note that, like the *action* method, you must return *true* if you intercept the event and *false* if you do not.

The WINDOW_DESTROY event is a special case in the awt, because stand-alone windows will not close automatically when you click on the window's Close box unless you intercept this event and specifically close the window, as shown in the code above.

The Controls Demonstration Program

The Controls demonstration program illustrates all of the controls we discuss in this chapter. The source is provided as controls.java in the \chapter7 directory on the Companion CD-ROM. The list box shows a record of all of the events on the other controls, and it can be cleared using the Clear button. The TextField edit box allows you to type in characters if the L(ocked) check box is not checked. If the P(assword) check box is checked, the characters are echoed as asterisks. The label above the edit field changes depending on the state of these two check boxes. It also changes when you click on an entry in the list box.

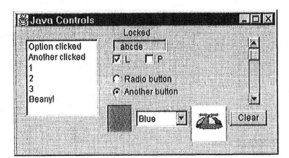

Figure 7-2: The Controls demonstration program.

You can click on either of the two radio buttons and have its label appear in the list box. There are two panels below the radio buttons, one flashing between blue and green and one displaying a beanie. The Choice box, a drop-down list box, allows you to switch between having blue—green and red—green flashing. If you click on the beanie, its name appears in the list box. The program window is shown in Figure 7-2.

Rather than going over the Controls demonstration program in this chapter, we will introduce the concepts of the controls one by one in the chapters that follow. However, you can examine the source code on the Companion CD-ROM.

The Button Control

The button control can have a label and can be clicked on with the mouse. It also can be enabled, disabled, shown, hidden, and have its caption changed. This basic button cannot have its background color changed (in Windows 95) or display an image, but we will see how to make an image button in Chapter 18, "Using the Mouse in Java." The methods for setting and reading the button labels are described in Table 7-4, but you usually set the button's text as part of the constructor:

```
Clearit = new Button("Clear");
```

Method	Description
setLabel(String)	Sets the button's label.
getLabel	Retrieves the button's label.

Table 7-4: Methods for the Button class.

The action Event

Usually, the only important button event is its *action* event, which occurs when the button is clicked. Since all of the clicks of all of the controls in a class will come to the same action method, you need to determine which control caused the event, as follows:

```
public boolean action(Event evt, Object arg)
{
 if (evt.target == Clearit)
   clickedClearit();          //call Clearit button's routine
}
```

Alternatively, you can catch the click event in the *handleEvents* method as follows:

```
public boolean handleEvents(Event evt)
{
   if (evt.id == ACTION_EVENT && evt.target == Clearit)
      clickedClearit();
}
```

And of course, you must write the actual action routine yourself:

```
private void clickedClearit()
{
//clear out list box when button pressed
 list1.delItems(0, list1.countItems() -1);
 }
```

The Label

The label is simply a place to display static text. It has only two constructors:

```
Label lbl = new Label();                 //create an empty label
Label lbl = new Label(String, align);//create label with text
             //align can be LEFT, CENTER or RIGHT
```

Method	Description
setAlignment(int)	Sets label alignment.
setText(String)	Sets label text.
getText	Returns label text.

Table 7-5: Methods for the Label control.

The label methods are equally simple (they are shown in Table 7-5). While you can set the font of a label, you can change its color only on the UNIX, Mac, and OS/2 implementations. The *setForeground()* method does not work in Java 1.0 on Windows 95.

TextFields & TextAreas

A TextField is a single line where you can type in text, and a TextArea is a multiline entry field. The constructors are:

```
//create text field with string displayed
TextField tf = new TextField(String);
//create empty text field n characters wide
TextField tf = new TextField(n);

//create text area of spec'd # of rows and columns
TextArea ta = new TextArea(rows, cols);
```

The most significant methods for these controls are shown in Table 7-6.

Method	Description
TextArea	
getText	Returns current text in box.
setText(String)	Sets text field to that string.
setEditable(boolean)	Sets whether text can be edited.
select(start, end)	Selects the text characters specified.
selectAll	Selects all the text.
TextField	
setEchoChar(char)	Set character to be echoed to allow password entry. To undo this, set the echo char to '\0'

Table 7-6: TextArea and TextField methods.

Events that you might wish to intercept include GOT_FOCUS, LOST_FOCUS, KEY_PRESS, KEY_RELEASE, and KEY_ACTION (the Enter key).

The List Box

A list box is a vertical list of single lines of text. You can add to it, select or change items, and delete items. If you add more items than can be displayed, a scroll bar appears on the right side. There are two constructors for the List control:

```
//create new list with no visible rows
List list1 = new List();
//create new list with n visible rows
//and whether to allow multiple selections
List list1 = new List(n, boolean);
```

The important methods are described in Table 7-7.

Method	Description
addItem(String)	Adds an item to the end of the list.
addItem(String, n)	Adds an item at position *n* in the list.
clear	Clears the list (but for Windows 95, see below).
delItem(n)	Deletes item *n*.
delItems(i, n)	Deletes *n* items starting at *i*.
countItems	Returns number in list.
deselect(n)	Deselects item *n*.
getSelectedIndex	Returns index of selected item.
getSelectedItem	Returns text of selected item.
getItem(n)	Returns text of item *n*.
isSelected(n)	Returns *true* if item is selected.
replaceItem(n,String)	Replaces item *n* with next text.
select(n)	Selects item *n*.
setMultipleSelections (boolean)	Sets list to allow or not allow multiple selections.

Table 7-7: Important list box methods.

In addition to adding items to list boxes and seeing what line or lines are selected, you might want to change some program feature when the user selects a line in a list box. You do this by catching the LIST_SELECT event in the *handleEvents()* method for the class that contains the list box.

In Java 1.0, there are three known bugs in the Windows 95 implementation of the list box:

◈ Java version 1.0 for Windows 95 does not implement the *clear()* method correctly. You should use the *delItems(0, countItems()-1)* method instead.

◈ If you create a list box as single-select box and convert to a multiple-select box, it will shorten by one line (only once). You can work around this by resetting the size afterward.

◈ If you create a list box as a multiselect list and add terms to it, the scroll bar will never appear. You can work around this by creating the list box as a single-select box, adding the lines, and then setting multiselect mode. However, beware of the single-select-to-multiselect conversion bug above if you do this.

The Choice Box

The Choice box is a single-line window with a drop-down arrow revealing a drop-down list box. It has the same constructors and methods as the list box. The events for a Choice box are slightly different: selecting an item from a Choice box generates an *action* event, while clicking on an item in a list box generates a LIST_SELECT event.

The Choice box is not a Windows-style combo box where you can type or select from the top line, but you could easily construct such a combo box from a text field, a button, and a hidden list box.

The Scroll Bar

While list boxes contain their own scroll bars, it is sometimes useful to have scroll bars for selecting other kinds of variable input. The Scrollbar control can be constructed as a horizontal or vertical scroll:

```
scroller = new Scrollbar(orient); //HORIZONTAL or VERTICAL

scroller = new Scrollbar(orient, value, visible, min, max);
```

You interact with the scroll bar by intercepting the events SCROLL_LINE_UP, SCROLL_LINE_DOWN, SCROLL_PAGE_UP, SCROLL_PAGE_DOWN, and SCROLL_ABSOLUTE. The methods you can use are explained in Table 7-8.

Method	Description
getValue()	Returns position of scroll relative to min and max.
setValue(int)	Sets position of slider.
setValues(val, posn, min, max)	Sets parameters for scroll bar.
setLineIncrement(int)	Sets how much to move on one click.
setPageIncrement(int)	Sets how much to move on page up/down increment.

Table 7-8: Scroll bar methods.

If you click on the arrows at each end of a scroll bar, you'll generate a SCROLL_LINE_UP or SCROLL_LINE_DOWN event. If you click just below the scroll bar's "elevator," you'll generate the SCROLL_PAGE_UP and SCROLL_PAGE_DOWN events. Finally, if you drag the elevator with your mouse, you'll generate the SCROLL_ABSOLUTE event.

Check Boxes

A check box is a square box that you can click on or off. Unlike the check box in Visual Basic, it does not have a third grayed-out state. Check boxes operate independently from each other; you can check or uncheck as many as you like. When a check box is checked, it returns as state of *true*; if unchecked it returns *false*. The important methods are described in Table 7-9. The constructors are:

```
//create checkbox with label
Checkbox cb = new Checkbox(String);
```

Method	Description
getState	Returns state of checkbox.
setState(boolean)	Sets state of checkbox.
getLabel	Gets label of checkbox.
setLabel(String)	Sets label for checkbox.

Table 7-9: Important Checkbox methods.

In Windows 95, the *setLabel()* method for check boxes does not work in Java 1.0.

Radio Buttons

Radio buttons (or in Visual Basic terms, Option buttons) are in fact a special case of check boxes in Java. Radio buttons have all the same methods as check boxes, but appear as circles where only one of a group can be selected if the check box items are made members of a *CheckboxGroup*.

In Visual Basic, you can have only one set of option buttons on a form, unless you put one or more of the groups inside frames. In Java, you can have as many groups of radio buttons on a page as you like, as long as you make each set a member of a different *CheckboxGroup*.

The following Java statements create a pair of radio buttons belonging to a single *CheckboxGroup*:

```
//First create a new Check box group
CheckboxGroup cbg = new CheckboxGroup();

//then create check boxes as part of that group
Checkbox Female = new Checkbox("Female", cbg, true);
Checkbox Male = new Checkbox("Male", cbg, false);
```

Note that it is the use of this kind of *Checkbox* constructor that causes the boxes to be displayed as rounded radio buttons.

Colors

Colors in Java can be specified as RGB hexadecimal numbers or as named constants. Each of the red, green, and blue color components can vary between 0 and 255. You usually use them in *setBackground* and *setForeground* statements, and often using the following predeclared constants:

black	green	lightGray
orange	blue	cyan
darkGray	grey	pink
red	yellow	white

Table 7-10: Predeclared color constants.

Since these constants are all part of the *Color* class, you refer to them using the class name:

```
setBackground(Color.blue);
```

You can also create specific colors using a single integer to represent the RGB values or by using a group of three byte values:

```
setForeground(new Color(0xff00dd));
setBackground(new Color(255, 0, 0xdd));
```

Fonts

There are six basic fonts that Java supports on all platforms:

- Times Roman
- Helvetica
- Courier
- Dialog
- DialogInput
- ZapfDingbats

For any given platform, you may also use any font that you know is available.

The default font for Java applets and applications is Roman. Since sans serif fonts are more readable for window labels and text, you should always switch the font of any class containing visual controls to Helvetica using the *setFont* method:

```
setFont(new Font("Helvetica", Font.PLAIN, 12));
```

where the styles may be:

```
Font.PLAIN
Font.BOLD
Font.ITALIC, or
Font.ITALIC + Font.BOLD.
```

The symbol font ZapfDingbats is not rendered the same on all platforms, and as of this writing, you should not count on any specific symbolic characters being available on the various platforms.

FontMetrics

The *FontMetrics* class contains methods to find out the size of the current font or the width of a string drawn in that font. It is not related to or contained in the Font class itself, but is instead dependent on where you are drawing the font. The Graphics class contains the call *getFontMetrics*(), which returns an instance of the class for that graphics object. For this reason, you can only determine the actual size of a font with a *paint* or related method, where the current graphics context is available.

Moving On

In this chapter, we've looked at the set of visual controls that the Java abstract window toolkit (awt) uses. We've listed their events and their methods and talked a little about how event-driven programming works. You can't really appreciate how to use these controls to build real programs unless we take you through some examples. We'll do so in the next couple of chapters.

8

Writing a Simple Visual Application in Java

In this chapter, we're going to begin writing Java programs that utilize the visual controls we've introduced. We'll also see how we can interact with events the user can generate by clicking the mouse on these controls.

Windows in Java

When you write visual applications in Java, you are writing programs that use and manipulate windows. All Java windows inherit from the *Container* class, but the inheritance tree beyond that has two branches. For applications, the hierarchy starts with the *Window* class, which is an undecorated square on the screen. The *Frame* class, derived from the *Window* class, is the one we usually see on the screen. It contains a title bar and may contain a menu.

Applets are also a kind of window derived from the *Panel* class. Panels are designed to be regions inside another container where you draw or arrange components in a particular way. Applets are a kind of panel with specific methods that the Web browser can call to initialize and start them running. The inheritance tree for applets and frames is shown in Figure 8-1.

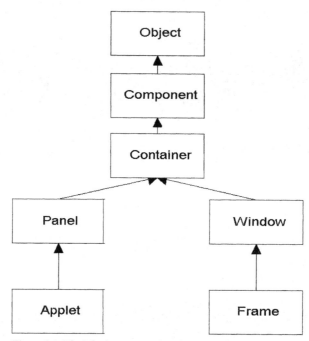

Figure 8-1: The inheritance tree of applets and frames.

Since both applets and frames are kinds of containers, it is not surprising that we add the visual controls that we wish to use into these containers. It is important to recognize that creating instances of these graphical objects is only part of our job. We also have to tell the window that it is going to contain them, so the window can display the objects by calling their *paint* methods. How and where it will display the controls really depends on the window's layout manager, and we will consider several ways of laying out a window in this chapter.

Building a Temperature Conversion Applet

Now that we've outlined the common controls in a Java application, let's build one. We are going to build a temperature conversion program that will allow us to convert temperatures between Fahrenheit and Celsius. This program will consist of a text field, two labels, two radio buttons, a Compute button, and a Quit button.

Writing the Program in Visual Basic

To start, let's write the program in Visual Basic so we can see the similarities in how VB and Java work. We start by using the VB form designer to draw and align a label ("Enter temperature"), an empty edit box, a blank label for the result, two radio buttons, and two pushbuttons. This layout is shown in Figure 8-2.

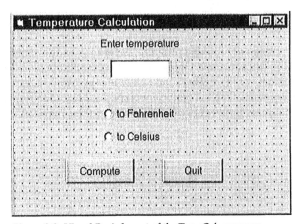

Figure 8-2: Visual Basic layout of the TempCalc program.

Next, we write the code for the program. The code consists primarily of the actions to take when the Compute button is clicked:

```
Option Explicit
'------------------------------
Private Sub Compute_Click()
Dim temp As Single, newtemp As Single

temp = Val(TempEntry.Text)
If Fahr.Value Then
  newtemp = temp * 9 / 5 + 32
Else
  newtemp = 5 * (temp - 32) / 9
End If

result.Caption = Str$(newtemp)
End Sub
'------------------------------
Private Sub Quit_Click()
  End
End Sub
```

When we run this program, we get the window shown in Figure 8-3. You can enter a temperature into the edit box, click on "to Fahrenheit" or "to Celsius," and have the program display the converted temperature in the results label caption. The code for this VB application is in the \chapter8 directory on the Companion CD-ROM.

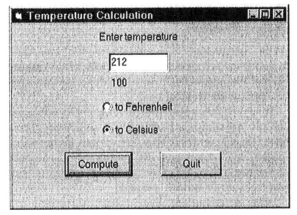

Figure 8-3: The Visual Basic version of TempCalc running.

Writing the Java Version

We are going to write this conversion program as an *applet*: a program that runs inside a Web browser. In this example, we are going to create a class called *TempCalc* in a file called tempcalc.java. We will compile this into an applet called tempcalc.class, which we will run from an HTML file called tempcalc.html. The structure of the applet consists of:

* The public class initializer routine where we initialize variables.

* Layout of controls on the screen.

* Routines to process user events: usually *action*, *handleEvent*, or both.

Laying Out Controls on the Screen

At the current stage in the development of Java, there are two methods for laying out visual controls: those that use a visual builder like Visual Basic does and those that use *layout managers* to arrange the controls for us.

The layout-manager approach means that the positions of the controls are computed dynamically so that they never overlap, based on rules embedded in the various layout manager objects. Further, layout manager–driven applications are independent of screen resolution and allow the layout to expand and stretch dynamically as a window is resized.

Some visual builders like Symantec Café allow you to set the layout manager to *null* and set the controls by absolute pixel position. The advantage of this latter approach is that you can get a good, professional-looking screen with the controls where you want them. The disadvantage is that the absolute pixel values of controls generated for different platforms at different screen resolutions may not look as good as on the original platform. Our experience so far, however, has been that visual builders produce code that works perfectly well on all the platforms we have tried.

In this chapter we are first going to write the program using no layout manager, and then we will revisit it using a layout manager class. One way to lay out controls is to simply sketch the screen on quadrille paper and compute the pixel coordinates from their layout on the page. We did essentially that here, resulting in the coordinates for the labels, option buttons, and command buttons you will see in Table 8-1 below.

Control	Location	Size
Window		360 x 25
Label1 "Enter temperature"	100, 25	135 x 20
TempEntry entry field	125, 55	75 x 25
Result label	125, 85	90 x 20
Option button "to Fahrenheit"	125, 100	100 x 15
Option button "to Celsius"	125, 135	100 x 15
Compute button	75, 170	65 x 30
Quit button	175, 170	65 x 30

Table 8-1: Layout coordinates for the controls in our TempCalc *class.*

All of the initialization we have performed in applications so far has been in the class's constructor. Applets are launched by the Web browser which displays the Web page, and the interface between the Web browser and the applet is well defined.

The init() Method

After the applet is loaded and its constructor called, the browser calls its *init()* method. This is the time when connection is first made to the run-time environment and the earliest time that making references to the layout of graphical objects is meaningful. So, for applets, rather than doing our initialization inside the constructor, we do it inside the *init()* method. However, we'll see later in the "Applets vs. Applications" section that writing a program which can run either as an applet or as an application is quite straightforward.

TIP

Does this mean that applets and applications are forever separated? Can we write a single program that is both an applet and an application? Yes, we can, by having the main() *method call the* init() *method and a couple of others. We'll see this later in the chapter.*

The start() & stop() Methods

What happens if we display an applet on a Web page and then scroll down or switch pages so it is no longer showing? Does it continue to run? Can it be restarted?

The Web browser calls the *init()* method only once. Then it calls the applet's *start()* method. The applet runs until that part of the Web page is obscured either by scrolling away from it or by moving to another page. Then the browser calls the applet's *stop()* method. If you scroll or switch back to the applet again, the browser again calls the *start()* method.

While you may not need to override these methods and write any actual code for many applets, they can be useful when you write animation programs.

Laying Out Our Applet

The private variables in our TempCalc applet consist of the graphical controls on the screen and the CheckboxGroup object:

```
private CheckboxGroup Temper;   //group radio buttons
private Label label1;
private TextField TempEntry;     //edit box
private Checkbox Fahr;           //radio button
private Checkbox Celsius;        //radio button
private Label result;            //result shown here
private Button Compute;          //compute when clicked
private Button Quit;             //exit when clicked
```

We then initialize the applet's layout manager to *null*, define the default font to be Helvetica-12, and define the size of the window:

```
setLayout(null);
setFont(new Font("Helvetica", Font.PLAIN, 12));
resize( 360, 225);
```

In general, windows look better with a sans serif font like
Helvetica, so we will always change the default font to Helvetica.
The default in Java is Times Roman, which is somewhat more
cluttered looking than Helvetica.

Creating Objects

Let's consider that *Font* statement above for a minute:

```
setFont(new Font("Helvetica", Font.PLAIN, 12));
```

What do we mean by this? Well, if you look at the constructor for
the *Font* class, you will find that it is:

```
public Font(String name, int style, int size);
```

Then, if you look for the method *setFont* under the *Applet* class,
you won't find it. If you start going down the inheritance tree, you
will pass through *Panel* and *Container* before you find the method
in the base *Component* class:

```
public void setFont(Font  f);
```

So in order to set the font to the new style or size, we have to
create a Font object. We could do this as follows:

```
Font newfont = Font("Helvetica", Font.PLAIN,12);
setFont(newfont);
```

Or we could do it by creating a new Font object right in the *setFont*
method call, which is what we have done here:

```
setFont(new Font("Helvetica", Font.PLAIN, 12));
```

Initializing the Controls

Next we begin initializing the controls. For each control, we create
an instance of it using the *new* operator. Note that while we declared a variable *label1* of type *Label* above, we didn't create an
object to put in that variable. This is where objects differ from

simple numeric types such as *float* or *int*. Objects are some sort of unspecified data structure containing data and pointers to methods. In order to use an object, you have to allocate space for it using *new*.

So in the case of the label1 object, we create a label using the *label* constructor which specifies the text of the label. Then we use the applet's *add* method to add each control to the applet container:.

```
label1 = new Label("Enter temperature:");
add(label1);
label1.reshape(100, 25,135,20);
```

Finally, since we aren't using a layout manager here, we position the label using its *reshape* method.

We do pretty much the same thing for each of the other controls. However, the option (radio) buttons are a little different since they are a special kind of check box. First we need to create a CheckboxGroup object and then refer to it in the constructor of each of the option buttons that we want to have work together as a unit:

```
Temper = new CheckboxGroup();
Fahr = new Checkbox("to Fahrenheit",Temper, false);
add(Fahr);
Fahr.reshape(125, 100,100,15);

Celsius = new Checkbox("to Celsius",Temper, false);
add(Celsius);
Celsius.reshape(125, 135,100,15);
```

The Button Click Event

Now that we have initialized the controls and started the applet, we need to take action when the Compute or Quit button is clicked. As before, clicking on a button causes the *action* method to be called. So we subclass this method and have it make calls to our *clickedCompute()* method or to the *System.exit()* method:.

```
public boolean action(Event evt, Object obj)
  {
    if (evt.target == Compute)
    {
    clickedCompute();
    return true;
    }
  else
    if (evt.target == Quit)
    {
    System.exit(0);
    return true;
    }

  return super.action(evt, obj);
  }
```

As before, we note that the *action* method returns either *true* or *false*. If you handle a particular event, you should return *true* to indicate that it has been handled and should not be passed up the chain to further parent classes. Otherwise you can either return *false* or return the results of calling the parent's *action* method.

The clickedCompute Method

Now to the crux of the program. We need to read the value in the TextField box TempEntry, see whether the Fahr button is selected, and then perform one calculation or the other. We will need two local variables:

```
float temp, newtemp;
```

Then we convert the text in the text box into a float as follows. First we convert the string into a Float object:

```
Float flt = new Float(TempEntry.getText());
```

Then we obtain the float numerical value from the Float object using that class's *floatValue()* method:

```
temp = flt.floatValue();
```

Or we can do the whole thing in one statement:

```
temp = new Float(TempEntry.getText()).floatValue();
```

So our entire *clickedCompute* method is as follows:

```
public void clickedCompute()
  {
  float temp, newtemp;
  temp = new Float(TempEntry.getText()).floatValue();
  if (Fahr.getState())
    newtemp = 9 * temp / 5 + 32;
  else
    newtemp = 5 * (temp - 32) / 9;
  result.setText(new String().valueOf(newtemp));
  }
```

As you see, it looks a lot like the *Compute_Click* method in Visual Basic. The running program for computing and displaying temperatures is illustrated in Figure 8-4.

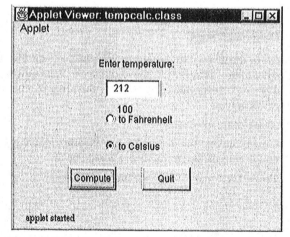

Figure 8-4: The TempCalc program running in the appletviewer.

The listing is as given below:

```
//Simple temperature calculator
//will run either as applet or application

import java.awt.*;
import java.applet.*;

public class TempCalc extends Applet
{
private CheckboxGroup Temper;      //group buttons
private Label label1;
private TextField TempEntry;        //edit box
private Checkbox Fahr;              //radio button
private Checkbox Celsius;           //radio button
private Label result;              //result shown here
private Button Compute;             //compute when clicked
private Button Quit;                //exit when clicked
//---------------------------------------------------
public void init()
{
//initialize applet
setLayout(null);
setFont(new Font("Helvetica", Font.PLAIN, 12));
resize( 360,  225);

label1 = new Label("Enter temperature:");
add(label1);
label1.reshape(100, 25,135,20);

TempEntry = new TextField(7);
add(TempEntry);
TempEntry.reshape( 125,55,75,25);

Temper = new CheckboxGroup();
Fahr = new Checkbox("to Fahrenheit",Temper, false);
add(Fahr);
Fahr.reshape(125, 100,100,15);

Celsius = new Checkbox("to Celsius",Temper, false);
```

```java
        add(Celsius);
        Celsius.reshape(125, 135,100,15);

        result = new Label(" ");
        add(result);
        result.reshape( 125, 85,90,20);

        Compute = new Button("Compute");
        add(Compute);
        Compute.reshape(75, 170,65,30);

        Quit = new Button("Quit");
        add(Quit);
        Quit.reshape(175,170,65,30);

        super.init();
        }
//----------------------------------------------------
public boolean action(Event evt, Object obj)
  {
     if (evt.target == Compute)
     {
      clickedCompute();
      return true;
     }
    else
     if (evt.target == Quit)
     {
      System.exit(0);
      return true;
     }
    return super.action(evt, obj);
  }
//----------------------------------------------------
  public void clickedCompute()
    {
      float temp, newtemp;
      temp = new Float(TempEntry.getText()).floatValue();
       if (Fahr.getState())
```

```
            newtemp = 9 * temp / 5 + 32;
        else
            newtemp = 5 * (temp - 32) / 9;
        result.setText(new String().valueOf(newtemp));
    }
//------------------------------------------------------
}        //end of class
```

Applets vs. Applications

An applet is always a visual program. It lives inside a Web page and comes into existence when the Web browser calls its *init* and *start* methods.

By contrast, applications need no visual components. If you want to display something in a window, you must provide an initialized window. The basic displayable unit is the *Window* class, but the *Frame* class, which extends *Window*, provides borders and a title bar. It is usually the *Frame* that we use to construct windows in applications.

If we add a *main* routine to the *TempCalc* class, we can create a program that will run either as an application or as an applet. We need only create a frame, which is just another kind of container, add the *TempCalc* class to it, resize it, and display it:

```
public static void main(String arg[])
    {
    //create instance of applet
    Applet app = new TempCalc();

    //create a frame window
    Frame fr = new Frame("Temperature Calculator");
    fr.add(app);        //add the applet to the frame
    fr.resize(364, 225);
    fr.show();          //display the frame window

    app.init();         //initialize the applet
    app.start();        //and start it
    }
```

If we compile and run the *TempCalc* class with this *main* method included, it will run as a stand-alone window. This *main* method is included in the tempcalc.java program in the \chapter8 directory of the Companion CD-ROM. The TempCalc program, running as an application, is shown in Figure 8-5.

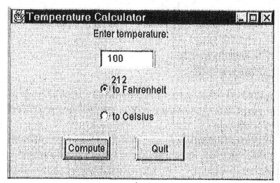

Figure 8-5: The same TempCalc program, running as an application.

Stopping Your Application From the System Close Button

If you tried to close the application we show above by clicking the system close button at upper right, it would not close. This is because, by default, the WINDOW_DESTROY event is not handled by the Frame object. You must include a specific *handleEvent* method in your application that receives this close message:

```
public boolean handleEvent(Event evt)
  {
  switch (evt.id)
    {
    case Event.WINDOW_DESTROY:
      System.exit(0);
      return true;
```

```
    default:
      return super.handleEvent(evt);


   }
  }
```

However, if you have an applet that is also going to be run as an application, you can't just insert this trap for the WINDOW_DESTROY event into the applet, because it is not a Frame and will not receive the message. Remember that we created a Frame in the *main* method, and it is that Frame that will receive the *destroy* event. In order to trap this event, you must create a new class that extends *Frame* and does trap for this *destroy* event.

This class is simply:

```
class pubFrame extends Frame
{
 public pubFrame(String caption)
 {
 super(caption);    //pass caption to parent Frame
 }
//-------------------------------------------------
 public boolean handleEvent(Event evt)
 {
 switch (evt.id)
   {
   case Event.WINDOW_DESTROY:
     System.exit(0);//exit if destroy
     return true;
   default:
     return super.handleEvent(evt);
   }
 }
} //end pubFrame class
```

Then we modify the *main* method of the *Applet* class to create this new type of Frame rather than an ordinary Frame:

```
public static void main(String arg[])
  {
  Frame fr = new pubFrame("Temperature Calculator");
  Applet app = new tempcalh();
  fr.add(app);
  fr.resize(364, 225);
  fr.show();
  app.init();
  app.start();
  }
```

This modified version of the program is called tempcalh.java on the Companion CD-ROM.

Exit From action & handleEvents

While it is accurate to say that we must return *true* if we handle an event and *false* if we do not, it is more important to note that if we do not handle an event, we should pass it on to the parent class. This is why we show the last statement in these methods above as:

```
return super.action(evt, arg);
```

and:

```
return super.handleEvents(evt);
```

The return from the parent class will then be the desired *true* or *false* value.

Subclassing the Button Control

One of the great strengths of Java is that because it is an object-oriented language, you can extend nearly any class to add function to it. We just saw a useful reason to extend the *Frame* class. Now let's consider the *Button* class.

As Visual Basic programmers, we are most familiar with the idea that every button-click generates its own private subroutine where we can carry out the operations we require:

```
Private Sub Compute_Click()
Dim temp As Single, newtemp As Single

temp = Val(TempEntry.Text)
If Fahr.Value Then
   newtemp = temp * 9 / 5 + 32
Else
   newtemp = 5 * (temp - 32) / 9
End If

result.Caption = Str$(newtemp)
End Sub
```

Here we don't require any awkward *action* or *handleEvents* method to make the program more confusing to read. Clicking on the button generates a call to the *Compute_Click* routine, and we simply fill in the code there.

How could we go about doing the same thing in Java? If we derived a new class from Button, we could put a derived *action* method inside that class and know that only one possible event could cause the method to be called. Then the *action* method inside that derived *Button* class would be the equivalent of the VB *Compute_Click* event we show above.

Unfortunately, one of the reasons this works is that VB is not thoroughly object oriented; you can call any subroutine you want from within a *click* event subroutine. In a fully object-oriented system, only methods of a particular object could be called from within that object. In Java, if we extended our *Button* class, it would be a separate class that would not have direct access to the *clickedCompute* method of our *Applet* class. In order to make it available, we need to make sure it is a public method and that we pass a reference to this instance of the *Applet* class into the *Button* class. We do this using the special reserved word *this*, which refers to the current instance of a class.

Our final drawback to this approach is that we have to create a separate subclass for each separate button on the form. Here, since there are only two buttons, creating the subclasses is not particularly difficult. We declare our two buttons as new classes:

```
private ComputeButton Compute;    //compute when clicked
private QuitButton Quit;          //exit when clicked
```

Then we create instances of these classes during *init*, as usual, but passing a reference to this instance of the *TempCalc* class into the button as part of the constructor:

```
Compute = new ComputeButton("Compute", this);
Quit=new QuitButton("Quit", this);
```

Now our button classes are pretty simple, since we can have the base *Button* class do most of the work:

```
class ComputeButton extends Button
{
private tempcal2 app; //local copy of applet ref

public ComputeButton(String caption,tempcal2 ap)
 {
 super(caption);
 app = ap;               //save reference to calling applet
 }
public boolean action(Event evt, Object obj)
 {
 app.clickedCompute();     //call method in applet
 return true;
 }
}
//=================================================
class QuitButton extends Button
{
private tempcal2 app; //local copy of applet ref

public QuitButton(String caption, tempcal2 ap)
 {
 super(caption);
 app= ap;               //save reference to calling applet
 }
```

```
public boolean action(Event evt, Object obj)
  {
  System.exit(0);   //Call exit method directly
  return true;      //so the app reference
                    //wasn't really needed here

  }
}
```

The complete program is called tempcal2.java and is in the
\chapter8 directory on the Companion CD-ROM.

Using Symantec Café to Lay Out Applications

Symantec Café provides an integrated application-building environment where you can lay out and align fairly complex controls
on the screen using the Café Studio GUI builder. Figure 8-6 shows
this GUI builder in use.

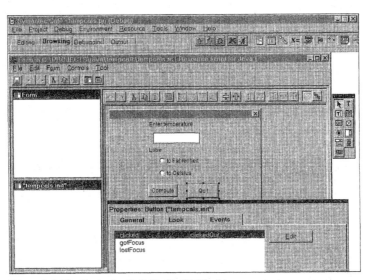

Figure 8-6: The Symantec Café Studio GUI builder.

Once you have generated your screen layout, you can select the events you wish to respond to and have Café generate the code in *handleEvent*, which calls your class's methods. It then provides a syntax-highlighted editor where you can enter the code for these methods. In addition, it generates all of the code to produce the control layout you design. If you use the *null* layout, your program will look exactly the same as you drew it in the GUI builder.

This is the generated code for a version of TempCalc laid out using Café:

```java
public void init() {

//{{INIT_CONTROLS
setLayout(null);
addNotify();
resize(insets().left + insets().right + 354, insets().top +
        insets().bottom + 180);
 group1= new CheckboxGroup();
 label1=new Label("Enter temperature");
 add(label1);
 label1.reshape(insets().left + 75,insets().top + 9,112,15);
 tempentr=new TextField(12);
 add(tempentr);
 tempentr.reshape(insets().left + 200,insets().top + 99,22);
 result=new Label("result");
 add(result);
 result.reshape(insets().left + 148,insets().top +38,91,15);
 Fahr=new Checkbox("to  Fahrenheit",group1, false);
 add(Fahr);
 Fahr.reshape(insets().left + 127,insets().top + 52,119,23);
Celsius=new Checkbox("to Celsius",group1, false);
add(Celsius);
Celsius.reshape(insets().left + 127,insets().top +75,98,22);
Compute=new Button("Compute");
add(Compute);
Compute.reshape(insets().left + 127,insets().top+105,77,22);
 //}}

 super.init();
 }
```

Café generates code for all events inside the *handleEvent* method, rather than catching *action* events in a separate *action* routine. This method can become a long if-else list. Here it is quite short:

```
public boolean handleEvent(Event event)
{
if (event.id == Event.ACTION_EVENT &&
                    event.target == Quit)
 {
clickedQuit();
return true;
 }
 else
  if (event.id == Event.ACTION_EVENT &&
         event.target ==                 Compute)
   {
   clickedCompute();
   return true;
   }
  return super.handleEvent(event);
 }
```

Symantec now also has a follow-on product called Visual Café, which allows even more sophisticated manipulation of layout and control properties from a VB-like interface. It generates similar code to that shown above.

Moving On

Now that we have built some real visual applications in Java, we have all the fundamentals in hand. We've learned about applets and applications, about laying out screens, and about using Café to lay out your controls. We've seen how to derive new classes from the *Frame* class and from the *Button* class and have begun to write some significant Java code.

In the next chapter, we'll look at the other way to lay out Java code: using layout managers. Then we'll continue to build on our knowledge by taking up images and files in the chapters to come.

9

Layout Managers

As we discussed in Chapter 8, laying out controls in a Java window can be done by absolute pixel positioning or by using a layout manager class. While most Visual Basic programmers probably started in the PC world where visual GUI builders are more common, Java started in the UNIX world where specifying a program to do your layout is more common. In fact, many UNIX programmers believed that if it was hard to write, it should be hard to use.

Before Java came along, the most popular high-level language for creating GUI applications was TCL/TK, a language system developed almost entirely by John Osterhout. Since he had to deal with any number of different UNIX platforms as well as screens varying from 640 X 480 to thousands of pixels across, he developed the concept of a layout manager that would allow you to tell it something about the relative positions of the controls and would then figure out how to achieve it.

The great advantage of layout managers is that they allow you to write programs that are independent of the screen size and the operating system. Further, if you resize a window controlled by a layout manager, the components will move apart in a sensible fashion. The great disadvantage is that layout managers take a good deal of programming by the user to achieve this screen independence.

Java Layout Managers

Java provides five layout manager objects:

* **FlowLayout**—controls flow from left to right and onto new lines as needed.

* **BorderLayout**—controls can be added to North, South, East, West, and Center. Any space not used by the four borders goes into the Center. Controls can also be explicitly added to the Center.

* **CardLayout**—allows you to display one of several card areas a time, as Hypercard or a tabbed container does.

* **GridLayout**—a layout of n rows by m columns, where you specify m and n.

* **GridBagLayout**—a complex layout where each object can take up several rows or columns.

For the most part, you can lay out simple screens using the Flow, Grid, and Border layouts. The other layout managers are for more involved cases.

In Java applications, a Frame is the top-level window that you display on the screen. It has a title bar and may have a menu. Layouts apply to the Frame where you add controls in either an applet or an application.

A *Panel* is a logical, but unmarked, region of a screen where you can group controls. You can add one or more Panels within the frame area, each of which can then have its own layout. The default layout manager for a Frame is BorderLayout and the default for a Panel is FlowLayout. Rather than trying to remember this, we will always set the layout we need in our example programs.

For simple programs, you can do a fairly good job using the GridLayout to divide your window into regions and then inserting panels in the grid cells. Each grid cell has a FlowLayout so that the components within a cell are spaced apart and do not touch. You can use the BorderLayout if you want some component to be along one of the edges of the window.

The FlowLayout Manager

A FlowLayout allows you to add components to a panel in a simple, left-to-right fashion using the following constructors:

```
public FlowLayout();
```

When one row is full, the next component starts a new row. When you select the FlowLayout, you have the option of specifying the alignment and gap between components. However, the default alignment is CENTER, and the default gap is a reasonable-looking 10–20 pixels:

```
public FlowLayout(int align);
   public final static int CENTER;
   public final static int LEFT;
   public final static int RIGHT;
public FlowLayout(int align, int hgap, int vgap);
```

The FlowLayout is primarily for laying out rows of buttons, although you can use it for check or text boxes or any other kind of component you wish. The following code produces the layout shown in Figure 9-1:

```
import java.awt.*;

class flow1 extends Frame
{
 public flow1()
 {
 super("Flow Layout 1");
 setLayout(new FlowLayout());
 add(new Button("Button 1"));
 add(new Button("Button 2"));
 add(new Button("Button 3"));
 add(new Button("Button 4"));
 add(new Button("Button 5"));
 reshape(100,100,200,100);
 show();
```

[internal image]

```
    }
    public static void main(String arg[])
    {
    new flow1();
    }
    }
```

This program is flow1.java in the \chapter9 directory of this book's Companion CD-ROM.

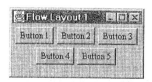

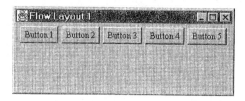

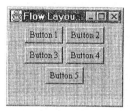

Figures 9-1a, 9-1b, 9-1c: The FlowLayout of five buttons showing how three different screen widths automatically affect the layout.

If you want to align the components along the left edge, use the third version of the constructor, as shown in the code that follows:

```
class flow2 extends Frame
{
public flow2()
{
super("Flow Layout 2");
setLayout(new FlowLayout(FlowLayout.LEFT, 30, 30));
add(new Button("Button 1"));
add(new Button("Button 2"));
add(new Button("Button 3"));
add(new Button("Button 4"));
add(new Button("Button 5"));
reshape(100,100,200,100);
show();
}
```

This program is flow2.java on the Companion CD-ROM. It is illustrated in Figure 9-2.

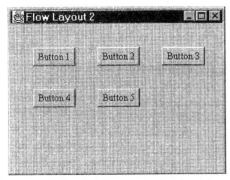

Figure 9-2: The FlowLayout using left alignment and a 30-pixel horizontal and vertical gap.

FlowLayouts can also produce mixed-control layouts that are fairly reasonable looking. Each row must be the same height all the way across, but different rows may have different heights to accommodate different kinds of components. For example, the following code leads to the layout shown in Figure 9-3:

```
class flow3 extends Frame
{
public flow3()
{
super("Flow Layout 3");
setLayout(new FlowLayout(FlowLayout.LEFT,30, 30));
add(new Button("Button 1"));
add(new Button("Button 2"));
add(new Checkbox("Display spelling errors"));
add(new List(8, false));
add(new Button("Button 5"));
reshape(100,100,200,100);
show();
}
}
```

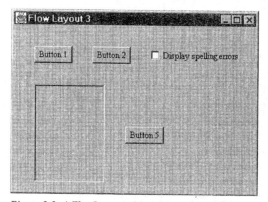

Figure 9-3: A FlowLayout of a mixed group of components.

The GridLayout Manager

The GridLayout manager organizes the container into a specified number of rows and columns. While they need not be the same size, all cells in a row must be the same height and all cells in a column must be the same width.

The constructors are:

```
public GridLayout(int rows, int cols);
public GridLayout(int rows, int cols, int hgap, int vgap);
```

So for example, if you want to lay out five controls in two rows, you could use the GridLayout:

```
class grid1 extends Frame
{
  public grid1()
  {
  super("Grid Layout 1");
  setLayout(new GridLayout(3,3));
  add(new Button("Button 1"));
  add(new Button("Button 2"));
  add(new Button("Button 3"));
  add(new Button("Button 4"));
  add(new Button("Button 5"));
  reshape(100,100,200,100);
  show();
  }
```

This program, grid1.java in \chapter9 of the Companion CD-ROM, produces the display shown in Figure 9-4. It is clearly not particularly elegant to have the buttons touching each other without any space between them. However, by simply changing the GridLayout constructor to:

```
setLayout(new GridLayout(3, 3, 30, 5));
```

you can have the somewhat more pleasant spacing shown in Figure 9-5.

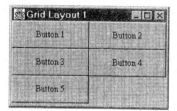

Figure 9-4: The GridLayout using a grid of 3 X 3 with five buttons. No spacing between buttons was specified.

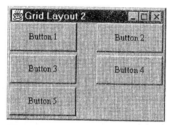

Figure 9-5: The GridLayout using a grid of 3 X 3 with five buttons and a spacing of x=30 and y=5.

The BorderLayout Manager

The BorderLayout manager allows you to divide the screen into five regions named "North," "South," "East," "West," and "Center." Like the other managers, it has two constructors:

```
public BorderLayout();
public BorderLayout(int hgap, int vgap);
```

When you add a component to a BorderLayout, you specify the edge name as part of the add method:

```
add("North", Button1);
```

Each component is given the amount of space it naturally requires; there is no requirement that the layout manager distribute the space equally. For example, the following program produces the layout shown in Figure 9-6:

```
class border1 extends Frame
{
public border1()
{
super("Border Layout 1");
setFont(new Font("Helvetica", Font.PLAIN, 16));
setLayout(new BorderLayout(5, 5));
add("West",  new Button("Button 1"));
add("North", new Button("Button 2"));
add("East",  new Button("Btn 3"));
add("South", new Button("Button 4"));
add("Center",new Button("Button 5"));
reshape(100,100,300,200);
show();
}
```

The program is called border1.java in \chapter9 of the Companion CD-ROM.

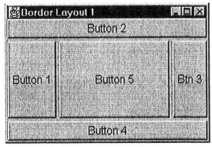

Figure 9-6: A frame using the BorderLayout manager. Note that the right and left border areas are unequal in width.

Since we labeled the West button as "Button 1," but the East button as "Btn 3," the left and right panels are not of the same width. Programmers generally use the BorderLayout manager to set aside part of the window at one side or another, and then put a panel containing another type of layout manager in the remaining space.

For example, we could divide the screen in half, putting a list box in one part and a series of buttons in the other. Since the center always takes up "what's left," we will put the list box in the center and the buttons on the right side. We will add the list box to the Center part of the border layout and then create a panel to add to the East side of the border layout.

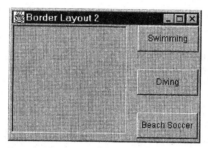

Figure 9-7: Using a BorderLayout to divide the screen into two parts.

The following code shows the program for laying out the controls in two columns:

```
class border2 extends Frame
{
public border2()
{
super("Border Layout 2");
setFont(new Font("Helvetica", Font.PLAIN, 12));
setLayout(new BorderLayout(15, 1));
Panel rpanel = new Panel();
add("East", rpanel);

add("Center", new List(10, false));
rpanel.setLayout(new GridLayout(3, 1, 30,25));
rpanel.add(new Button("Swimming"));
```

```
rpanel.add(new Button("Diving"));
rpanel.add(new Button("Beach Soccer"));
reshape(100,100,300,200);
show();
}
```

Figure 9-7 shows the window the code generates. This program is called border2.java in \chapter9 on the Companion CD-ROM.

Padding a Layout Using Panels

One problem with the layout as shown in the previous section is that the buttons are too fat and take up too much of the right-hand screen area. It would be better if the spacing between the buttons stayed the same, but more space was added both above the top button and below the bottom button.

The easiest way to accomplish this is to make the GridLayout 1 X 5 instead of 1 X 3. But how will we fill just the middle three cells? Simple. We'll just insert a Panel control in the top and bottom cells:

```
public border3()
  {
  super("Border Layout 3");
  setFont(new Font("Helvetica", Font.PLAIN, 12));
  setLayout(new BorderLayout(15, 1));
  Panel rpanel = new Panel();
  add("East", rpanel);

  add("Center", new List(10, false));
  rpanel.setLayout(new GridLayout(5, 1, 30, 5));
  rpanel.add(new Panel());  //fill top cell
  rpanel.add(new Button("Swimming"));
  rpanel.add(new Button("Diving"));
  rpanel.add(new Button("Beach Soccer"));
  rpanel.add(new Panel());  //fill bottom cell
  reshape(100,100,300,200);
  show();
  }
```

This layout is shown in Figure 9-8, and the program is called border3.java in \chapter9 on the Companion CD-ROM.

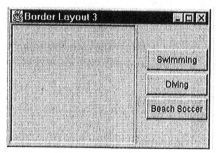

Figure 9-8: A BorderLayout divided with a 1 X 5 GridLayout on the right side. Top and bottom grid cells contain an empty panel.

Layout for the Temperature Conversion Program

Now, before we move on to the last two types of layout managers, let's consider how we could have written the Temperature Conversion program we started with in Chapter 8 using layout managers instead of absolute pixel positioning.

To lay out the controls for this program, we'll need to put the controls into five rows and one column to contain:

* A label, "Enter Temperature," and an entry field.
* A label where the result is to be displayed.
* The "to Fahrenheit" option button.
* The "to Celsius" option button.
* A Compute button and a Quit button on a single line together.

We create the layout using the following steps:

1. Create a 6 X 1 grid.
2. Add an empty panel to the top line of the grid for spacing purposes.

3. Add a panel to the second line and add a label and a TextField to that panel.

4. Add a panel to the third line and add the Results label to it.

5. Add a panel to the fourth line and add the "to Fahrenheit" option button to it.

6. Add a panel to the fifth line and add the "to Celsius" option button to it.

7. Add a panel to the sixth line and add the two push buttons to it.

The code for accomplishing this is:

```
public class TempLayout extends Frame
{
Label lbl, Result;        //labels used on screen
TextField tempval;        //the entry field
Checkbox Cels, Fahr;      //the radio buttons
Button Compute;           //the Compute pushbutton
Button Quit;              //the Quit pushbutton

public TempLayout()
{
  super("Temperature Conversion");
  setFont(new Font("Helvetica",Font.PLAIN, 12));

  //5 rows, 1 column plus empty cell at top
  setLayout( new GridLayout(6, 1));
  add(new Panel());
  //top row has label and text field

  Panel p1 = new Panel();
  add(p1);
  p1.setLayout(new FlowLayout());
  //create label
  lbl = new Label("Enter temperature:");
  tempval = new TextField(8);//text field 8 chars wide
  p1.add(lbl);
  p1.add(tempval);
```

```
//2nd row has result label
//Default layout for panel is Flowlayout, centered
//so use panels to center controls
Panel p2 = new Panel();
add(p2);
Result = new Label(" result "); //put label in panel
p2.add(Result);

//Third and fourth rows are two radio buttons
CheckboxGroup cbg = new CheckboxGroup();
Fahr = new Checkbox("to Fahrenheit", cbg, true);
Panel p3 = new Panel(); //use panels
Panel p4 = new Panel(); //to center controls
add(p3);
add(p4);
p3.add(Fahr);
Cels = new Checkbox("to Celsius", cbg, true);
p4.add(Cels);

//Fifth row is two pushbuttons
Panel p5 = new Panel();
add(p5);
p5.setLayout(new FlowLayout(FlowLayout.CENTER,
        10, 0));
Compute = new Button("Compute");
p5.add(Compute);
Quit = new Button("Quit");
p5.add(Quit);
reshape(100, 100, 250, 300);
show();
    }
}
```

The program is called TempCalc.java in \chapter9 of the Companion CD-ROM, and the displayed window is shown in Figure 9-9.

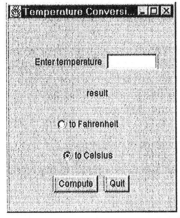

Figure 9-9: The TempCalc program designed using the GridLayout manager.

Creating a Java panel in this manner may seem like a lot of work, especially compared with Visual Basic, where you can create the layout using a visual builder. However, if you consider that such code produces a resizeable window that will execute on any platform at any resolution, it may frequently be worth it to use layout managers once you get the hang of it.

If you look at the code at the top of any VB Form module, it is rather analogous to the code in the last example, except that it was generated for you by VB's visual builder. A number of vendors are at work on visual builders for Java that generate code like that. For example, RogueWave's JFactory generates layouts using its own layout manager, and Sun's Java Workshop generates code using the GridBagLayout that we will discuss shortly. In addition, Symantec's Café and Visual Café allow you to draw your components and have them produce very nice-looking screens, using either the *null* layout or the standard layout managers.

The CardLayout Manager

The CardLayout manager allows you to create a number of components, usually panels containing controls, but to show only one of them at a time. It can provide a basis for designing a tabbed dialog or a Hypercard-like program. The constructors are the same as for the other layout classes:

```
public CardLayout();
public CardLayout(int hgap, int vgap);
```

However, when you add components to the layout, you give each of them a name:

```
pcard.setLayout(new CardLayout());
pcard.add("Panel 1", list);
```

You can use any kind of name you like, but when you wish to switch to displaying that particular card, you must use that same name. To display a card, you use the CardLayout manager's show method:

```
cardlay.show(pcard, "Panel 1");
```

You can also cycle through the cards in the layout by using these methods:

```
public void first(Container parent);
public void last(Container parent);
public void next(Container parent);
public void previous(Container parent);
```

A Simple Card Layout Example

In the example below, you see that we construct a Frame window with a BorderLayout. We then put four buttons across the top of the layout labeled "Panel 1" through "Panel 4." Finally, we add a panel to the remainder of the window (the Center), create a CardLayout, and set that panel's layout to the card layout instance. We save a variable containing that instance of the card layout because we need to be able to reference it when we want to switch between cards.

In this simple example, we create four controls: a list box, a text area, a button, and a scroll bar; and add one to each of four cards in the card layout, naming these cards as "Panel 1" through "Panel 4."

Now we have an easy way to switch between cards. When you click on one of the buttons, an action event occurs and the argument in that action event is the label on the button. Thus, we can simply choose the right card to display by executing a show method on the card layout, passing it the String in the arg:

```
cardlay.show(pcard, (String)arg);
```

Figure 9-10 shows one card displayed using this card1.java program.

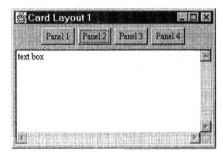

Figure 9-10: A simple program using the CardLayout manager.

The complete program for displaying cards in a card layout is as follows:

```
import java.awt.*;

class card1 extends Frame
{
Panel pcard;      //panel in center which uses cardlayout
List list;        //a list box
Button btn;       //a button
Scrollbar sbr;    //a scrollbar
```

```java
TextArea ta;              //a text area
CardLayout cardlay;       //the card layout manager object
//-----------------------------------------------
 public card1()
 {
 super("Card Layout 1");          //set title bar
 setLayout(new BorderLayout()); //border layout
 Panel p0 = new Panel();          //line of buttons

 //put panel containing line of buttons along the top
 add("North", p0);                //put panel along top
 p0.add(new Button("Panel 1")); //4 labeled buttons
 p0.add(new Button("Panel 2"));
 p0.add(new Button("Panel 3"));
 p0.add(new Button("Panel 4"));

 //create controls and assign values to them
 list = new List(5, false);
 list.addItem("ListItem");
 list.setBackground(Color.white);
 btn = new Button("Click Me");
 sbr =
   new Scrollbar(Scrollbar.HORIZONTAL, 10, 1, 0, 20);
 ta = new TextArea(4, 10);
 ta.setText("text box");

 //Now create CardLayout in rest of screen
 pcard = new Panel();             //panel for rest of window
 add("Center", pcard);
 cardlay = new CardLayout();      //create layout object
 pcard.setLayout(cardlay);        //set card layout
 pcard.add("Panel 1", list);      //now add named cards
 pcard.add("Panel 2", ta);
 pcard.add("Panel 3", btn);
 pcard.add("Panel 4", sbr);
 reshape(100,100,300,200);
 show();
 }
 //-----------------------------------------------
```

```
public boolean action(Event evt, Object arg)
//display panel based on name from button label
//which is stored in arg
{
cardlay.show(pcard, (String)arg);
return true;
}
//-------------------------------------------
public static void main(String arg[])
{
new card1();
}
}
```

A Card Layout Program Using Panels

You will see from Figure 9-10 (and if you run the card1.java program) that the controls expand to fill the entire screen area of each card. This is hardly an aesthetic approach, and you will find that the best way to use the card layout manager is to insert a panel for each card and lay out controls inside the panels, much as we would do if there were only one screen of controls.

We illustrate how to do this in the card2.java program, a fragment of which follows:

```
pcard.setLayout(cardlay);

//now create 4 panels, add controls to them
//and add the panels to the card layout
//naming them "Panel 1" through "Panel 4"
Panel p1 = new Panel();        //create panel
p1.add(list);                  //add list to it
pcard.add("Panel 1", p1);      //add to layout

Panel p2 = new Panel();        //create panel
p2.add(ta);                    //add textarea to it
pcard.add("Panel 2", p2);      //add to layout
```

```
Panel p3 = new Panel();        //create panel
p3.add(btn);                   //add button to it
pcard.add("Panel 3", p3);      //add to layout
//etc.
```

Figure 9-11 shows Panel 2 of this card layout, illustrating that if you insert a panel inside each card of the layout, each panel will have the more usual FlowLayout provided by default within panels.

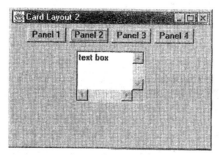

Figure 9-11: The CardLayout manager program card2.java. Each card has a Panel to which the controls are added.

The GridBagLayout Manager

Of the layout managers provided with Java, the GridBagLayout manager is the most complex as well as the most versatile. The underlying assumption of this layout manager is that you can have controls that span more than one row or column:

```
public void GridBagLayout();
public void GridBagConstraints();
```

Each element that you add to a container managed by a GridBagLayout has its drawing controlled by an instance of the *GridBagConstraints* class. Since the values of this class are copied into the GridBagLayout along with a reference to the control, you only need one instance of the *GridBagConstraints* class as well.

The GridBagConstraints class has a number of publicly accessible variables that tell the GridBagLayout class how to position that component (see Table 9-1). You can change these fields before adding each new component to the layout.

Variable	Description
gridx	X grid position of the component.
gridy	Y grid position of the component.
gridwidth	The number of x cells the component spans.
gridheight	The number of y cells the component spans.
fill	Which dimensions should grow if the space is larger than the component: NONE, BOTH, HORIZONTAL, or VERTICAL.
ipadx	Extra space in pixels added to the width of the component.
ipady	Extra space in pixels added to the height of the component.
insets	Margins to appear around component: part of inset class.
anchor	How the component should be aligned within the grid cells: CENTER, EAST, NORTH, SOUTH, WEST, NORTHEAST, NORTHWEST, SOUTHEAST, SOUTHWEST.
weightx	How much weight a given cell should be given relative to others if window is wider than needed. Default is 0.
weighty	How much weight a given cell should be given relative to others if window is higher than needed. Default is 0.

Table 9-1: Publicly accessible variables of the GridBagConstraints class.

To position a component using the GridBagLayout, we have to create an instance of both the GridBagLayout and GridBagConstraints, add the component, and then set the constraints for that component:

```
gbl = new GridBagLayout();        //create layout mgr
gbc = new GridBagConstraints();   //and constraints
setLayout(gbl);                   //set layout
```

```
Button b1 = new Button("One");    //create button
gbc.gridx = 4;                    //fourth row
gbc.gridy = 0;                    //first column
gbc.gridwidth = 2;             //two cells wide
gbc.gridheight =1;             //one cell high
add(b1);                       //add button into layout
gbl.setConstraints(b1, gbc);    //set constraints for b1
```

Since most controls will have just their positions set as they are added, we can put most of the above into a private method that operates on *gbl* and *gbc*:

```
private void add_component(Component c, int x,
       int y, int w, int h)
  {
  gbc.gridx = x;                    //set x and y positions
  gbc.gridy = y;
  gbc.gridwidth = w;             //and sizes
  gbc.gridheight =h;
  add(c);                        //add component
  gbl.setConstraints(c, gbc);    //set constraints
  }
```

A Simple GridBagLayout Example

Now let's write a simple program using a list box and three buttons. The list box will occupy three horizontal cells and four vertical ones. The push buttons will be one cell each: two in row 0 and one in row three. The complete program for laying out the buttons is:

```
public class gblay extends Frame
{
private GridBagLayout gbl;
private GridBagConstraints gbc;
private List lb;
//----------------------------------------------
  public gblay(String caption)
  {
```

```
super(caption);
gbl = new GridBagLayout();       //set layout mgr
gbc = new GridBagConstraints(); //set constraints
setLayout(gbl);

lb = new List(5,false);          //add in list box
lb.setBackground(Color.white);
add_component(lb, 0, 0, 3, 4); //3 x 4

Button b1 = new Button("One");   //button
add_component(b1, 4, 0, 2, 1); // at 4,0

Button b2 = new Button("Two");
add_component(b2, 6, 0, 2, 1); //at 6,0

Button b3 = new Button("Three"); //at 5,3
add_component(b3, 5, 3, 2, 1);

reshape(20, 20, 200, 150);
show();
}
//--------------------------------------------
private void add_component(Component c, int x, int y,
                int w, int h)
{
gbc.gridx = x;
gbc.gridy = y;
gbc.gridwidth = w;
gbc.gridheight =h;
add(c);
gbl.setConstraints(c, gbc);
}
//--------------------------------------------
public boolean action(Event evt, Object arg)
{
lb.addItem((String)arg);
return true;
}
```

```
/--------------------
public static void main(String arg[])
 {
 new gblay("GridBag Layout");
 }
}
```

The resulting layout is illustrated in Figure 9-12. The program is called gblay.java in \chapter9 of the Companion CD-ROM.

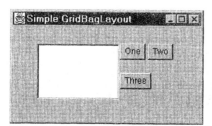

Figure 9-12: Simple GridBagLayout of list box and three buttons.

Improving on Our Simple GridBagLayout

If you stretch the window in the gblay.java program, the buttons and list box will stay the same size and stay clustered in the center of the window. Further, the buttons seem a bit crowded. Let's see what we can do to unclutter the layout slightly.

First, we can make the buttons a bit bigger on either side of their captions by making *ipadx* and *ipady* larger than their default, 0:

```
gbc.ipadx = 5;        //make buttons wider
gbc.ipady = 3;        //make buttons higher
```

Then we can add a little more space between the buttons by
adding a few pixels to the *insets* class. This class has four direction
names, and we add four pixels to each:

```
gbc.insets.left =    4;
gbc.insets.right =   4;
gbc.insets.bottom = 4;
gbc.insets.top =     4;
```

Finally, let's experiment with the *weightx* variable to see what it
does. It should give that column more space as the window expands. We'll use it on Button b2:

```
Button b2 = new Button(" Two ");
gbc.weightx = 1;      //this column gets more space
add_component(b2, 6, 0, 2, 1);
```

The complete program gblay2.java is in \chapter9 of the Companion CD-ROM. It contains only the changes we have just discussed. Figure 9-13 shows the window displayed by this program
at its normal width, and Figure 9-14 shows the same window
stretched horizontally. As you can see, Buttons One and Three stay
near the list box, but Button Two moves outward as the window is
expanded.

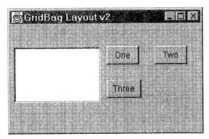

Figure 9-13: GridBagLayout gblay2.java, showing the effects of increasing
ipadx *and* ipady *and adding values for insets.*

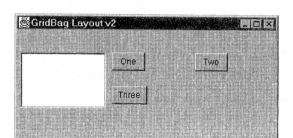

Figure 9-14: GridBagLayout gblay2.java, stretched horizontally. This illustrates the effect of setting weightx *to 1 for Button Two.*

A GridBagLayout for the TempCalc Program.

When we look at the layout of the TempCalc program we constructed using flow and grid layouts (see Figure 9-10), it looks adequate but not that professional. Let's see how it will look using the GridBagLayout manager to arrange the controls. We'll arrange them using the grid layout illustrated in Figure 9-15.

(blank)	(blank)	(blank)	(blank)
Enter temperature:		TempEntry TextField	
	Result label		
	O - To Fahrenheit		
	O - to Celsius		
(blank)	(blank)	(blank)	(blank)
Compute			Quit

Figure 9-15: Layout of cells to be used for the final layout of the TempCalc program.

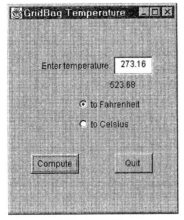

Figure 9-16: The TempCalc program as laid out using the GridBagLayout manager.

The complete program is shown below and is named gbTemp.java on the Companion CD-ROM. The window it displays is shown in Figure 9-16.

```
public class gbTemp extends Frame
{
private GridBagLayout gbl;        //layout mgr
private GridBagConstraints gbc;   //and constraints

private Label label1;             //label
private TextField TempEntry;      //entry field
private Label result;             //result label
private CheckboxGroup cbg;
private Checkbox Fahr;            //radio buttons
private Checkbox Celsius;
private Button Compute;           //compute button
private Button Quit;             //quit button
```

```java
public gbTemp(String caption)
{
super(caption);
setFont(new Font("Helvetica",Font.PLAIN, 12));
gbl = new GridBagLayout();
gbc = new GridBagConstraints();
setLayout(gbl);
gbc.ipadx = 5;          //make buttons wider
gbc.ipady = 5;          //make buttons higher


label1 = new Label("Enter temperature:");
add_component(label1,0,1,2,1);

TempEntry = new TextField(5);
add_component(TempEntry,2,1,1,1);

result = new Label(" result ");
add_component(result,1,2,2,1);


cbg = new CheckboxGroup();
//left align check boxes in cell 1
gbc.anchor = GridBagConstraints.WEST;
Fahr = new Checkbox("to Fahrenheit", cbg, true);
add_component(Fahr,1,3,2,1);

Celsius = new Checkbox("to Celsius", cbg, false);
add_component(Celsius,1,4,2,1);

//return to center alignment
gbc.anchor = GridBagConstraints.CENTER;
add_component(new Label(""),1,5,1,1); //leave space
Compute = new Button("Compute");
add_component(Compute, 0,6,1,1);

Quit = new Button("  Quit   ");
add_component(Quit, 2,6,1,1);
```

```
        reshape(20, 20, 250, 300);
        show();
        }
    //----------------------------------------
    private void add_component(Component c, int x, int y,
                        int w, int h)
        {
    gbc.gridx = x;
    gbc.gridy = y;
    gbc.gridwidth = w;
    gbc.gridheight =h;
    add(c);
    gbl.setConstraints(c, gbc);
        }
//----------------------------------------
    public boolean action(Event evt, Object arg)
        {
    if (evt.target == Compute)
        {
        clickedCompute();
        return true;
        }
    else
    if (evt.target == Quit)
        {
        System.exit(0);
        return true;
        }
    else
        return super.action(evt, arg);
        }
//----------------------------------------
private void clickedCompute()
{
float temp, newtemp;
// get the entered value:
// we assume it is valid for program simplicity
temp = new Float(TempEntry.getText()).floatValue();
if (Fahr.getState())
```

```
    newtemp = 9 * temp / 5 + 32;
else
    newtemp = 5 * (temp - 32) / 9;
result.setText(" "+new String().valueOf(newtemp)+" ");
}
//----------------------------------------
public static void main(String arg[])
  {
  new gbTemp("GridBag Temperature");
  }
}
```

Moving On

In this chapter, we've looked at all the ways Java provides for laying out components in windows. We've looked at the FlowLayout, the GridLayout, the BorderLayout, the CardLayout, and the venerable GridBagLayout. We've seen how you can use the *GridBagConstraints* class to position almost anything anywhere. In the next chapter, we're going to talk first about graphics and then about how Java uses files.

10

Using Graphics Methods

Graphics methods in Java are very easy to use. While they are similar to the graphics methods in Visual Basic, they are actually more versatile. In this chapter we'll briefly remind you of what VB graphics are like and then explain how to do similar things in Java.

Graphics in Visual Basic

In Visual Basic, you can draw a line or a rectangle with the *line* method:

```
line(x1,y1)-(x2,y2),color, BF
```

where if *B* is included, a box is drawn, and if *F* is included the box is filled with the current color. Drawing can take place on a form or in a picture box within a form.

You can draw a circle, oval, or arc with the *circle* method:

```
circle (x, y),radius, color, start, end, aspect
```

where *start* and *end* determine the amount of arc drawn in radians. Whether the arc or circle is filled is determined by the current form or picture's *FillStyle* and *FillColor* properties.

VB also provides the Shapes control, which allows you to place a permanent rectangle, circle, rounded rectangle, or arc on a form as a decoration. These shapes are not generally used to draw current program data, but only to enhance the form's appearance.

Java, on the other hand, does all drawing through the Graphics object. It has more versatility in the number of kinds of shapes available, but has no line style and fill style options.

The Graphics Object

You've probably noticed that we have referred to a Graphics object and a *paint* method when we drew rectangles on the screen. In this chapter, we'll cover most of the properties of this powerful object, and you'll see what sort of drawing you can easily do in Java.

The Graphics object is a member of the *awt* class and is an abstraction of the graphical methods available on all of the supported platforms and operating systems. It gives you a way to draw lines, text, and shapes, as well as setting the drawing and clipping modes.

When you create a Frame or Applet window, it has a graphics object associated with it. You can obtain a reference to this object using the *getGraphics()* method of any graphical control or container. However, you don't need to do this in most programs, because the *paint()* method always passes a reference to the graphics object to that routine:

```
public void paint(Graphics g)
```

Thus, you almost always do all your drawing from within the *paint* method.

The *paint* method is called whenever the screen needs refreshing, such as when a window is exposed after being hidden or when it is resized. You never call the *paint* method yourself, of course, because you don't usually have a copy of the graphics object to pass to it. Instead, if you want to force a window to be repainted, simply call that window's *repaint()* method; this will cause the *update()* method to be called, which in turn calls the *paint* method.

All drawing with a graphics object uses the current color and the current font, as well as the current paint mode (paint or XOR), and all drawing is done only within the current clipping region. Usually the clipping region is the entire window, although you can specify a smaller region.

In the Rect1 program in Chapter 4, we used the *getGraphics* method in the constructor to obtain a copy of the current graphics object (sometimes also called the graphics *context)*. If there is no such object, because one has not yet been created, this method will return *null*. We made sure this would work in this simple example program by specifically calling the *addNotify()* method before calling the *getGraphics()* method:

```
public Rect1()
{
 super("Rect1 Window");
 addNotify();
 rect1 = new Rectangl(getGraphics());
```

The *addNotify()* method connects the Java graphics context to the actual underlying windowing system. While this connection is made automatically during startup of a Java Window, we make sure it has been made by the time we want to obtain a graphics context by calling the *addNotify()* method. Normally, you would seldom need to use this method. In that case, we used it so that each of our rectangle objects already has a copy of the graphics context stored.

Graphics Methods

Remember that all of the major graphics methods (see Table 10-1) require that you call them as methods of the graphics object, not just as subroutines, as you might easily assume. Thus, we draw the rectangle in Chapter 4 using:

```
g.drawRect(x, y, w, h);
```

Method	Description
clearRect(x,y,w,h)	Clears rectangle region.
clipRect(x,y,w,h)	Sets new clipping region.
copyArea(x,y,w,h,dx,dy)	Copies rectangle to new region offset by dx and dy.
create(x,y,w,h)	Creates new graphics context where origin is offset by x,y and w,h specify the clipping region.
dispose()	Deletes this graphics context.
draw3Drect(x,y,w,h,raised)	Draws 3D rectangle with shading raised or indented.
fill3Drect(x,y,w,h,raised)	Fills 3D rectangle in current color.
drawArc(x,y,w,h,startAngle, endAngle)	Draws arc at x,y; size is w,h starting at angle startAngle and ending at endAngle.
drawBytes(data[], offset, length, x,y)	Draws characters from byte array.
drawChars(data[], offset, length,x,y)	Draws characters from character array.
drawLine(x1,y1,x2,y2)	Draws a line.
drawOval(x,y,w,h)	Draws an oval.
fillOval(x,y,w,h)	Draws a filled oval.
drawPolygon(x[],y[],n)	Draws a polygon from array.
drawPolygon(polygon)	Draws a polygon from an object.
fillPolygon(x[], y[], n)	Draws a filled polygon from array.
fillPolygon(p)	Draws a filled polygon from an object.
drawRect(x,y,w,h)	Draws a rectangle.
fillRect(x,y,w,h)	Draws a filled rectangle.
drawRoundRect(x,y,w,h, arcw, arch)	Draws a rounded rectangle.
fillRoundRect(x,y,w,h, arcw, arch)	Draws a filled, rounded rectangle.
drawString(str, x,y)	Draws characters from a String.
Rectangle getClipRect()	Gets clipping region.

Method	Description
Color getColor()	Gets current color.
Font getFont()	Get current font.
setFont(Font)	Sets current font.
FontMetrics getFontMetrics()	Gets current font size and shape.
FontMetrics getFontMetrics (font)	Gets font size and shape.
setPaintMode()	Sets drawing mode to write over.
setXORMode(color)	Sets drawing mode to XOR.

Table 10-1: Major graphics methods in Java.

Lines

The *drawLine* method draws a line between the coordinates you specify in the current line color. In Java 1.0, there are no line thickness or style (dashed, dotted) line types, but these are expected to be provided in later versions. To simulate a thicker line, just draw it again transposed by one pixel:

```
g.drawLine(x1, y1, x2, y2);
g.drawLine(x1+1, y1+1, x2+1, y2+1);
```

It is not an error to draw a line or other graphical element that extends outside the current window boundary.

Graphics Drawing Modes

There are two drawing modes in Java: *draw over* and *XOR* mode. You choose them using the two methods:

```
g.setPaintMode();
g.setXORMode(color);
```

These modes are complementary. The normal *setPaintMode()* drawing mode is the "draw over" method in which everything is replaced by the new drawing element. When the XOR mode is set, the current color is replaced by the color specified in the *setXORMode* method. All other colors are replaced with their logical XOR. The replacement color is not predictable, but XORing them twice will restore the original colors.

Shapes

The awt contains definitions for the Rectangle and Polygon shapes. They are simple classes that allow you to specify shapes easily.

Rectangles

The *Rectangle* class provides a convenient way to refer to a four-cornered object, and for the most part, you can treat the Rectangle as if it has the four public properties of x, y, width, and height, although it has a number of other methods. You can draw a rectangle either by specifying its dimensions as part of the *drawing* method:

```
g.drawRect(100,100,200,300);
```

or by passing it a rectangle object:

```
Rectangle r = new Rectangle(100,100,200,300);
g.drawRect( r);
```

or finally, you could set the rectangle properties yourself:

```
Rectangle r = new Rectangle();
r.x = 100;          r.y = 100;
r.width = 200;      r.height = 300;
g.drawRect(r);
```

In each case, you could also draw the rectangle in filled mode by replacing the above methods with the method:

```
g.fillRect(r);
```

The *draw3DRect* method is supposed to draw a shaded 3D rectangle, with a raised look if the *raised* parameter is true and with an inset look if it is false. It does not appear to be implemented in Windows 95, but works in most UNIX versions.

The *drawRoundRect* method:

```
g.drawRoundRect(x,y,w,h, arcwidth, archeight);
```

draws a rectangle with the specified shape and with arcwidth and archeight equal to the horizontal and vertical diameter of the arc at each corner.

Polygons

The *Polygon* is a class that contains arrays of *x* and *y* data points comprising the coordinates of each vertex of the polygon. You can add points to it in pairs:

```
Polygon p = new Polygon();
addPoint(100, 100);
addPoint(300, 400);
```

You can then draw a polygon by specifying a *Polygon* class or the *x* and *y* arrays specifically:

```
int x[] = new int[2];
int y[] = new int[2];
x[0] = 100;  y[0] = 100;
x[1] = 300; y[1] = 400;
g.fillPolygon(x, y, 2);    //draws closed filled polygon
```

In Java 1.0, however, to draw an unfilled polygon, you must specify an additional last point equal to the first point:

```
int x[] = new int[3];
int y[] = new int[3];
x[0] = 100;  y[0] = 100;
x[1] = 300; y[1] = 400;
x[2] = 100;  y[2] = 100;

g.drawPolygon(x, y, 3);    //draws closed unfilled polygon
```

Ovals & Arcs

You can draw ovals and circles with the *drawOval* method:

```
g.drawOval(x,y,w,h);
```

If *w* and *h* are the same size, the shape is a circle. The *drawArc* method allows you to draw either a round or elliptical arc:

```
g.drawArc(x, y, width, height, startAngle, endAngle);
```

The center point of the arc is at (x,) and if width and height are equal, the arc is circular. The arc is drawn from the *startAngle* to the *endAngle*, where both angles are in degrees (not radians). An angle of zero degrees is at three o'clock.

Drawing Text

Java provides several methods for drawing text in a window. In all cases, the drawing is done in the current font and color. The most commonly used method is:

```
g.drawString("foo", x, y);
```

but you can also draw text from an array of chars (16-bit) or of bytes (8-bit):

```
g.drawBytes(data[], offset, length, x, y);
g.drawChars(data[], offset, length, x, y);
```

where *data* is an array of bytes or chars, respectively, *offset* is the index in the array where drawing is to start, and *length* is the number of characters to draw. The (x, y) position is where the baseline of the character string will be drawn, not the top or lower limit of the descenders. Text strings are drawn in a single line, if you include newline characters ("\n") the text is not drawn on a new line.

Drawing Lines Around Text

In order to find out how much space a string occupies, you must use the FontMetrics object returned from the graphics context using the *getFontMetrics* method. You can then use the *getHeight* and *getStringWidth* methods to find out the size of the string you are drawing. You can obtain the string dimensions and draw lines as follows:

```
String s = "Here is a string";
g.drawString(s, 150, 120);
FontMetrics fm = g.getFontMetrics();
int height = fm.getHeight();
int width = fm.stringWidth(s);
g.drawRect(150, 120 - height, width, height);
```

Note that you draw the string at (x, y) where *y* represents the baseline of the font, but that you draw lines starting at the top of the string (120 - height).

The Clipping Rectangle

The clipping rectangle of a window is that part of the entire area in which graphics operations actually draw something. Graphics operations outside that area are ignored. Normally, the entire window constitutes the clipping rectangle. However, you can set a different clipping rectangle using the *clipRect* method, and you can obtain the current clipping rectangle using the *getClipRect* method.

The *translate(x,y)* method provides a convenient way to change the graphics origin. Normally, the upper left corner is (0,0), but the *translate* method makes the current position (x,y) into the new coordinate (0,0). However, since the positive y-direction remains down (as it normally is in Visual Basic), this is less useful for drawing technical graphs where we would have preferred that the y-direction were upward.

A Graphic Demonstration

The program GrDemo.java in the \chapter10 directory on the Companion CD-ROM contains examples of most of the figures and methods we have discussed here. Figure 10-1 shows the displayed window for this program.

Figure 10-1: The GrDemo.java program, showing most graphics elements.

The GrDemo program illustrates the drawing of a filled hexagon, a hollow, rounded rectangle, a filled 3D rectangle, and an arc drawn in XOR mode. When you click on the Clip button, the clipping region is changed from full scale to the center of the screen (Figure 10-2), and when you click on the Translate button, the entire display is shifted by 50 pixels in both the x and y directions.

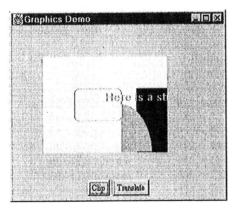

Figure 10-2: The GrDemo program with the smaller clipping region selected.

This program is listed below:

```
import java.awt.*;
public class GrDemo extends Frame
{
//arrays for polygons
final int rect_points = 7;
int xpoints[] = new int[rect_points];
int ypoints[] = new int[rect_points];
boolean clip, trans;   //flags to indicate what to do during
paint
Button Clip, Translate; //command buttons
Font font;              //font to draw strings in
/---------------------
  public GrDemo(String caption)
  {
  super(caption);        //create frame with title bar
  setFont(new Font("Helvetica", Font.PLAIN, 12));
  setBackground(Color.white);
  clip = false;          //no clipping on
  trans = false;         //translation not on
  setLayout(new BorderLayout());
  Clip = new Button("Clip");
  Translate = new Button("Translate");
```

```java
        Panel p1 = new Panel();          //to Southern border
        add("South", p1);
        p1.add(Clip);
        p1.add(Translate);
        //create x and y arrays for polygon
        xpoints[0] = 120;        ypoints[0] = 30;
        xpoints[1] = 140;        ypoints[1] = 30;
        xpoints[2] = 160;        ypoints[2] = 50;
        xpoints[3] = 140;        ypoints[3] = 70;
        xpoints[4] = 120;        ypoints[4] = 70;
        xpoints[5] = 100;        ypoints[5] = 50;
        xpoints[6] = 120;        ypoints[6] = 30; //must close

        reshape(100,100,350,300);
        font = new Font("Helvetica", Font.BOLD, 18);
        show();
        }
//--------------------------------------------------
    public void paint (Graphics g)
    {
    g.setPaintMode();                        //set to draw over
    if (clip)
        {
        g.clipRect(50,50,200,150);        //clip rectangle
        g.setColor(Color.yellow);
        Rectangle r = g.getClipRect();
        g.fillRect(r.x, r.y, r.width, r.height);
        }
    if (trans)
        {
        //translate graphics context by 50 x and y units
        g.translate(50, 50);
        trans = false;                       //but only once
        }
    //draw red filled hexagon
    g.setColor(Color.red);
    g.fillPolygon(xpoints, ypoints, rect_points);
    //draw green rounded rectangle
    g.setColor(Color.green);
```

```
            g.drawRoundRect(100, 100,75,50,15,15);
            //draw blue filled 3D rectangle
            g.setColor(Color.blue);
            g.fill3DRect(200,100,75,100,false);
            //draw blue arc in XOR mode
            g.setXORMode(Color.red);          //overlap orange
            g.fillArc(125,125,100,150,0,90);
            //Draw text, still in XOR mode
            g.setFont(font);
            String s = "Here is a string";
            g.drawString(s, 150, 120);
            FontMetrics fm = g.getFontMetrics();
            int height = fm.getHeight();
            int width = fm.stringWidth(s);
            g.setColor(Color.black);
            g.setPaintMode();
            g.drawRect(150, 120 - height, width, height);
            }
//----------------------------------------------
   public boolean action(Event evt, Object arg)
   {
   if (evt.target == Clip)          //set clip variable
     {
     clip = ! clip;
     repaint();
     return true;
     }
   else
   if(evt.target == Translate)      //sets translate
     {
     trans = true;
     repaint();
     return true;
     }
 else
   return false;
   }
//----------------------------------------------
```

```
public boolean handleEvent(Event evt)
{
if (evt.id == Event.WINDOW_DESTROY)
  {
  System.exit(0);
  return true;
  }
else
 return super.handleEvent(evt);
  }
//-------------------------------------------
public static void main(String argv[])
{
new GrDemo("Graphics Demo");
  }
//-------------------------------------------
}
```

Moving On

In this chapter, we've learned about the powerful Graphics context and how to use it to draw various hollow and filled shapes. We've also discussed using the paint and XOR drawing modes and how to obtain a copy of the Graphics context.

In the next chapter, we'll take up a slightly more complicated program that requires that we allow objects to communicate between two different windows and makes use of some of the graphics methods we have discussed in this chapter.

11

Writing a Program With Two Windows

In Visual Basic, we often write programs that contain a number of windows, or *forms*, that need to communicate data entered between them. In VB 3.0, we did this somewhat awkwardly with global variables. In VB 4.0, it became possible to give each form some public subroutines or methods that would allow us to set the values of the new form before you displayed it. We can do the same sort of thing in Java, but in an even more rigorously object-oriented fashion.

A Temperature Plotting Program

In Chapter 8, we wrote a simple program for converting temperatures between Fahrenheit and Celsius, but the program had no memory of past data points. In this chapter, we'll write a program that keeps an array of data points and then allows us to display a plot of them on the screen.

While an array would be a likely candidate to store a list of data points, one drawback is that we won't know ahead of time how many data points the user might enter. Rather than reserving some large, unnecessary amount of memory, in VB we have the option of using the *ReDim Preserve* to expand memory arrays as needed:

```
max = 10      'define array size
ReDim x(max) 'dimension array
i  = 1
While Not Eof(f)
  Input #f, x(i)    'read in data point
  i = i + 1         'next array element
  If i > max then
    max = max +10   'redimension if needed
    ReDim Preserve x(max)
  EndIf
Wend
```

In Java, we have a somewhat simpler way of doing the same thing using the *Vector* class. An instance of a *Vector* class can hold any number of objects (although not primitive data types) and expands as needed. While there is no requirement that the objects all be of the same type, if you intermingle objects it is up to you to make sure you obtain objects of the correct type, or a run-time error will occur. The major *Vector* methods are:

```
Vector v = new Vector();     //pick default size
Vector v = new Vector(n);    //estimate size
v.addElement(obj);           //any object type
obj = v.elementAt(i);        //return an element
v.removeElement(i);          //remove an element
v.insertElementAt(obj,i)     //insert element
n = v.size();                //return number in use
```

Since *Vectors* always return objects of type Object, you must cast them to the correct type of object on return:

```
v.addElement(Float(x));            //add Float object
Float Fx = (Float)v.elementAt(I); //retrieve one
```

In this plotting program, we will accumulate the data to be plotted in a Vector, and then, when we want to plot it, we'll pass a reference to the entire vector to the plotting window. Our main entry screen is shown in Figure 11-1. The complete program is on the Companion CD-ROM as TempPlot.java in the \chapter11 directory.

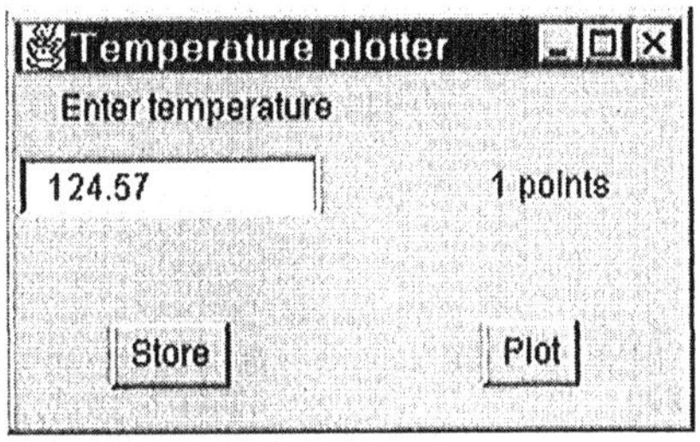

Figure 11-1: The TempPlot entry screen.

The program screen is laid out using the Border and Grid layout managers as follows:

```
public class TempPlot extends Frame
{
private Vector Plotpoints;        //data stored here
private TextField edit1;
private Label label1;
private Label counter;
private Button Store;
private Button Plot;
//--------------------------------
public TempPlot(String caption)
{
 super(caption);
 setFont(new Font("Helvetica", Font.PLAIN, 12));
 //layout using border layout for top line
 //and Grid Layout for panel inserted in center
 setLayout(new BorderLayout());
 label1=new Label("Enter temperature");
 add("North", label1);
 Panel p0 = new Panel(); //put panel in center
 add("Center", p0);
 //create 2 x 2 Grid
 p0.setLayout(new GridLayout(2,2, 20, 20));
```

```
//create 4 panels to force flow layouts
 Panel p1 = new Panel();
 Panel p2 = new Panel();
 Panel p3 = new Panel();
 Panel p4 = new Panel();
 p0.add(p1);                //add them into grid slots
 p0.add(p2);
 p0.add(p3);
 p0.add(p4);

 edit1 = new TextField(13);      //entry field
 p1.add(edit1);                  //edit in 1,1

 counter = new Label("0 points");   //label in 1,2
 p2.add(counter);

 Store=new Button("Store");      //store push button
 p3.add(Store);                  //Store in 2,1

 Plot=new Button("Plot");        //plot push button
 p4.add(Plot);                   //Plot in 2,2

 Plotpoints = new Vector();      //create vector
 resize(250,150);
 show();
 //request focus does not work before show method
 edit1.requestFocus();           //set focus to edit
 }
```

Note that if we want to set the focus to the text entry field edit1 using the *requestFocus* method, we must do so *after* the window's *show* method has been executed.

We can enter any number of data points by typing them in and clicking on Store. Each time we store data, we clear the text box and place the cursor back there for the next data point:

```
public void clickedStore()
{
//create Float object from fp data
Float temp = new Float(edit1.getText());
Plotpoints.addElement(temp);     //add to vector
```

```
//change label to show new number of points
counter.setText(new String().valueOf(Plotpoints.size())
                           + " points");
edit1.setText("");        //clear entry field
edit1.requestFocus();     //reset focus here
}
```

It would be convenient to be able to enter data using the Enter key rather than having to click on Store each time. In Visual Basic, we would have done this by making Store the default button. In Java, we can do something analogous because pressing the Enter key generates an action event. Then we need only test for where it came from and call the *clickedStore* procedure:

```
public boolean action(Event evt, Object arg)
{
 if (evt.target == Plot)
 {
   clickedPlot();            //plot button starts plot
   return true;
 }
 else
 if ((evt.target == Store) || (evt.target == edit1))
 {
   clickedStore();           //store button adds point
   return true;
 }
 else
 return super.action(evt, arg);
}
```

When we have accumulated enough data points, we click on Plot and it creates an instance of the *Plotit* class:

```
public void clickedPlot()
{
//create instance of Plotit class to display data
 Plotit pl = new Plotit(Plotpoints); //pass in vector
 pl.show();             //and display it
}
```

The Plotit display is shown in Figure 11-2.

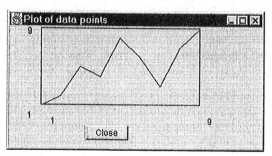

Figure 11-2: A plot of the data entered using the TempPlot *class.*

The Plotit Display

The Plotit display window contains a Close button, four label fields, and a Panel control that we have subclassed to plot x-y data. When we create an instance of the *Plotit* class, we pass it a reference to the vector of x,y points. Then, when we define the size of the panel using the *reshape* method, the *plotPanel* class extends this method to calculate the x- and y-scaling factors. Once the class has determined the maximum and minimum y-values as part of this scaling process, we can use its public *Ymax* and *Ymin* methods to obtain the values we will put in the ymin and ymax axis labels. We can determine the x-axis labels from the number of points in the vector. The *Plotit* class constructor is as follows:

```
// The plotit class plots an array of yvalues
// against the x-index in a rectangle drawn in a panel

public class Plotit extends Frame
{
private Panel panel1;
private Label ytop;
private Label ybottom;
private Label xleft;
```

```java
private Label xright;
private Button Closit;
private plotPanel  plp;
//-------------------------
public Plotit(Vector v)
{
 super("Plot of data points");
 setFont(new Font("Helvetica", Font.PLAIN, 12));
 setLayout(null);
 resize( 380,  200);        //size of window

 //size of plot box-area where graph is drawn
 plp = new plotPanel(v);
 add(plp);
 plp.reshape(50,25,235,110);
 //axis labels
 ytop=new Label("");
 add(ytop);
 ytop.reshape(14, 22, 35, 15);
 ybottom=new Label("");
 add(ybottom);
 ybottom.reshape( 14,142,35,15);
 xleft=new Label("");    //always start with point 1
 add(xleft);
 xleft.reshape( 49,150,35,15);

 xright = new Label("");
 add(xright);
 xright.reshape(280, 150,35,15);
 // close button closes window
 Closit = new Button("Close");
 add(Closit);
 Closit.reshape( 117, 165,63,20);
 //set text for labels
 xleft.setText("1");
 xright.setText(new String().valueOf(v.size()));
 ybottom.setText(new String().valueOf(plp.getYmin()));
 ytop.setText(new String().valueOf(plp.getYmax()));
 }
```

```
//----------------------
public boolean action(Event event, Object arg)
{
//Receive click for close button
if (event.target == Closit)
{
 clickedClosit();
 return true;
}
else
 return super.handleEvent(event);
}
//----------------------
    public void clickedClosit()
    {
     dispose();
    }
}
```

The *plotPanel* class does most of the work in this display. It receives a copy of the vector of plot points in its constructor:

```
//=================================================
class plotPanel extends Panel
{
//this panel class plots an array within its boundaries
//and draws an outline in black
private Vector plotpnts;
private float xmin, xmax, ymin, ymax;
private int pwidth, pheight;
private int pleft, ptop;
private float xscale, yscale;
//----------------------
public plotPanel (Vector pl)
{
 plotpnts = pl;           //save vector inside object
}
```

During its *reshape* method, the *plotPanel* class calculates the scale for the plot based on the size of the window. The method calculates the maximum and minimum *y* values, and, from the number of y-pixels, computes the *y* scale. Since (0,0) is in the upper left corner in Java graphics, the yscale is computed as a negative, and during plotting, this value is added to the height to determine the absolute y-pixel position:

```
public void reshape(int xpos, int ypos,
          int width, int height)
{
Dimension sz;
xmin = 1;
xmax = plotpnts.size();
ymin = 1e35f;
ymax= -1e35f;

//find max and min to scale plot
for (int i = 0; i < plotpnts.size(); i++)
{
  float y = ((Float)plotpnts.elementAt(i)).floatValue();
  if ( y > ymax)
      ymax = y;
  if (y < ymin)
      ymin = y;
 }
//compute scale for plots
 xscale = width/((xmax-1));
 yscale = height/(-(ymax - ymin));
super.reshape(xpos, ypos, width, height);
}
//-------------------------
public float getYmin()
{
return ymin;
}
//-------------------------
public float getYmax()
{
return ymax;
}
```

The *paint* routine is where the plotting actually takes place. The plot Panel determines its size and draws a border around that region. Then it computes the *x* and *y* pixel position of each data point and draws a line to it from the last point:

```java
public void paint (Graphics g)
{
  float x, y;
  int xpix, ypix, xold=0, yold=0;
//draw black rectangle for border
  g.setColor(Color.black);
  Dimension sz = size();       //get window size
  g.drawRect(0,0,sz.width-1,sz.height-1);
//plot data in blue
  g.setColor(Color.blue);
  for (int i=0; i< plotpnts.size(); i++)
    {
    x = i + 1;
    //get each floating value from Vector
    y = ((Float)plotpnts.elementAt(i)).floatValue();
    //convert to pixel values
    xpix = (int)((x -xmin) * xscale ) ;
    ypix = (int)((y- ymin) * yscale ) + sz.height ;
    if (i>0)
      g.drawLine(xold, yold, xpix, ypix);
    //note that these values are save even for the
    //first point
    xold = xpix;     //save for next line
    yold = ypix;
    }

}
}
```

Moving On

In this brief chapter, we've tackled a real-world problem: entering an array of data and plotting it on the screen using Java. Most significantly, we saw how we could use a *public* method to pass a reference to the entire vector to the plotting window. In addition, we saw how we could subclass *Panel* to have it plot x-y data and how subclassing the *reshape* method allowed us to compute the plotting scale.

In the next chapter we'll take up how to read and write files and make use of exceptions to handle I/O error conditions.

12 |

Files & Exceptions

J ava applications have the ability to handle files in a large number of ways that make them as powerful as applications written in any other language. By contrast, Java *applets*, of course, cannot read or write files on any of your computer's disk drives. They do have the ability to read files from the Web server machine, as we will see later.

Java has a large number of classes in the java.io package that can be useful in reading and writing files. The complete list is shown below, but we will be discussing only a few of them in this chapter. You can read about the capabilities of each of these classes in the reference documentation.

```
BufferedInputStream
BufferedOutputStream
ByteArrayInputStream
ByteArrayOutputStream
DataInputStream
DataOutputStream
File
FileDescriptor
FileInputStream
```

```
FileOutputStream
FilterInputStream
FilterOutputStream
InputStream
LineNumberInputStream
OutputStream
PipedInputStream
PipedOutputStream
PrintStream
PushbackInputStream
RandomAccessFile
SequenceInputStream
StreamTokenizer
StringBufferInputStream
```

The File Class

The *File* class provides you with a convenient system-independent way to manipulate files and directories. It has the two constructors:

```
public void File(String filename);
public void File(String path, String filename);
```

as well as one using the *File* class itself:

```
public void File(File dir, String name);
```

The methods in the *File* class provide most of the convenient ways to check for a file's existence and find its directory, create directories, rename a file and find its length, and list the contents of the directory.

However, the *File* class has no open, read, or write methods. In fact, all of the classes that do actual input or output make use of the *File* class as an underlying object. Before we can actually open a file and write to it, we need to understand how *Exceptions* work.

Exceptions

An *Exception* is a class of objects representing various kinds of fatal and near-fatal errors that require special handling in your program. When you perform an illegal operation, such as trying to read a file that doesn't exist or trying to write a file to a write-protected device or volume, the Java system is said to *throw* an exception.

Most operations surrounding file handling throw exceptions. Since the fact that they throw exceptions is included in the method definition, the compiler issues errors if you do not test for exceptions when using these methods. For example, the *RandomAccessFile* constructor is declared like this:

```
public RandomAccessFile(String name, String mode)
                    throws IOException
```

To catch such exceptions, you must enclose them in a *try* block:

```
RandomAccessFile f = null;
  try
    {
    f = new RandomAccessFile("people.add", "r");
    }
  catch (IOException e)
    {
    System.out.println("no file found");
    }
  finally
    {
    System.out.println("File processing completed");
    }
```

Try blocks may be followed by zero or more *catch* blocks, each catching a different exception, and may be further followed by one *finally* block. The try, catch, and finally blocks are one or more lines of code following the keywords *try, catch,* and *finally,* each enclosed in braces.

The program proceeds as follows. The statements within the *try* block are executed sequentially, and if no error occurs, the program exits from the *try* block and executes any statements in the finally block. If an error occurs, the Java system looks for the first *catch* block whose arguments match or are derived from the class of exceptions specified in the argument list. It executes that *catch* block and then, if a *finally* block exists, goes on to execute that code as well.

Note the unusual syntax of the *catch* block:

```
catch (IOException e) { statements; }
```

The exception *e* is, of course, an object, with methods you can use to obtain more information. The two most useful methods are:

```
String e.getMessage();      //obtain a descriptive message
e.printStackTrace();        //print stack trace to output
```

Kinds of Exceptions

Java I/O classes throw exceptions for most of the kinds of errors you might expect for files: file not found, read errors, and write errors:

```
EOFException
FileNotFoundException
IOException
InterruptedIOException
UTFDataFormatException
```

Another class of exceptions are thrown by the run-time system, but the compiler does not require you to catch them since they are usually fatal to the program in any case:

```
ArithmeticException
ArrayIndexOutOfBoundsException
ArrayStoreException
ClassCastException
ClassNotFoundException
CloneNotSupportedException
Exception
```

```
IllegalAccessException
IllegalArgumentException
IllegalMonitorStateException
IllegalThreadStateException
IndexOutOfBoundsException
InstantiationException
InterruptedException
NegativeArraySizeException
NoSuchMethodException
NullPointerException
Class NumberFormatException
RuntimeException
SecurityException
StringIndexOutOfBoundsException
```

However, you can wrap any sequence of statements you like in a *try* block and catch any of these exceptions as well, if you believe your program can deal with them.

Reading Text Files

Now that we've discussed exceptions, let's see how we use them in reading files. We'll start by considering the *RandomAccessFile* class. Now this class is quite powerful and versatile and allows you to read and write data from and to any position in a file. It allows you to read binary integers and floating point numbers as well as text. But most useful to us as Visual Basic programmers is the method:

```
public final String readLine();
```

which allows us to read lines of text from a text file. This method returns the entire line, including the newline character (in some cases you may want to remove this while processing the string). The *readLine* method does not throw an *EOFException* if you try to read past the end of the file (you will almost always read past the end, not knowing the file length in advance). Instead, it returns a string value of null when no more lines can be read.

Let's assume that we have a series of comma-separated lines of text representing a series of customers:

```
Fred, Fump, 437 Old Farkle Way, Neenah, WI, 65432, 517-443-5555
Janey, Antwerp, 22 Dilly Drive, Darlington, MO, 66789, 217-445-6789
Franz, Bloviate, 1456-23 Bafflegab Pl, Bilgewater, CT, 06401, 203-222-3333
Anthony, Quitrick, 42 Kwazulan Ave, American Samoa, USA, 12345, 222-333-4444
Daniel, Night-Rider, 52 Cartalk Plaza, Arfaircity, MA, 02133, 555-444-2220
Newton, Fig-Nottle, 43 Glimway Close, Blandings, NE, 76543, 777-666-5432
Fillippa, Phontasy, 521 Fink Tower Pl, Arduos, AL, 55678, 444-555-8998
```

We can read these in as lines of text and parse them later using the following program:

```java
import java.awt.*;
import java.io.*;
class ftest
{
//---------------------------------------------
 public ftest()
  {
  String s = "";            //initialize s
  RandomAccessFile f = null;     //and file
  try
    {
    //open file
    f = new RandomAccessFile("people.add", "r");
    }
  catch (IOException e)
    {System.out.println("no file found");}
  do
    {
    try
     {
      s = f.readLine();
     }
    catch (IOException e)
     {System.out.println("File read error");}
```

```
        if (s != null)
            System.out.println(s);
        }
    while (s != null);
    }
//-------------------------------------------
public static void main(String argv[])
    {
    new ftest();
    }
}
```

Note that both the instantiation (creation of an instance) of the *File* class and the *readLine* method require that you surround them with try blocks. However, you don't ever have to worry about which lines to surround with try blocks: the compiler will tell you if they are required.

However, we see here some unusual code initializing both the string and the file object to some value before we enter the try block:

```
String s = "";              //initialize string
RandomAccessFile f = null;    //and file
```

Why do we do this? If we simply declared the variables without initializing them:

```
String s;
RandomAccessFile f;
try
    {
    f = new RandomAccessFile("people.add", "r");
    }
try
    {
    s = f.readLine();
    }
catch (IOException e)
    {System.out.println("File read error");}
System.out.println(s);
```

the compiler would detect that the statements inside the try block may not be executed, and thus that *f* and *s* had not been initialized:

```
ftest.java(23): Variable f may not have been initialized
ftest.java(27): Variable s may not have been initialized
2 error(s), 0 warning(s)
```

Then the statements:

```
s = f.readline();
```

and:

```
System.out.println(s);
```

would be illegal since neither *s* nor *f* have been initialized to any value. Therefore, by simply initializing both to any value, including null, you can avoid this compiler error message.

This program is called ftest.java and is in the \chapter12 directory on the Companion CD-ROM.

Multiple Tests in a Single Try Block

Obviously, the code in the previous section is somewhat cluttered and confusing to read. However, there is no reason why you can't enclose all of the statements that might throw exceptions in a single try block and make the program easier to code and easier to read. We revise the program to do this in the program ftest2.java:

```
import java.awt.*;
import java.io.*;
class ftest2
{
//------------------------------------
public ftest2()
{
String s = "";
RandomAccessFile f = null;
try    //enclose everything in one try block
  {
  f = new RandomAccessFile("people.add", "r");
  do
```

```
      {
        s = f.readLine( );
      if (s != null)
        System.out.println(s);
      }
    while (s != null);
    }    //end of try block

  catch (IOException e)
      {
      System.out.println(e.getMessage( ));
      e.printStackTrace( );
      }
  }
//------------------------------------
public static void main(String argv[])
  {
  new ftest2( );
  }
  }
```

Catching More Than One Exception

Since we have enclosed more than one method that can throw an exception in our try block, we might expect that we'll need to catch more than one type of exception. It turns out that most of the exceptions you will need to catch are of the class *IOException*, so this doesn't happen that often. However, let's modify the program so that it generates a *null pointer* exception.

As you may recall, the *readLine* method *RandomAccessFile* class does not throw an *EOFException*, but instead simply returns a null for any string once the end of the file is reached. Now the output routine *System.out.println()* handles virtually all data types correctly and converts the reference null to the string null. This does not cause an error.

But suppose we modify the loop to print out the length of each line as well as its contents:

```
do
    {
    s = f.readLine();
    System.out.println(s.length() + " " + s);
    }
while (s != null);
```

Then, when the *f.readLine()* method returns a null, the *s.length()* method will fail on a null pointer. We can trap this by catching both kinds of exceptions in a loop, as follows:

```
try
    {
    f = new RandomAccessFile("people.add", "r");
    do
        {
        s = f.readLine();
        System.out.println(s.length() + " " + s);
        }
    while (s != null);
    }
catch (IOException e)                //file errors here
    {
    System.out.println(e.getMessage());
    e.printStackTrace();
    }
catch (NullPointerException e)   //pointer error here
    {
    System.out.println("exception: "+e.getMessage());
    e.printStackTrace();
    }
```

This final version of the program is called ftest3.java and when run, it prints out the error:

```
exception: null
java.lang.NullPointerException
```

Creating Your Own Exceptions

You can also create your own exceptions by deriving them from the base *Exception* class. Then you can define any method as one that throws that type of exception, and as part of your error checking, simply throw that exception rather than returning an error condition. This sounds very appealing at first, but you should only use this approach if the odds of the exception occurring are *very* unlikely. If this is not the case, your program will perform quite slowly, since the cost of throwing exceptions is quite high.

Building an Input File Class

Even though the *RandomAccessFile* class is fairly powerful, it still doesn't give us the flexibility we are used to in Visual Basic. It is fairly simple, however, to encapsulate all of the functions of this class inside one class with the usual file-reading capabilities.

We would like to build a class that hides all of the exception handling and simulates the Visual Basic statements:

```
input #f, s$        'read to next comma or end of line
line input #f, s$   'read entire line
```

Note that we said we would *encapsulate* the function of the class rather than *extend* the class. We make this distinction because Java does not allow you to extend a class whose constructor methods throw exceptions (except as a new class whose constructor methods throws exceptions).

Java enforces this restriction because of its requirement that the first line in a derived constructor be the call to the *super* method, the constructor of the parent class. Since it must be first, it is not possible to enclose it in a try block. Thus the following is not allowed by Java compilers:

```
public class MyInput extends RandomAccessFile
{
public MyInput(String file)
{
```

```
try
 {
 super(file);      //this is not allowed by the compiler
 }
catch(IOException e)
 {System.out.println("Error");}
 }
```

Instead, we will write a new class that *contains* the *RandomAccessFile* class and then specifically expose the methods from this class that we plan to use. Note that this is similar to the way we derive classes in Visual Basic 4.0, which does not allow inheritance.

We will create a class called *InputFile*, which has a *readLine* and a *read* method. As in the *RandomAccessFile* class, *readLine()* will read to the next newline character, but read will read to the next comma or newline character. Our constructor is:

```
class InputFile
{
RandomAccessFile f = null; //embedded file type
boolean errflag;                   //errors stored here
String s = null;                   //strings read in here
 public InputFile(String fname)
 {
 errflag = false;                  //start with error false
  try
    {
    //open file
    f = new RandomAccessFile(fname, "r");
    }
  catch (IOException e)
    {
    //print error if not found
     System.out.println("no file found");
     errflag = true;    //and set flag
    }
 }
```

Since we are not extending *RandomAccessFile* directly, we will have to write our own *readLine()* method. Fortunately all we have to do is call this method in the embedded class:

```
public String readLine()
 {
//read in a line from the file
s = null;                  //initialize
try
 {
 s = f.readLine();      //could throw error
 }
catch (IOException e)
{
errflag = true;
System.out.println("File read error");
}
return s;
 }
```

With this simple class, we can then rewrite our ftest.java program to be merely:

```
//opens a file and reads it a line at a time
class fclass
{
 public fclass()
 {
String s = "";
InputFile f = new InputFile("people.add");
while ((! f.checkErr()) && (s != null))
 {
   s = f.readLine();          //read one field at a time
   if (s != null)             //only print non-nulls
  System.out.println(s);      //and print it out
 }
 f.close();
 }
```

This is clearly much easier to write and much more readable.

If we want to read in data a field at a time, where the fields on a single line are separated by commas, we simply read in a line at a time as before. We then search for commas, returning the text between commas until none remain, and then returning the remainder of the line:

```java
public String read()
{
//read a single field up to a comma or end of line
String ret = "";
if (s == null)              //if no data in string
   {
   s = readLine();          //read next line
   }
if (s != null)             //if there is data
 {
 s.trim();                 //trim off blanks
 int i = s.indexOf(",");   //find next comma
 if (i <= 0)
   {
   ret = s.trim();         //if no commas go to end of line
   s = null;               //and null out stored string
   }
 else
   {
   //return left of comma
   ret = s.substring(0, i).trim();
   s = s.substring(i+1);   //save right of comma
   }
 }
else
   ret = null;
return ret;                //return string
}
```

Now we can rewrite our calling program only slightly, and we can print out the fields in the file one by one:

```java
class fclass
{
 public fclass()
```

```
{
String s = "";
InputFile f = new InputFile("people.add");
while ((! f.checkErr()) && (s != null))
  {
    s = f.read();           //read one field at a time
    if (s != null)
      System.out.println(s);     //and print it out
  }
f.close();
}
```

Tokenizer Classes in Java

Java has two classes which you can use to break up text into
words or *tokens*. The *StringTokenizer* class takes a String and returns individual tokens, while the *StreamTokenizer* class reads from
a file input stream.

Using the StringTokenizer Class

We could also break a line apart into tokens using the
StringTokenizer class. This class returns groups of characters, or
tokens, separated by any combination of characters you specify. In
this case, we want to return tokens separated by commas and the
newline character:

```
StringTokenizer tok = new StringTokenizer(s, ",\n");
```

Then we return tokens as long as any remain:

```
public String read()
{
 if (tok.hasMoreTokens())
   return tok.nextToken();
 else
   return null;
}
```

The StreamTokenizer Class

The *StreamTokenizer* class is much like the *StringTokenizer* class, but somewhat more powerful. You create a *StreamTokenizer* class using an *InputStream*, such as might come from a file:

```
f = new FileInputStream(new File("people.add"));
    stok = new StreamTokenizer(f);
```

Then you set up the formats you wish to represent using the following methods:

Method	Description
lowerCaseMode(flag)	If flag is true, return all strings converted to lower case
parseNumbers()	tells class to detect and parse numbers
resetSyntax()	sets all characters to "ordinary" so that numbers are not parsed
slashSlashComments(flag)	if flag is true, Java-style // comments are skipped
slashStarComments(flag)	if flag is true, C-style /* comments are skipped

Then to use this class, you obtain each token. The *nextToken()* method returns the type of the token as TT_NUMBER or TT_WORD, and the value of the token is found in the constant fields *nval* or *sval*. The following program illustrates how to use this class:

```java
import java.io.*;

public class fstream
{
FileInputStream f;
```

```
StreamTokenizer stok;
 public fstream()
  {
 int type=0;
//open the file and the tokenizer
 try
   {
  f = new FileInputStream(new File("people.add"));
  stok = new StreamTokenizer(f);
   }
 catch (IOException e)
   {System.out.println("stream open failure");}

//get tokens until EOF is returned
    while (stok.ttype != StreamTokenizer.TT_EOF)
      {
      try {
      type = stok.nextToken();}
      catch (IOException e)
      {System.out.println("bad token");}
      switch (type)          //check type of token
        {
        case StreamTokenizer.TT_WORD:
          System.out.println("s:" + stok.sval);  //word
          break;
    case StreamTokenizer.TT_NUMBER:
          System.out.println("n:" + stok.nval);  //number
          }
       }
   }
  //------------------------------------
  public static void main (String argv[])
   {
  new fstream();
   }
 }
```

Building an Output File Class

Just as we built an *InputFile* class to provide the functionality of the Visual Basic *Input* statement, we can build an Output File class that allows us to print numeric and string data to a file. We will include the ability to space data apart in columns in a manner similar to the VB *Tab(n)* function. Since many word processors prefer tab-separated columns to import data into tables, we will put in the ability to write an actual tab character to a file.

You might assume that we could simply extend the same *RandomAccessFile* class we used for input, but this class is intended primarily for reading and writing binary data. The *PrintStream* class, however, contains *print* methods for all of the standard data types, and it is quite simple to enclose this class inside a new object that will have all of these *output* methods.

However, if you look at the constructors for the *PrintStream* class, you discover that it requires an instance of the *OutputStream* class:

```
public PrintStream(OutputStream  out);
```

And if we look at the *OutputStream* class constructors, we discover that it is a very low-level class that has no connection to data files. Fortunately, the *FileOutputStream* class is derived from the *OutputStream* class and it allows a filename in its constructor:

```
public FileOutputStream(String  name);
```

Thus, the constructor for our *OutFile* class will create an instance of the *FileOutputStream* class that will be used to create an instance of the *PrintStream* class. We will use the instance of the *PrintStream* class within the class whenever one of our methods generates output:

```
public class OutFile
{
  FileOutputStream f;
  PrintStream p;
  boolean errflag;
  int tabcolumn;
//--------------------------------
```

```
public OutFile(String filename)
{
errflag= false;
tabcolumn=0;
try
  {
 //create file output stream
  f= new FileOutputStream(filename);
  }
 catch(IOException e)
  {
  errflag = true;
  }
//create PrintStream using the file output stream
 p = new PrintStream(f);
 }
```

PrintStream Methods

The methods shown below are the *PrintStream* methods we will be wrapping. Each delivers a particular data type to the output stream:

```
public void flush();
public void print(boolean  b);
public void print(char  c);
public void print(char  s[]);
public void print(double  d);
public void print(float  f);
public void print(int  i);
public void print(long  l);
public void print(Object  obj);
public void print(String  s);
public void println();
public void println(boolean  b);
public void println(char  c);
public void println(char  s[]);
public void println(double  d);
```

```
public void println(float  f);
public void println(int  i);
public void println(long  1);
public void println(Object  obj);
public void println(String  s);
```

Again, note that we will have to explicitly name all the methods we wish to use in our *OutFile* class since we aren't extending *PrintStream* but instead wrapping another class around it. However, this is not on onerous task, because we need to count the characters delivered by each method anyway. This will allow us to keep out columns lined up.

In this class, we will convert each kind of variable directly to a string and then use our own *print* method for strings to keep count of the number of characters to the next tab column:

```
public void print(String s)
{
 p.print(s);
 tabcolumn += s.length();
}
```

Then, when we need to print spaces up to a specified column, we know how many are required:

```
public void tab(int tb)
{
if (tb > tabcolumn)
 {
 print(space(tb - tabcolumn));
 }
else
  println("");
}
```

The *space* method above emulates VB's *Space$* function; it returns a string containing the number of spaces you specify. In Java, the *String* class produces constant strings; you can't change them after they are directed.

However, you can create strings whose contents you can change using the *StringBuffer* class, which has an *insert* method. Our *space* method is:

```
public String space(int n)
{
 StringBuffer sb = new StringBuffer(n);
 //put spaces into string buffer
 for (int i=0; i < n; i++)
  {
  sb.insert(i, ' ');
  }
 return sb.toString();
}
```

The program outclass.java in the \chapter12 directory on the Companion CD-ROM prints a few lines to a file. It is merely:

```
public class outclass
{
  public outclass()
  {
  OutFile p = new OutFile("foo.txt");
  p.print("fooie");
  p.tab(12);
  p.println(123.45);
  p.close();
}
//-----------------------------------
public static void main(String argv[])
  {
  new outclass();
  }
}
```

The actual *OutFile* class is in the separate file OutFile.java in the same directory. Since it is in your classpath and referred to by the outclass program, it is automatically compiled when you compile outclass and loaded when you run the Java interpreter. The following code shows the complete *OutFile* class:

```java
import java.io.*;
//=================================
//Output file class
public class OutFile
{
 FileOutputStream f;
 PrintStream p;
 boolean errflag;
 int tabcolumn;
 int width;
//----------------------------------
 public OutFile(String filename)
 {
 errflag = false;
 tabcolumn = 0;
 width = 0;
 try
  {
  f= new FileOutputStream(filename);
  }
  catch(IOException e)
   {
   errflag = true;
   }
 p = new PrintStream(f);
 }
//----------------------------------
public void tab()
{
//put a tab in the output file
p.print("\t");
}
//----------------------------------
public String space(int n)
{
 StringBuffer sb = new StringBuffer(n);
 //put spaces into string buffer
```

```
  for (int i=0; i < n; i++)
   {
   sb.insert(i, ' ');
   }
  return sb.toString();
}
//-----------------------------------
public void setWidth(int n)
{
width = n;
}
//-----------------------------------
public void tab(int tb)
{
if (tb > tabcolumn)
 {
 print(space(tb - tabcolumn));
 }
else
  println("");
}
//-----------------------------------
public void println(String s)
{
 p.print(s+"\r\n");
 tabcolumn = 0;
}
//-----------------------------------
public void println(int i)
{
 p.print(i+"\r\n");
 tabcolumn = 0;
}
//-----------------------------------
public void println(double d)
{
 tabcolumn = 0;
 p.print(d+"\r\n");
}
```

```java
//-----------------------------------
public void print(String s)
{
 if (s.length() < width)
   print(space(width-s.length()) );
 p.print(s);
 tabcolumn += s.length();
}
//-----------------------------------
public void print(int i)
{
String s=new Integer(i).toString();
print(s);
}
//-----------------------------------
public void print(float f)
{
 String s=new Float(f).toString();
 print(s);
}
//-----------------------------------
public void print(double d)
{
 String s=new Double(d).toString();
 print(s);
}
//-----------------------------------
public void close()
{
p.close();
}
//-----------------------------------
public void finalize()
{
close();
}
//-----------------------------------
}
```

Using the File Class

The *File* class allows you to manipulate files and directories on any of your disk drives. Using the *File* class, you can move through directories, create new directories, and delete and rename files. While you can determine the "current directory" from which the program was launched, Java does not have the concept of changing to a new current directory. You can move to new directories and determine their absolute path to use in reading or writing files.

File Methods

When we create an instance of a File object, we can then utilize any of the following methods to determine its properties:

```
public boolean canRead();
public boolean canWrite();
public boolean delete();
public boolean equals(Object  obj);
public boolean exists();
public String getAbsolutePath();
public String getName();
public String getParent();
public String getPath();
public int hashCode();
public boolean isAbsolute();
public boolean isDirectory();
public boolean isFile();
public long lastModified();
public long length();
public String[] list();
public String[] list(FilenameFilter  filter);
public boolean mkdir();
public boolean mkdirs();
public boolean renameTo(File  dest);
```

While some operating systems allow you to use either the backslash \ or the forward slash / character for separating directory and subdirectory names, others are less forgiving. Fortunately the separator string for your system is stored in the static string *File.separator* and you can use it completely independent of the actual platform your program is running on:

```
String fl = f.getAbsolutePath() + File.separator + st;
```

Probably the most useful method in the *File* class is the *exists()* method. You can create a file object and find out if it exists without causing an error or exception:

```
File f = new File("nail.txt");
if (f.exists())
  System.out.println("The file exists");
```

You can also delete or rename such a file just as easily:

```
if (f.exists())
  {
f.renameTo("file.txt");    //either rename
f.delete();                //or delete
  }
```

Moving Through Directories

You must start by finding out what directory your program is running in. This information is available as *user.dir*, one of 15 named system properties that Java saves when the interpreter starts:

```
String thisdir = System.getProperty("user.dir");
```

Once you have the name of any directory, you can obtain either:

◆ a list of files (and subdirectories) in that directory, or

◆ the name of the parent directory.

The list of files in that directory is available using the File object's *list()* method. You can examine each name and determine whether it is a file or a subdirectory using the *isDirectory()* method. The *isFile()* method is not an exact complement. System files and hidden files will return false from the *isFile()* method.

If you want to open a new directory, just create a file object having that path and reload the list boxes using the *list()* method.

Figure 12-1 shows a simple, visual program for exploring files and directories. The code for this program is shown below and is on the Companion CD-ROM as filedir.java:

```java
import java.awt.*;
import java.io.*;
//displays a file and directory list box
//and an "up directory" button
//clicking on a directory entry causes the
//program to open that directory
public class filedir extends Frame
{
List fdir;                //directory list
List flist;               //filename list
Button updir;             //up directory button
File f;
String[] filelist;        //list of files
//---------------------------------------------
public filedir()
{
super("File and directory list");   //title
setLayout(new BorderLayout());
updir = new Button("Up Dir");   //button
Panel p0 = new Panel();
add("North", p0);
p0.add(updir);                      //panel for button
Panel p1 = new Panel();             //panel for lists
add("Center", p1);
fdir = new List(10, false);
p1.add(fdir);
flist = new List(10, false);
p1.add(flist);

//start with current directory
loadlists(System.getProperty("user.dir"));
reshape(100, 100,400,300);
show();
}
//---------------------------------------------
public boolean action (Event evt, Object arg)
```

```java
   {
   //if button is clicked move up one directory
   String p =f.getParent();
   if (p == null)
     p = f.pathSeparator;
   loadlists(p);                    //and reload list boxes
   return true;
   }
//----------------------------------------------
   private void loadlists(String p)
   {
   f = new File(p);                 //create new obj each time
   setTitle(f.getAbsolutePath());
   filelist =f.list();
   //clear out lists
   fdir.delItems(0, fdir.countItems()-1);
   flist.delItems(0, flist.countItems()-1);

   for (int i = 0; i < filelist.length; i++)
     {
     File file = new
File(f.getAbsolutePath()+"\\"+filelist[i]);
     //put in one list or the other
     if ( file.isDirectory())
       fdir.addItem(filelist[i]);
     else
       flist.addItem(filelist[i]);
     }
   }
//----------------------------------------------
public boolean handleEvent(Event evt)
{
 if (evt.id == Event.WINDOW_DESTROY)
   {
   System.exit(0);
   return true;
   }
```

```
else
 if ((evt.id == Event.LIST_SELECT) && (evt.target == fdir))
  {
  //open directory that was clicked on
  String st =fdir.getSelectedItem();
  loadlists(f.getAbsolutePath() + File.separator + st);
  return true;
  }
else
return super.handleEvent(evt);
}
//-----------------------------------------
 public static void main(String argv[])
  {
  new filedir();
  }
//-----------------------------------------
 }
```

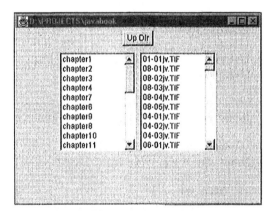

Figure 12-1: The display of files and directories from the filedir.java program.

The FilenameFilter Interface

The FilenameFilter is an interface that you can use to create a class to filter filenames, returning only those of interest to your application. You can write any kind of class you want as long as it implements the FilenameFilter interface. This interface amounts to only one method:

```
public boolean accept(File dir, String name)
```

You write any sort of method you want to examine the directory and filename and return either *true* or *false*. Then you tell the *list* method of the *File* class the name of the class you created. It passes every filename through the *accept* method of your class and receives either *true* or *false* back.

To use a FilenameFilter, we create a class that implements that interface:

```
class FileFilter implements FilenameFilter
{
Vector extnlist;
 public FileFilter(String s)
 {
 extnlist =new Vector();
 extnlist.addElement(s);
 }
//------------------------------------------
 public boolean accept(File dir, String name)
 {
 boolean found = false;
 for (int i =0; i< extnlist.size(); i++)
   {
   found =found ||
       (name.endsWith((String)extnlist.elementAt(i)));
   found = found ||
       new File(dir+File.separator+name).isDirectory();
   }
 return found;
 }
```

```
//-------------------------------------------
 public void addExtension(String s)
 {
 extnlist.addElement(s);
 }
 //--------------------------------------------
 }
```

Our *FileFilter* class has a constructor that saves one type of file extension. We also include an *addExtension* method to add additional ones. Then, in the *accept* method, we filter each filename against a list of possibilities. Here we allow any file extension in the vector *extnlist* and also allow any name that is a directory.

We modify our calling program to make use of this filter as follows:

```
private void loadlists(String p) {
 //first create file filter:
 FileFilter filter = new FileFilter("class");
 filter.addExtension("java");
 f = new File(p);            //create new obj each time
 filelist =f.list(filter); //create filtered list
```

The remainder of the program is the same as in the previous example. The complete program is filedir2.java on the Companion CD-ROM.

File Selection

The above two programs work on a single disk drive. Java does not currently provide a way to obtain the names of other drives on your computer or attached over the network. If you need to move between drives, however, Java provides a method to call the operating system's file dialog box. The FileDialog object allows you to bring up a File/Open or a File/Save As dialog using the following simple constructor:

```
public FileDialog(Frame  parent, String  title,
            int  mode);
```

where *mode* can be either FileDialog.LOAD or FileDialog.SAVE. You simply create the object and execute it's *show* method. The file dialog is shown as a *modal* dialog, meaning that no other windows can get the focus until it is closed:

```
fdlg = new FileDialog(this, "Open a File", FileDialog.LOAD);
fdlg.show();
System.out.println(fdlg.getDirectory());
System.out.println(fdlg.getFile());
```

The *getDirectory* and *getFile* methods return the directory and filename you selected. The FileDialog is supposed to support use of a FilenameFilter, but it has not been implemented in Java 1.0 in either Windows or in OS/2. If you bring up the file dialog in Save mode and select an existing filename, it asks if you want to replace that file and only exits if you answer by clicking on Yes. The program filedlg.java on the Companion CD-ROM illustrates the use of the file dialog. This program is illustrated in Figures 12-2 and 12-3.

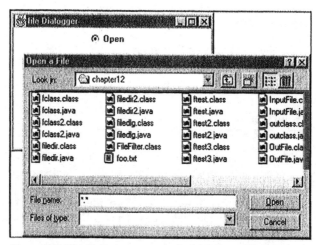

Figure 12-2: The filedlg.java program for initiating a file dialog.

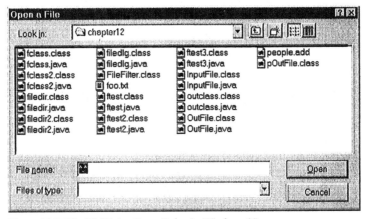

Figure 12-3: The FileDialog Open dialog in Windows 95.

Moving On

We've covered quite a number of ways to use files in Java in this chapter. To make using files easier, we created *InputFile* and *OutputFile* classes, basing them on the *RandomAccessFile* and *PrintStream* classes, respectively. We also learned how to navigate through directories in Java and how to use the FilenameFilter interface. Finally, we learned how to bring up the standard File/Open and File/Save dialogs.

Next we're going to take up displaying images and using threads in Java. Then we'll look into some more elaborate applications and applets.

13

Using Threads in Java

One of the most powerful features of Java is its ability to execute several threads within the same program. When you think of a multitasking system like Windows 95 or UNIX, you recognize that you can start several programs at the same time and have them all appear to be running "at once." Of course, what is really happening is that each program takes a turn receiving a fraction or *slice* of the available time from the underlying operating system's scheduler. Thus, it is not unusual for Windows 95 users to keep a mail program, a Web browser, and a word processor all running at once. Each program or *process* gets time successively if it has work to do.

In the same manner, you can subdivide a program into little processes called *threads* and have them execute simultaneously, each getting successive time slices from your operating system. The difference is that within your program, you must somehow tell the operating system how you want to break up your program into threads and when you want them to start executing.

One of the great strengths of Java over most other languages is that you can write a multithreaded program very simply by making just a few changes to a single-threaded program. In fact, Java makes this kind of multitasking trivially simple compared to almost any other language.

The Thread Object

Of course, in Java, a thread is an object with a set of methods associated with it. Below we list the most important *Thread* methods.

```
public void checkAccess();
public void destroy();
public static int enumerate(Thread tarray[]);
public final String getName();
public final int getPriority();
public final ThreadGroup getThreadGroup();
public void interrupt();
public static boolean interrupted();
public final boolean isAlive();
public final boolean isDaemon();
public boolean isInterrupted();
public final void join();
public final void join(long millis);
public final void resume();
public void run();
public final void setDaemon(boolean on);
public final void setName(String name);
public final void setPriority(int newPriority);
public static void sleep(long millis);
public void start();
public final void stop();
public final void suspend();
public static void yield();
```

As you can see, you can start, stop, suspend, and resume threads, as well as create and destroy them. The most important of these methods is the *run* method, although you never call it yourself. Instead, the operating system calls it for you when it is that thread's turn to receive a time slice.

Making a Class Into a Thread

There are two ways to make a class into a thread. You can either extend the *Thread* class:

```
class Timer extends Thread
```

or if your class is already the descendent of another class, you can simply indicate that it implements the Runnable interface:

```
class ThreadList extends Frame implements Runnable
```

Now the Runnable interface simply indicates that that class has a *run* method:

```
public interface java.lang.Runnable
{
    public abstract void run();
}
```

and in fact, all you need to do is include a *run* method and that method will execute in a separate thread.

Reasons for Using Threads

The trouble with most explanations of threads is that they never tell you what they're for, unless you want to use them to write little animation programs. While such animations are diverting, they are by no means the most significant purpose of threads. Threaded programs allow you to take their time-consuming parts and execute them as background processes while the user interface remains lively and interactive.

To illustrate this point, let's consider a program that needs to load a large number of names into a list box. This program will essentially freeze until the data are completely read from the input file. We'll first write this program using a single process without threads so you can see how easy it is to change and so you can try both versions on the Companion CD-ROM. We are going to read in a list of names from the file spnames.txt and add them to the list box. We'll use the *InputFile* class we developed in Chapter 12 to save time:

```java
import java.awt.*;
class LoadList extends Frame
    {
    private List namelist;          //listbox
    private Button openit, closit;  //and two buttons
    //-------------------------------------
    public LoadList()
        {
        super ("Normal List loader"); //title bar
        setLayout(new BorderLayout());
        namelist = new List(15, false); //create list
        openit = new Button("Open");    //and buttons
        closit = new Button("Close");
        Panel p1 = new Panel();
        add("Center",namelist);         //add list to middle
        add("South", p1);               //and panel to bottom
        p1.add(openit);
        p1.add(closit);                 //add buttons to panel
        reshape (100, 100, 250,300);
        show();
        }
    //-------------------------------------------
    public boolean action (Event evt, Object arg)
        {
        if (evt.target == openit)
            {
            clickedOpenit();       //open and load file
            return true;
            }
        else
        if (evt.target == closit)
            {
            clickedClosit();       //exit on close
            return true;
            }
```

```
else
return super.action(evt, arg);
}
//------------------------------------
private void clickedClosit()
{
System.exit(0);
}
//------------------------------------
public void clickedOpenit()
{
//read in data file
InputFile f = new InputFile("spnames.txt");
String s = "";
while (s != null)
  {
  s = f.readLine();      //read a line at a time
  if (s != null)
    namelist.addItem(s);//and add to list
  }
f.close();
}
//------------------------------------
public static void main(String argv[])
 {
 new LoadList();
 }
}
```

The significant part of this program is the *clickedOpenit*
method, which is executed when the user clicks on Open. It
opens the file and reads it a line at a time, loading it into the
list box. The display it produces is shown in Figure 13-1. The
program is called LoadList.java, and it is in the \chapter13
directory of the Companion CD-ROM.

During the time the file is being read in, you can click on Close
and it will appear to press in, but nothing will happen; the program
will not exit. There is no response because the graphics methods
run in their own thread in Java, and have no effect on the program
execution thread, which is busy reading the file.

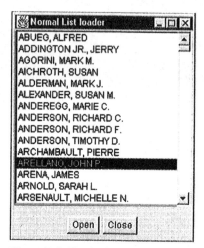

Figure 13-1: The single-threaded version of the LoadList program.

Adding Threads to the LoadList Program

Now let's consider how we could make a small change in this program that will allow it to react to other user commands while it is reading in the list of names. In the program above, all the time-consuming activity is localized in the *clickedOpenit* method. If we could make that method run in another thread, we could make the program respond at once to other button clicks.

In order to convert this program, we need to do only three things:

◈ Add *implements Runnable* to the class definition.

◈ Put the time-consuming code in a *run* method.

◈ Create an instance of the *Thread* class within this class, and call its *start* method.

This simple set of changes gives us the following program (changes indicated in **bold**):

```
import java.awt.*;
class ThreadList extends Frame implements Runnable
{
private List namelist;        //listbox
private Button openit, closit; //and two buttons
private Thread filler;        //here is the thread
//-------------------------------------
public ThreadList()
{
super ("Threaded List loader"); //title bar
setLayout(new BorderLayout());
namelist = new List(15, false); //create list
openit = new Button("Open");    //and buttons
closit = new Button("Close");
Panel p1 = new Panel();
add("Center",namelist);         //add list to middle
add("South", p1);               //and panel to bottom
p1.add(openit);
p1.add(closit);                 //add buttons to panel
reshape (100, 100, 250,300);
show();
}
//---------------------------------------------
public boolean action (Event evt, Object arg)
{
if (evt.target == openit)
  {
  filler = new Thread(this); //instance of thread
  filler.start();   //same as clickedOpenit
  return true;
  }
else
if (evt.target == closit)
  {
  clickedClosit();        //exit on close
  return true;
  }
else
return super.action(evt, arg);
```

```
}
//------------------------------------
private void clickedClosit()
{
System.exit(0);
}
//------------------------------------
public void run()
{
//read in data file
InputFile f = new InputFile("spnames.txt");
String s = "";
while (s != null)
  {
  s = f.readLine();     //read a line at a time
  if (s != null)
    namelist.addItem(s);//and add to list
  }
f.close();
}
//------------------------------------
public static void main(String argv[])
 {
 new ThreadList();
 }
}
```

Let's consider how these changes work. By including *implements Runnable*, we are simply saying that the class will have a *run* method. Then, when someone clicks on Open, we create an instance of a thread with:

```
filler = new Thread(this);  //instance of thread
```

This creates a thread that can be started within the current instance of this class. Note that we use the reserved word *this* to indicate that we mean the current instance of *ThreadList*, not some new instance. Then, to launch code that will run in a separate thread, all we have to do is start the thread:

```
filler.start();
```

You might find these last two operations confusing. The only instance of the *ThreadList* class is running as a main thread. How can we also have it running in another thread? We don't, of course. The code that runs in the new thread is contained in this class's *run* method. The rest of the code continues to run in the main thread. Again, note that we never call the *run* method. We launch the thread by calling *start*: the Java thread system calls the *run* method when that thread is to be given a time slice.

This version of the program is called ThreadList.java in the \chapter13 directory of the Companion CD-ROM. The running program display is shown in Figure 13-2. The only difference is that if you click on Close while the list is loading, the program will exit immediately. Note that since Visual Basic has no direct analog to threads or multitasking in general, there is no exact way to carry out this sort of multithreaded program in VB.

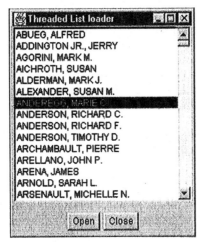

Figure 13-2: The multithreaded ThreadList program. You do not have to wait for the list box to fill before the buttons become active.

Another Syntax for Starting a Thread

The Java documentation suggests that you create a thread for the current instance of the class using the code:

```
new Thread(this).start();        //start the thread
```

This is really the same thing as the ThreadList code in more compressed and less readable form. We create a thread and start it in one statement instead of two. This is just an example of how to write unclear code, like the ternary operator we discussed in Chapter 3. The compiler will generate the same code for either of them. A program using this terser method is provided as ThreadList2.java on the Companion CD-ROM.

Several Threads in the Same Program

You can also write programs in which a single class is used for several threads at once. Most of the examples of running several instances of the same class in threads come from visual effects such as animation. Let's suppose we want to write a program where two squares blink on and off at different rates. To compare Java with Visual Basic, we'll start by writing the program in VB.

The Visual Basic Program

Our VB form will consist of two picture boxes and a Start push button. In order to have the boxes swap colors at different rates, we'll also need two Timer controls. The layout for this program is shown in Figure 13-3 and the executing program is shown in Figure 13-4.

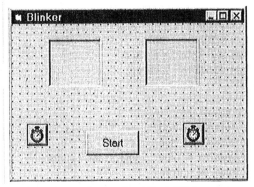

Fig 13-3: Layout for the Visual Basic Blinker program.

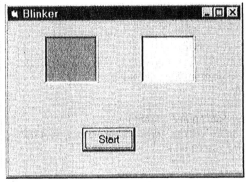

Fig 13-4: Executing the Visual Basic Blinker program showing the two boxes that blink.

While we could make some sort of a class out of our Timer control *tick* event and have two instances of it, there is no real advantage since we can't make the timer and its related picture box part of the same class. The program code for this VB version of our Blinker program is:

```
Option Explicit
Private color1 As Long   'colors for pictures
Private color2 As Long
'-------------------------------------
```

```
Private Sub Form_Load()
color1 = vbRed            'starting colors
color2 = vbBlue
Picture1.BackColor = color1
Picture2.BackColor = color2
End Sub
'----------------------------------------
Private Sub Start_Click()
Timer1.Interval = 500    'set intervals
Timer2.Interval = 300
Timer1.Enabled = True    'and start timers
Timer2.Enabled = True
End Sub
'----------------------------------------
Private Sub Timer1_Timer()
If color1 = vbRed Then  'swap colors at tick
  color1 = vbGreen
Else
  color1 = vbRed
End If
Picture1.BackColor = color1
End Sub
'----------------------------------------
Private Sub Timer2_Timer()
If color2 = vbBlue Then  'swap colors at tick
  color2 = vbYellow
Else
  color2 = vbBlue
End If
Picture2.BackColor = color2
End Sub
```

In this program, we create two picture boxes and two Timer
controls and use one timer for changing the color of each picture
box. Then we need the two timer *tick* routines shown above to
switch the colors of the two picture boxes. We'll soon see that the
Java version is somewhat more elegant.

A Java Version of the Blinker Program

In the Java Blinker program below, we create a panel class with the Runnable interface. Then the instances of this class are run as separate threads to allow them to blink between two colors at different rates; in this case, 0.5 sec and 0.3 sec.

Rather than using anything like the *Timer* class approach of Visual Basic, we use the thread's *sleep* method to delay execution within that thread for a specified interval. The *run* method is just a continuous loop with the *sleep* method delaying its execution each time:

```
//almost all of the run method
while (true)
  {
  if (thiscolor == color1)
    thiscolor = color2;
  else
    thiscolor = color1;
  setBackground(thiscolor);
  repaint();                        //redraw in thiscolor
  Thread.sleep(interval);           //almost all
  }
```

You will note that we inserted a couple of caveats in the comments for this routine. Since it is possible that the *sleep* method could be interrupted, the Java compiler requires that we catch exceptions surrounding the *sleep* method:

```
try {
    Thread.sleep(interval);
    }
catch(InterruptedException e) {};
```

The complete Java version of the blinker program is on the Companion CD-ROM as Blinker.java and is shown on the next few pages. The running program is shown in Figure 13-5.

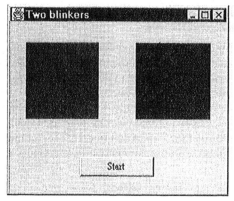

Figure 13-5: The Java Blinker program.

```java
import java.awt.*;
import java.util.*;
//Blinks two squares at different rates
public class Blinker extends Frame
{
Button start;   //start pushbutton
Blinky b1, b2;  //timed panels
//----------------------------------------
 public Blinker()
 {
 super("Two blinkers");          //title bar
 setLayout(null);
 //create two instances of panel class that
 //is a runnable thread
 b1 = new Blinky(Color.red, Color.green, 500);
 b2 = new Blinky(Color.blue, Color.yellow, 300);
 b1.reshape(25, 50, 100,100);
 b2.reshape(175, 50, 100,100);
 add(b1);
 add(b2);
 //add start button
 start = new Button("Start");
 add(start);
```

```
 start.reshape(100,200,100,25);
 reshape(100,100,300,250);
 show();
 }
//-------------------------------------
public boolean action(Event evt,Object arg)
{
 b1.start(); //Start button clicked
 b2.start();
 return true;
}
//-------------------------------------
public boolean handleEvent(Event evt)
  {
 if (evt.id == Event.WINDOW_DESTROY)
   {
   System.exit(0);  //exit
   return true;
   }
else
  return super.handleEvent(evt);
  }
//-------------------------------------
public static void main(String argv[])
  {
 new Blinker();
  }
}
//=================================
class Blinky extends Panel implements Runnable
{
Color color1, color2, thiscolor;
int interval;
Thread blinkit;

public Blinky(Color c1, Color c2, int intval)
 {
 color1 = c1;            //store colors
 color2 = c2;
```

```java
  interval = intval;     //store interval
  thiscolor= color1;
  setBackground(color1);
  }
//-------------------------------------
public void start()
{
  blinkit = new Thread(this);    //create a thread
  blinkit.start();               //and start it
  }
//-------------------------------------
public void run()
{
  while (true)
  {
  if (thiscolor == color1)
    thiscolor = color2;
  else
    thiscolor = color1;
  setBackground(thiscolor);
  repaint();
  try {
    Thread.sleep(interval);
      }
  catch (InterruptedException e) {};
  }
 }
//-------------------------------------
 }
```

Building a Timer Class

You can also build classes that are derived directly from the *Thread* class. Even in these classes you must override the *run* method and include the code you want to have executed in a separate thread. Let's build a class like the Visual Basic Timer control, which you can set to "tick" at a specified rate.

This class will delay and then execute a tick at a specified interval. The question is, how will it tell the parent class that it has ticked, and how can we make this a general feature? This is where the idea of an *interface* becomes extremely useful. We'll define an interface *Ticker* as follows:

```
interface Ticker
  {
  public abstract void tick();
  }
```

Now all this says is that whatever class implements the Ticker interface must have a method called *tick()*. This is very useful because we now can have a way for the parent class of our timer to tell the *Timer* class where to notify that the time for a tick occurs. The *Timer* class itself is just the following:

```
class Timer extends Thread
  {
  int interval;
  Ticker parent = null;
  //-----------------------------------
  public Timer(Ticker obj, int intval)
    {
    interval = intval;
    parent = obj;
    }
  //-----------------------------------
  public void run()
    {
    while (true)
      {
      parent.tick();
      try  {
        sleep(interval);
        }
      catch(InterruptedException e) {};
      }
    }
  }
```

Note that this *Timer* class is derived from Thread and therefore has all of its methods without any special interface or reference to the *Thread* class. Thus, we can call the *sleep()* method directly.

The class constructor passes in a reference to the parent class that creates Timer and the value of the timing interval. Note that the type of the parent is declared to be Ticker, meaning that the parent class has a *tick()* method. It doesn't matter that the parent class is really of type TimerBox and that it only implements the interface Ticker. The advantage of this approach is that a parent class of any type at all can use the *Timer* class, as long as it implements the Ticker interface.

Then the timer's *run* method simply loops forever, calling tick in the parent class and then sleeping for the specified interval. Now let's discuss how we can use this *Timer* class in a real program.

The TimerBox Program

The TimerBox program, included on the Companion CD-ROM as TimerBox.java, is another simple example program that causes a square to change color. You can start and stop the flashing using two buttons as shown in Figure 13-6.

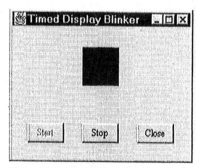

Figure 13-6: The TimerBox program.

```
class TimerBox extends Frame implements Ticker
{
private Button start, stop, close;  //three buttons
private Panel bpanel;
private Timer timer;
private Color color;
//------------------------------------
public TimerBox()
{
super ("Timed Display Blinker");  //title bar
setLayout(null);
addNotify();
start = new Button("Start");      //and buttons
stop = new Button("Stop");
close = new Button("Close");
bpanel = new Panel();             //create blinking
add(bpanel);                      //panel
bpanel.reshape(100,50,50,50);
add(start);
add(stop);                        //add buttons to panel
add(close);
start.reshape(25,150,50,25);      //start a timer
stop.reshape(100,150,50,25);      //stop a timer
close.reshape(175,150,50,25);     //close program
reshape (100, 100, 250,200);
color = Color.red;                //initial color
bpanel.setBackground(color);      //of blinking panel
show();
}
//--------------------------------------------
public void tick()
{
//called by Timer class
if (color == Color.blue)          //swap colors
  color = Color.red;
else
  color = Color.blue;
bpanel.setBackground(color);      //and chg color
bpanel.repaint();                 //of panel
}
```

```
//----------------------------------------------
public boolean action (Event evt, Object arg)
{
if (evt.target == start)    //start button
  {
  timer = new Timer(this, 200);        //create timer
  timer.start();              //begin timer ticking
  start.disable();            //turn off start button
  return true;
  }
else
if (evt.target == stop)   //stop button
  {
  timer.stop();        //stop timer
  start.enable();          //turn on start button
  return true;
  }
else
 if (evt.target == close) //close button
 {
 System.exit(0);          //program exit
 return true;             //for completeness
 }
return super.action(evt, arg);
}
//----------------------------------------
public static void main(String argv[])
 {
 new TimerBox();
 }
}
```

Note that our *TimerBox* class extends the *Frame* class and implements the Ticker interface. Then because it has an interface of type Ticker, the compiler will allow it to create an instance of *Timer* and pass in the current instance of *TimerBox* using *this*. When the *Timer* class ticks, it calls this class's *tick* method, which then switches the color of the panel and calls the *repaint()* method to change the color on the screen.

Since the *Timer* class is derived directly from *Thread*, it already has *start* and *stop* methods, and we use them with the push buttons on the user interface to start the timer. Since we create the timer when we click on Start, we destroy the timer when we click on Stop.

Synchronized Methods

A *synchronized* method can be called by only one thread at a time. If several threads try to call it at once, all but one are put on hold until the first one has left that method. This sort of method is needed when you need to make sure that two threads don't attempt to change data at the same time.

For example, whenever you are keeping numerical totals of any kind and a thread reads a value, increments it, and puts it back, you want to make sure that other threads aren't doing this at the same time. This sort of access protection is clearly needed in any sort of financial or accounting program where two threads should not attempt to modify a bank balance at the same time and write it back to the total.

The Model Town Bank

Let's consider a simple model of a town bank. To keep it really simple, we'll assume that there are five depositors who transact business only with each other. As the curtain rises, each depositor happens to have exactly $1,000 in his or her account. We employ one teller to fetch each person's records, withdraw from one person's account, and deposit to another person's account.

Now let's assume that business picks up suddenly: a casino opens or a Ponzi scheme begins to flourish and the depositors transact so much business in a day that the bank has to hire two more tellers to keep up. (Never mind where they keep *their* money.) Now it becomes more difficult: more than one teller may need access to a person's account at a time in order to withdraw or deposit money.

Let's represent our tellers by three threads and our accounts by an array of integers, to avoid accidental roundoff errors. If we write a program to illustrate this behavior, we simply use a random number generator to decide which two customers are transacting business, and in the interests of ever-increasing job specialization, we assign each teller a single transaction amount: one will do all one dollar transactions, one will do all five dollar transactions, and one will do only seven dollar transactions.

We give each teller access to the array of depositors' balances and start them working, moving money around like mad. The Balances.java program is on the Companion CD-ROM and is shown below.

```java
import java.awt.*;

class Balances extends Frame
{
  Label names[];          //array of customer name labels
  TextField sbalances[]; //displayed array of balances
  int balances[];          //integer array of balances
  Button start, stop;     //buttons to start and stop
  int sum;
  String s;
  Teller teller1, teller2, teller3;      //3 Tellers
  //----------------------------------
  public Balances()
  {
    super("Balance sheet");             //title bar
    setLayout(new BorderLayout());
    setBackground(Color.lightGray);
    Panel p1 = new Panel();     //holds names & balances
    Panel p2 = new Panel();     //holds buttons
    add("South", p2);
    add("Center", p1);
    p1.setLayout(new GridLayout(6, 2));
    balances = new int[5];          //array of balances
    sbalances = new TextField[6];   //displayed balances
    sum =0;
    names = new Label[6];
    names[0] = new Label("Alfie");
    names[1]= new Label("Bonnie");
```

```
              names[2] = new Label("Charlie");
              names[3] = new Label("Daphne");
              names[4] = new Label("Essie");
              names[5] = new Label("TOTAL");
              for (int i =0; i< 5; i++)
                {
                balances[i] = 1000;          //initialize balances
                sum += balances[i];
               s = new Integer(balances[i]).toString();
                sbalances[i] = new TextField(s);
                Panel p = new Panel();
                p1.add(p);
                p1.add(names[i]);
                p.add(sbalances[i]);
                p1.add(p);
                }
            s = new Float(sum).toString();
            sbalances[5] = new TextField(s);
             Panel p = new Panel();
             p1.add(names[5]);               //add in TOTAL and
             p1.add(p);
             p.add(sbalances[5]);            //display sum
             start = new Button("Start"); //add in buttons
             stop = new Button("Stop");
             p2.add(start);
             p2.add(stop);
             reshape(100,100,300,250);
             show();
             }
        //------------------------------------
        public void paint(Graphics g)
        {
        //repaint values each time
        float sum =0;
        for (int i=0; i< 5; i++)
           {
           String s = new Integer(balances[i]).toString();
           sbalances[i].setText(s);
           sum += balances[i];
           }
        sbalances[5].setText( new Float(sum).toString());
        }
```

```
//-------------------------------------
public void clickedStart()
{
//start tellers running about
 teller1 = new Teller(balances, 1);    //always $1
 teller2 = new Teller(balances, 5);    //always $5
 teller3 = new Teller(balances, 7);    //always $7
 teller1.start();
 teller2.start();                      //start your tellers!
 teller3.start();
 start.disable();                      //only once
 }
//-------------------------------------
public void clickedStop()
{
  teller1.stop();                      //stop tellers
  teller2.stop();
  teller3.stop();
  start.enable();                      //allow restarting
  repaint();
 }
//-------------------------------------
public boolean action(Event evt, Object arg)
{
if (evt.target == start)
 {
 clickedStart();
 return true;
 }
else
 if (evt.target == stop)
  {
  clickedStop();
  return true;
  }
else
  return super.action(evt, arg);
 }
//-------------------------------------
```

```java
    public static void main(String argv[])
    {
    new Balances();
    }
}
//=========================================
class Teller extends Thread
{
int count;
float amount;
int balances[];
 //-----------------------------------
 public Teller(int accounts[], float amt)
 {
 count = accounts.length;    //total number of customers
 amount = amt;                     //save amount to move
 balances = accounts;
 }
 //-----------------------------------
public void run()
{
 while (true)
 {
 //compute customer to move money from and to
 int from = (int)Math.round(Math.random() *(count-1));
 int to = (int)Math.round(Math.random() *(count-1));
if (from != to)
 {
//move money
 int fbalance = balances[from];
 int tbalance = balances[to];
 fbalance -= amount;
 tbalance += amount;
 balances[from] = fbalance;
 balances[to] = tbalance;
 }
 }
}
 //-----------------------------------
 }
```

Now, if we run this program, click on Start, let it execute for a minute or so, and then click on Stop, we find that the total is no longer $5,000! This is illustrated in Figure 13-7.

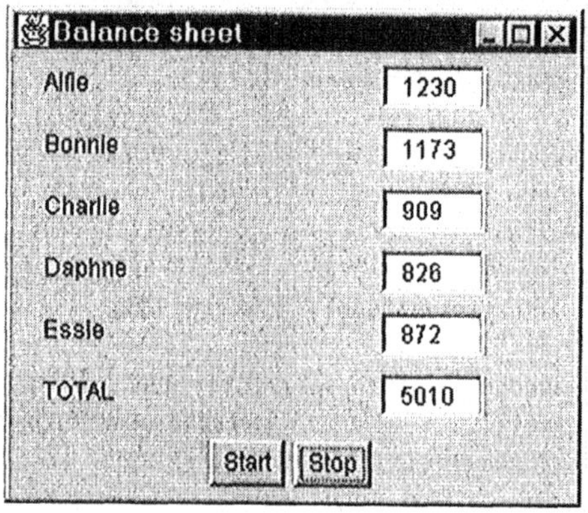

Figure 13-7: The Balances program, showing how parallel actions can result in out-of-balance accounts.

What happened? Is one of our tellers light-fingered? Well, if you look at the code in the *Teller* class, it laboriously fetches the balances, adds and subtracts the amount specified, and puts it back:

```
//move money
 int fbalance = balances[from];
 int tbalance = balances[to];
 fbalance -= amount;
 tbalance += amount;
 balances[from] = fbalance;
 balances[to] = tbalance;
```

If we consider what each teller is doing, we realize that it is perfectly possible for two tellers to be handing the same account at once, and both to be subtracting or adding money at the same time. This leads to the out-of-balance accounts shown in Figure 13-7.

A Bureaucratic Solution

The obvious bureaucratic solution is to prevent more than one teller from accessing the balances at a time. We could do this by creating a synchronized *moveMoney* method in the main program:

```
public synchronized void moveMoney(int from,
                   int to, float amt)
 //this routine moves money from customer "from"
 //to customer number "to"
 {
 if (from != to)              //but not if same person
 {
 int frombalance = balances[from]; //get each balance
 int tobalance = balances[to];
 frombalance -= amt;          //withdraw from one
 tobalance += amt;            //and deposit to other
 balances[from] = frombalance;  //put back
 balances[to] = tobalance;
 }
```

Then each teller receives a reference to the calling class and calls that *moveMoney* method as needed:

```
class Teller extends Thread
 {
 int count;
 Balances1 bank;          //calling class ref
 float amount;
 //-----------------------------------
 public Teller(Balances1 fr, int cnt, float amt)
 {
 count = cnt;    //total number of customers
 bank = fr;      //reference to parent class
 amount = amt;   //save amount to move
 }
 //-----------------------------------
public void run()
 {
   while (true)
```

```
{
//compute customer to move money from and to
int from = (int)Math.round(Math.random() *(count-1));
int to = (int)Math.round(Math.random() *(count-1));

//and ask bank to do it
bank.moveMoney(from, to, amount);
 }
 }
}
```

This program is available on the Companion CD-ROM as
Balances1.java.

Now the discerning reader, unlike the average bureaucrat, will
observe that using this approach means that only one teller can
move money at once. Logically, this is as if they had to stand in
line to move funds one at a time, thus augmenting customer lines
with teller lines. Clearly this is not satisfactory.

Objects in the Bank

A better solution to this teller overlap problem is to prevent two
tellers from accessing the same *account* at once rather than the
whole bank. We can do this by redesigning each customer account
as an object:

```
class Customer
{
int balance;
 //------------------------------------
 public Customer(int money)
 {
 balance = money;
 }
 //------------------------------------
 synchronized public void changeLedger(int value)
// public void changeLedger(int value)
 {
 balance += value;
 }
```

```
//------------------------------------
public int getBalance()
{
return balance;
}
}
```

Then we can create an array of these objects for the tellers to work on:

```
Customer customers[] = new Customer[5];
for (int i =0; i< 5; i++)
    {
    customers[i]= new Customer(1000);
    }
```

and within the Teller objects, we adjust the balances:

```
Customer custf, custto;

//compute two customers
 int from = (int)Math.round(Math.random() *(count-1));
 int to = (int)Math.round(Math.random() *(count-1));
 if (from != to)
  {
  custf =  (Customer)cust[from];         //get customers
  custto = (Customer)cust[to];
  custf.changeLedger(-amount);           //move money
  custto.changeLedger(amount);
  }      //end if
```

Since the *changeLedger* method is declared synchronized, the balances will never get out of alignment. You can try this in the program ObjBalances.java; if you remove the *synchronized* modifier, you will see that the teller threads again can interfere with each other. This program is on the Companion CD-ROM as ObjBalances.java, and the resulting display is shown in Figure 13-8.

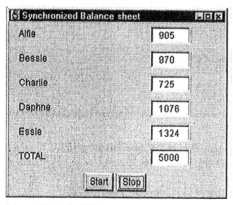

Figure 13-8: *The ObjBalances program produces correct balances by preventing teller threads from interfering with each other.*

Well, Hardly Ever

There is still a case where the balance will not total $5,000. Can you guess what it is? Here's a hint: the balance will always be one, five, or seven dollars *too small* if this unlikely event occurs.

If the balances in the display are only updated when you click on Stop, then the balances are dependent on *when* you click this button. If, by dint of skilled fingers or dumb luck, you manage to click on Stop after a balance is *removed* from one account but not yet *placed* in the other account, the total will be too small by the amount of the missing transaction. This is the equivalent of telling the tellers to go home for the day without finishing the transaction they started working on and trying to balance the books anyway.

The easiest way to solve this would be to subclass the thread's *stop* method and make sure that the thread is not stopped too soon. Unfortunately, this method is declared as final so that you can't subclass it. Instead, we'll create a *stoppit* method, which sets a flag telling the thread it is quitting time:

```
public void stoppit()
{
 stop_flag = true;        //stop at end of transaction
}
```

Then we call this method for all the threads when Stop is clicked:

```
public void clickedStop()
 {
   teller1.stoppit();
   teller2.stoppit();
   teller3.stoppit();
   start.enable();
   repaint();
 }
```

and check this flag inside the *run* method:

```
public void run()
{
Customer custf, custto;
 while (true)
 {
 //compute two customers
 int from = (int)Math.round(Math.random() *(count-1));
 int to = (int)Math.round(Math.random() *(count-1));
 if (from != to)
  {
  custf =  (Customer)cust[from];       //get customers
  custto = (Customer)cust[to];
  custf.changeLedger(-amount);         //move money
  custto.changeLedger(amount);
  }     //end if
  if (stop_flag)
     stop(); //stop only at end of loop
 }      //end while
}
```

Synchronizing Classes You Can't Change

If you don't have the source for a class you are using in one of your programs and for some reason can't derive a new class from it, you can synchronize *instances* of a class using the synchronized modifier as an operator:

```
public void run()
{
Customer custf, custto;
 while (true)
 {
 int from = (int)Math.round(Math.random() *(count-1));
 int to = (int)Math.round(Math.random() *(count-1));
 if (from != to)
  {
  custf = (Customer)cust[from];
  custto = (Customer)cust[to];
  synchronized(custf)
   {
   custf.changeLedger(-amount);
   }
  synchronized(custto)
   {
   custto.changeLedger(amount);
   }
  }     //end if
 if (stop_flag) stop();
 }     //end while
}
```

In the code above, we apply the synchronized operator to the class instances *custf* and *custto*. Then no other class can access these objects while this thread is using them. This version of the program is on the Companion CD-ROM as ObjBalances1.java.

Other Thread Properties

We've marched through most of the important features of threads in this chapter. However, to finish up we need to discuss daemon threads, thread priorities, and thread groups.

Daemon Threads

Daemon threads are threads that continue to run in the background throughout a program. However, if they are marked as daemon threads, you don't have to specifically shut them down for the program to terminate. If the only threads left running are daemon threads, the Java Virtual Machine will exit automatically.

To define a thread as a daemon thread, you must use the *setDaemon* method before you start the thread:

```
Thread t = new Thread();
t.setDaemon(true);
t.start();
```

Thread Priorities

In addition to starting threads, you can define the priority at which they will run, where higher-priority threads get proportionately more time than lower-priority threads. The *setPriority* method is used to define a thread's priority. The priorities values currently can be set between 1 and 10, with 5 being the default setting. However, the numerical values are not guaranteed to remain constant between Java releases, and we recommend that you use the following constants instead:

```
t.setPriority(Thread.NORM_PRIORITY);
t.setPriority(Thread.MAX_PRIORITY);
t.setPriority(Thread.MIN_PRIORITY);
```

Thread Groups

Java allows you to group threads into named groups rather like the CheckboxGroups we discussed earlier. The purpose of these groups is to allow you to destroy an entire group of threads at once. Since a thread group can itself contain thread groups, it is possible to build up a tree of threads that you can suspend, resume, stop, or destroy all at once. Typical code for creating and using thread groups is:

```
ThreadGroup grp = new ThreadGroup();
Thread th1 = new Thread(grp, "tom");    //put in group
Thread th2 = new Thread(grp, "disk");   //put in group
Thread th3 = new Thread(grp, "hery");   //put in group
grp.suspend();      //suspend all threads
```

Moving On

Now that we've looked into threads, we really can see the power of Java and how it can be used. We've looked at threads used for timing and threads used for delays. We've also looked at how we can use several threads running simultaneous parallel processes. Now that we understand how threads work, we can talk about how to read in and display images.

14

Images in Java Applets & Applications

Images are a primary part of building a professional-looking user interface. In this chapter, we'll look at loading and displaying images in applets and in applications as well as using some of the tools for constructing them.

The image classes and methods in Java can appear very confusing at first. There is an *Image* class as part of the awt package, and there is an awt.image package that contains ancillary classes that operate with and on images. The *Image* class consists of the following methods:

```
// Constructors
    public Image();

// Methods
public abstract void flush();
public abstract Graphics getGraphics();
public abstract int getHeight(ImageObserver  observer);
public abstract Object
    getProperty(String  name, ImageObserver  observer);
public abstract ImageProducer getSource();
public abstract int getWidth(ImageObserver  observer);
```

The awt.image package consists of the following classes:

```
class ColorModel
class CropImageFilter
class DirectColorModel
class FilteredImageSource
class ImageFilter
class IndexColorModel
class MemoryImageSource
class PixelGrabber
class RGBImageFilter
```

All versions of Java can display images in GIF (.gif) format and JPEG (.jpg) format. Some versions may allow you to display other formats, but these will not be portable to all platforms. Both applets and applications can display images, but they use different methods in different classes.

Displaying an Image in an Applet

Let's first consider how to display an image in an applet. The applet's *getImage* method returns an object of type *Image*, which you can display in the *paint* method using the *Graphics* method *drawImage*. The arguments to the *getImage* method are the URL where the image file is to be found and the image filename. You can find the server address from which you loaded the applet using the *applet* method *getCodeBase* and the URL that the document (.html) was loaded from using the *getDocumentBase* method. In summary, to load an image in an applet, the statement is:

```
Image image1;
image1 = getImage(getCodeBase(), filename);
```

Then, you draw the image on the screen in the *paint* method:

```
public void paint(Graphics g)
{
g.drawImage(image1, x, y, w, h, this);
}
```

The final *this* argument is a reference to the current applet as an instance of the ImageObserver interface. This provides a way for the thread that handles loading and drawing of images to notify the applet that the image is available. The complete applet for loading and drawing an image is:

```java
import java.awt.*;
import java.applet.*;
public class imgapplet extends Applet
{
private Image image;
//---------------------------------------
 public void init()
 {
 setLayout(null);
 image = getImage(getCodeBase(), "books05.gif");
 }
//---------------------------------------
 public void paint(Graphics g)
 {
 g.drawImage(image, 10, 10,  32, 32, this);
 g.drawImage(image, 100, 10, 64, 64, this);
 }
}
```

The applet displaying these images is show in Figure 14-1, and the code is imgapplet.java with a simple HTML file imgapplet.html on the Companion CD-ROM in the \chapter14 directory.

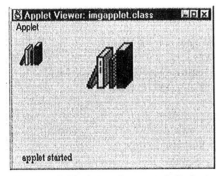

Figure 14-1: The imgapplet program displaying the same image at two sizes.

Note that we draw the image twice, once at 32 X 32 pixels and again as 64 X 64 pixels. The Java image drawing methods will stretch or compress the image as needed to fit the scale you specify.

Displaying an Image in an Application

The logic of loading and displaying an image in an application is similar to that of displaying an image in an applet, but you clearly do not need to reference a parent URL. However, the *Frame* inheritance tree does not have a direct *getImage* method for you to call. Instead, we have to delve a little way under the covers of Java for the *Toolkit* class, which contains the base methods that all implementations of Java must implement in order to produce a graphical user interface. You can obtain the current instance of the Toolkit for your platform using the component's *getToolkit()* method. Thus, to load an image in an application, you call:

```
image = getToolkit().getImage(filename);
```

A complete version of the imgapplet.java program as an application is given on the Companion CD-ROM as imgapp.java and is shown below:

```
import java.awt.*;
import java.applet.*;
public class imgapp extends Frame
{
private Image image;
//----------------------------------------
 public imgapp()
 {
 super("Image application");
 setLayout(null);
 image = getToolkit().getImage("books05.gif");
 reshape(10,10,200,150);
 show();
 }
//----------------------------------------
 public void paint(Graphics g)
```

```
        {
        g.drawImage(image, 10, 10,  32, 32, this);
        g.drawImage(image, 100, 10, 64, 64, this);
        }
//----------------------------------------
        static public void main(String argv[])
        {
        new imgapp();
        }
        }
```

Using the MediaTracker Class

When you execute a *getImage* method, the image is loaded in another thread. If you are writing a relatively passive applet, having one image drawn slowly so that it appears later than the rest of the controls is not much of a drawback. However, when there are several images in a window that are an integral part of the program, this can be quite disconcerting. Further, in applets, each image is loaded separately over the network, and while they may each be loaded in separate threads, the elapsed time for loading 10 icon images is still substantial.

If you want to make sure that images are fully loaded before beginning execution of an applet or application, you can add each of the images to a list contained in an instance of the *MediaTracker* class and then ask the class whether each is loaded before proceeding. This class has the following methods:

```
public void addImage(Image  image, int  id);
public void addImage(Image img, int  id, int w, int h);
public boolean checkAll();
public boolean checkAll(boolean  load);
public boolean checkID(int  id);
public boolean checkID(int  id, boolean  load);
public Object[] getErrorsAny();
public Object[] getErrorsID(int  id);
public boolean isErrorAny();
public boolean isErrorID(int  id);
```

```
public int statusAll(boolean  load);
public int statusID(int  id, boolean  load);
public void waitForAll();
public boolean waitForAll(long  ms);
public void waitForID(int  id);
public boolean waitForID(int  id, long  ms);
```

The *addImage* method of the MediaTracker object adds images to an internal array or collection along with an integer identifier:

```
track = new MediaTracker(this);
image = getImage(getCodeBase(), "books05.gif");
track.addImage(image, 0);
```

While these identifiers are most often simply sequential integers, they can be any values you choose. Then, when you have begun loading of all the images and you want to discover if they have completed, you can use any of the *wait* methods to check on any or all of the images. The example below follows from one given by Flanagan. It is on the Companion CD-ROM as TrackImage.java, and the result of this program is show in Figure 14-2.

Figure 14-2: The TrackImage.java program, showing the two images loaded and the final message displayed along the bottom.

The TrackImage program, illustrating the *MediaTracker* class, is:

```
import java.awt.*;
import java.applet.*;
public class TrackImage extends Applet
{
private Image images[];
private MediaTracker track;
//---------------------------------------
 public void init()
 {
 setLayout(null);
 images = new Image[2];
 track = new MediaTracker(this);

 //begin loading images
 images[0] = getImage(getCodeBase(), "books05.gif");
 images[1] = getImage(getCodeBase(), "beany.gif");

 //add images into tracker
 for (int i = 0; i < 2; i++)
    track.addImage(images[i], 0);

//check to see if they are done loading
 for (int i = 0; i < 2; i++)
   {
   showStatus("loading image: " + i);
   try
     {
     track.waitForID(i);
     }
   catch (InterruptedException e) {};
   if(track.isErrorID(i))
   showStatus("Error loading image: " + i);
  }
 }
//---------------------------------------
 public void paint(Graphics g)
 {
 int x, w, h;
```

```
//draw each image
 for (int i=0; i <2; i++)
   {
    x = 100*i + 10;
    w = images[i].getWidth(this);
    h = images[i].getHeight(this);
    g.drawImage(images[i], x, 10, w, h, this);
    }
  }
}
```

Now, it isn't always necessary to make sure that all of the images are loaded in the *constructor* or *init* routine. You just need to make sure they are loaded before you begin using them. This could happen somewhat later, depending on the nature of your application or applet.

Converting Between Image Types

Java allows you to display images in both JPEG and GIF formats. Both of these are compressed image formats, while bitmaps have at least one byte for each pixel. In general, JPEG compression is a little better than GIF and is usually better for pictures. GIF format is usually better for drawings.

Both of the images shown in Figure 14-2 are from the Visual Basic icon library, but they have been converted from icon format to GIF format using either HiJaak Pro Graphics Suite (www.quarterdeck.com) or Paint Shop Pro (www.jasc.com). HiJaak also provides convenient methods for screen capture and Paint Shop Pro excels at image manipulation.

If your images are to be downloaded over the Internet, it is sometimes useful to have them drawn in rough form and filled out later. You can do this by making an *interlaced* GIF file, where alternating lines from the entire image are stored in the first part of the file, and the remaining interlaced lines are stored in the last half of the file. As the image is received and drawn by your browser, it appears to draw the entire image in "rough draft" form and then go back and fill in the remaining lines. This gives the user faster feedback as to the nature of the image you are presenting.

To convert a VB icon file to a GIF file, you can use HiJaak Pro Graphics Suite. It allows you to read in icon files and then save them as noninterlaced GIF files. This File Save dialog is illustrated in Figure 14-3.

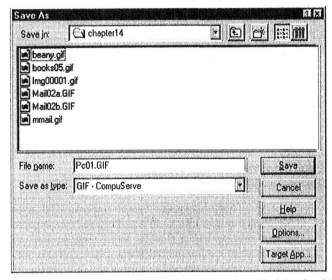

Figure 14-3: Converting a VB icon of a GIF file using HiJaak Pro Graphics Suite.

We have found that in the Win95 version of HiJaak, only the paint program will read in icons. The main program issues a file format error message.

To convert a GIF file into an interlaced GIF, load Paint Shop Pro and read in the icon file you wish to convert. Then select File | Save As (as shown in Figure 14-4), select the GIF89a file format, and select Interlaced. You now have a file with a .gif extension containing interlaced data.

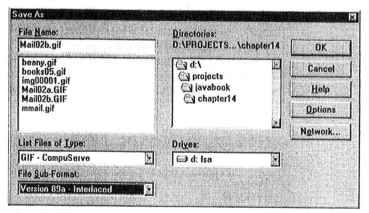

Figure 14-4: Using Paint Shop Pro to convert a noninterlaced GIF file into an interlaced GIF file.

Capturing Images Into Memory

The *PixelGrabber* class allows you to capture all or any part of a displayed image into an array of integers, where each integer represents one pixel. The lower three bytes represent the red, green, and blue intensities of that pixel, and the upper byte represents the transparency value. One reason to capture images in this format is that you can reload them to the screen much more rapidly than if they are in a compressed format like GIF or JPEG. In the next few sections, we'll illustrate how to do this.

To capture an image into memory, you compute the size of the array you need from the image's dimensions and create an integer array of that size:

```
w = images.getWidth(this);
h = images.getHeight(this);
int pix[] = new int[w * h];   //create array
```

Then, you create an instance of the *PixelGrabber* class, specifying the area of the image to capture:

```
PixelGrabber pxg =
  new PixelGrabber(images[j],0,0,w,h,pix,0,w);
```

and then execute the *grabPixels* method inside a *try* block:

```
//grab pixels
  try {
    pxg.grabPixels();
      }
    catch (InterruptedException e){}
```

Since interrupting this operation is quite unlikely, we won't bother to put any code inside the catch phrase. You can also make sure that the pixel capture is completed by checking the return value of the *status* method until the ALLBITS completion bit is set.

```
//make sure grab is completed
do
  {
  status = pxg.status();
  }
while ((status & ImageObserver.ALLBITS) == 0);
```

Saving the Data as a File

Once you have captured the data in memory, you can store it in a binary file and read it in quickly to display an image. While these binary files are quite a bit larger than GIF files or JPEG files, there is no processing delay while they are decompressed or checked for transmission and security errors.

One way we can decrease the transmission time and file size is to store all 3 colors in a single 8-bit byte. This is typically done by allocating 2 bits to green and 3 bits each to red and blue, in the form *ggrrrbbb*.

So we could write out the image data as a series of w*h bytes, (where *w* is the image pixel width and *h* its height) which we could read in and display rapidly. However, reading such an array tells us nothing about the shape of the image and we soon realize that we will have to design a format for storing the data that gives us this information.

One powerful way to store image data is to make it part of your program rather than a series of separate image files. By doing this, you are making sure that these images are transferred with your program and that each of several images is not downloaded separately over the network as they would be with individual *getImage* calls. Using these binary formats, the files will be larger but the overall load time will actually be less.

String Representation of Binary Data

You can store byte data in the lower byte of String characters by representing these bytes as octal (base-8) numbers. Java (and C) allows you to do this by prefixing each octal number with a backslash. Thus, we can store data very compactly by representing it as:

```
String bdata = "\223\004\047\146";
```

This generates a character string with the lower 8 bits of each character having the octal values 223, 004, 047, and 146. Be careful not to put spaces between these values as they will then become space characters in the string.

Now to make a class out of this, we simply make a static String within the class with methods to return the image arrays:

```
public class imagefile {
Vector imagelist;

static private String image0 ="377\377\377\377\377" + //etc.
etc.

static private String image1 = "\377\020\211"+ //etc.
```

The constructor to this class loads the vector with instances of an *image_cache* class that contains the binary data and the dimensions of the image:

```
public imagefile()
{
imagelist = new Vector(2);

image_cache c0 = new image_cache(image0, 32, 32);
imagelist.addElement(c0);

image_cache c1 = new image_cache(image1, 61, 61);
imagelist.addElement(c1);
}
```

This *image_cache* class contains the binary array and methods to retrieve the image and its size:

```
class image_cache
{
 String sbuf;
 int width, height;
 byte bytearray[];
 public image_cache(String s, int w, int h)
 {
 sbuf = s;
 width = w; height =h;
 bytearray = new byte[sbuf.length()];
 sbuf.getBytes(0, sbuf.length(), bytearray, 0);
 }
//-----------------------------------------------
public byte[] getBytes()
 {
 return bytearray;
}
//-----------------------------------------------
public int getWidth()
 {
 return width;
 }
//-----------------------------------------------
public int getHeight()
 {
 return height;
 }
}
```

The important methods are the *getBytes* method of the *String* class, which converts the low 8 bits of each string character into a binary byte in the specified array *bytearray*:

```
sbuf.getBytes(0, sbuf.length(), bytearray, 0);
```

The two zeroes represent the offset into the string array and the byte array.

Finally, we must design a method to return the byte array as an image. The *MemoryImageSource* class returns an image, given a byte or integer array. You must also specify the ColorModel, which defines how many bits of each byte or integer represent each color. Since we packed our image data into single bytes as *ggrrrbbb*, we need to describe this as an instance of the *DirectColorModel* class, where we specify the number of bits in a pixel word and the masks to obtain each color:

```
DirectColorModel cm =
new DirectColorModel(8, 0x38, 0xc0, 0x7);
```

Then we use this in the *MemoryImageSource* class as follows:

```
//Get image from Vector
image_cache c = (image_cache)imagelist.elementAt(i);
int w = c.getWidth();
int h = c.getHeight();
MemoryImageSource mis =
   new MemoryImageSource(w, h, cm, c.getBytes(),
      0, c.getWidth());
```

and return the image from the method as follows:

```
Image image = p1.createImage(mis);
return image;
}
```

The GrabImage.java program displays two images, as shown in Figure 14-5. When you click on Grab, it creates two 8-bit arrays describing the two images and writes out the code to create an *imagefile.java* class containing a vector of images and the *image_cache* class.

Figure 14-5: The GrabImage program. This program writes out the imagefile *class with both images as constant strings when you click on the Grab button.*

The memimage.java program uses the *imagefile* class and creates images from it as follows:

```
import java.awt.*;
import java.applet.*;
import java.awt.image.*;
//-----------------------------------------
public class memimage extends Applet
{
private Image image1, image2;
private imagefile img;
//-----------------------------------------
 public void init()
 {
 setLayout(null);
 img = new imagefile();
 image1 = img.getImage(0);
 image2 = img.getImage(1);
 }
//-----------------------------------------
 public void paint(Graphics g)
 {
 g.drawImage(image1, 10, 10,  image1.getWidth(this),
   image1.getHeight(this), this);
 g.drawImage(image2, 100, 10,  image2.getWidth(this),
   image2.getHeight(this),this);
 }
}
```

The data are read back in and displayed by the memimage program on the Companion CD-ROM and shown in Figure 14-6. The accompanying imagefile.java program generated by the GrabImage program is also on the Companion CD-ROM.

Figure 14-6: A display of the memimage program using the generated imagefile.class.

Making Blinking Alternating Images

Once of the simplest forms of animation is the blinking of an image between two or more related images. You can easily do this in Java by reading in the images and then displaying them alternately after a specified delay. The following program illustrates how we insert this delay:

```java
import java.awt.*;
import java.applet.*;
//blinks back and forth between 2 images
public class BlinkImage extends Applet implements Runnable
{
Image open, closed;      //two images
MediaTracker track;      //and tracker
Thread timer;            //timer for blinking
boolean openvis;         //flag for which to draw
 public void init()
```

```
  {
setLayout(null);
//read in the two images
open = getImage(getDocumentBase(), "mail02a.gif");
closed = getImage(getDocumentBase(), "mail02b.gif");
//make sure they are read in
<Computer Code> track = new MediaTracker(this);
track.addImage(open, 0);
track.addImage(closed, 1);
//check to see if they are done loading
for (int i = 0; i < 2; i++)
  {
  showStatus("loading image: " + i);
  try
    {
    track.waitForID(i);
    }
  catch (InterruptedException e) {};
  if(track.isErrorID(i))
  showStatus("Error loading image: " + i);
  }
//create a thread
timer = new Thread(this);
openvis = false;       //first display closed image
timer.start();         //start thread
  }
//-------------------------------------------
public void run()
//this method is called in new thread
  {
while (true)
  {
  openvis = ! openvis; //switch between images
  repaint(50,50,32,32);            //and redraw screen
  try
   {
   Thread.sleep(100);
   }
  catch (InterruptedException e){};
```

```
  }
}
//-----------------------------------------------
public void paint(Graphics g)
{
if (openvis)
  g.drawImage(open, 50,50, Color.lightGray, this);
else
  g.drawImage(closed, 50,50, Color.lightGray, this);
}
}
```

Note that to avoid flickering, we repaint only the area of the image itself. In this case, the two images are mail02a.gif and mail02b.gif, converted from the Visual Basic icon library of the same name and made transparent using Paint Shop Pro.

Animated GIF Files

If your animation needs are as simple as just cycling through two or more similar GIF files at the same position, you really don't have to write any Java code at all. The GIF89a specification includes a way to specify multiple frames, the time delay between them, and whether they are to run once or continuously. An increasing number of products allow you to create animated GIF files from pictures in several formats. For this example, we used GIF Construction Set for Windows from Alchemy Mindworks (www.mindworkshop.com). This package has a step-by-step

Animation Wizard which asks you all of the relevant details, allows you to add files to a list, and then constructs the animated GIF file for you (Figure 14-7). You can start with bitmap, GIF, or other common graphics files that you have imported or drawn and add them to a list, as shown in Figure 14-8.

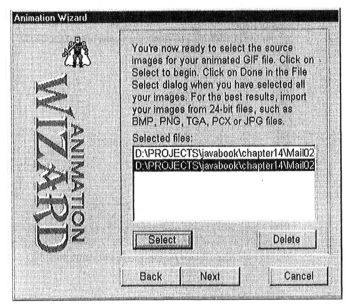

Figure 14-7: Using the GIF Construction Set to build an animated GIF file.

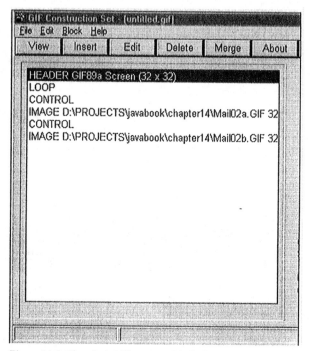

Figure 14-8: The selected files we used in building mmail.gif.

The GIF file mmail.gif on your Companion CD-ROM contains the two mail images we have been discussing and will display as a slowly changing pair of images when loaded into your Web browser. The file AnimImge.htm is provided so you can view the resulting image. While the delay time between images was selected as 100 msec, the image change appears much slower because Netscape Navigator imposes an additional delay at the start of each loop through the images.

Moving On

In this chapter, we've looked at how you can load and display images in both applets and applications and discussed how to use the *MediaTracker* class. We've also looked at how to capture and store images and make them part of classes rather than separate loadable files. Finally, we looked at image animation using both Java and GIF animation methods.

In the next chapter, we'll pick up on building user interfaces again, covering menus and dialog boxes, and go on from there to looking at how we can build our own controls.

15

Menus & Dialogs

So far, we've looked at the main visual controls you use in building applets and applications. Since visual applications are usually derived from the *Frame* class, they also allow you to add drop-down menus to these frame windows. You can, of course, create frame windows from applets as well, but this is done less frequently because of the somewhat inelegant "Unsigned Java Window" banner that appears along the bottom of such windows.

In this chapter, we'll take up how you can use these menu items in applications and in frame windows to launch program commands and to bring up dialog windows.

How Menus Are Used

A menu bar runs across the top of frame windows and contains the titles of categories of operations. By convention, the File menu is the leftmost menu on most menu bars, followed by the Edit menu. The menu next to the rightmost one will often be the Window menu and the rightmost menu is usually the Help menu. You can insert as many other menu categories between these as are necessary for your application.

Clicking on a menu always causes a list of menu options to drop down under the menu bar. You can then click on any of these options to cause the program to carry out some desired operation. Menus need not be only one level deep, of course; you can create menu items that expand to several more items to the right of the drop-down menu bar.

In the example illustrated in Figure 15-1, the menu bar consists of the two items: File and Setup. Clicking on File causes a menu to drop down consisting of Open, a horizontal separator line, and Exit. Clicking on Setup causes a two-item menu to drop down, consisting of the Appearance choice and the Preferences choice, where a right arrow appears to the right of Preferences. When you click on Preferences, the additional menu items Colors and Filetypes expand to the right of the arrow.

File	Setup	
Open...	Appearances...	
--------	Preferences -->	Colors...
Exit		Filetypes

Figure 15-1: A schematic representation of a simple two-item menu with expansion of the Preferences choice to two more items.

Menu Conventions

It is conventional to group items in a menu together using a horizontal separator bar between different logical types of operations. For example, the File menu has the usual Open menu choice and the Exit menu choice. Since exiting from the program is logically rather unlike opening or manipulating files, we separate the Exit choice from the Open choice using a horizontal bar. In more complex menus, it is not unusual to see three or four separator bars. If you require more than that, you might well reconsider your design, as it becomes confusing to the eye.

If a menu item brings up a new window where the user can select additional choices or enter data into fields, it should always have an ellipsis (...) following it. This indicates in advance to your users that they should expect a new window or dialog box to come up when they select this item.

In Windows programs, it is usual to allow users to select menu items from the keyboard as well as from the mouse by holding down the Alt key and pressing the underlined character in the menu. Thus, we open the File menu by pressing Alt+F. Then your user can select the item under it by pressing the underlined letters. To bring up the File | Open dialog, you should be able to press Alt+F and then O. It is not necessary to hold down the Alt key while pressing the O. We'll see that how you specify these special underlined menu characters is operating system–dependent and thus requires some awkward extra programming, since the conventions between operating systems differ. This inconsistency is scheduled to be corrected in Java 1.1.

Creating Menus

To add menus to a frame window, you create an instance of the *MenuBar* class and add it to the frame using the *setMenuBar* method:

```
MenuBar mbar = new MenuBar();    //create menu bar
setMenuBar(mbar);                //and add to Frame
```

Each menu item that runs across the menu bar is an object of type Menu, and each item under it is an object of type MenuItem.

Thus, to create the two-entry menu bar we drew in Figure 15-1, we just add two elements to our new menu bar:

```
//Create two top level menu items
File = new Menu("&File",true);
Setup = new Menu("&Setup",false);

//and add them to Menubar
mbar.add(File);
mbar.add(Setup);
```

To add items under the menu, we add *them* to the newly created menu objects:

```
//File menu is File->Open, separator, Exit
Open = new MenuItem("&Open...");
Exit = new MenuItem("E&xit");
File.add(Open);
File.add(new MenuItem("-"));     //separator
File.add(Exit);
```

To draw a menu separator, we simply add a new menu item whose caption is a single hyphen. You can also add a separator using the *addSeparator()* method. This gives us the left-hand menu, with the F, O, and x underlined, as shown in Figure 15-2. The methods you can use on a Menu object include:

```
public MenuItem add(MenuItem mi);
public void add(String label);
public void addNotify();
public void addSeparator();
public int countItems();
public MenuItem getItem(int index);
public boolean isTearOff();
public void remove(int index);
public void remove(MenuComponent item);
```

Because Java allows you to add and remove menu elements dynamically during a program, you can change some of the menu elements depending on the nature of the processes your program is carrying out. You need to be careful, however, not to do too much of this as menus that constantly vary can be extremely confusing to navigate.

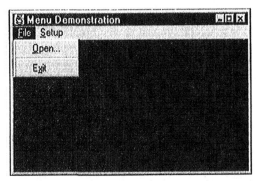

Figure 15-2: The File menu.

MenuItem Methods

Once you have created menu items under the menu bar, you can use the following methods on them:

```
public void disable();
public void enable();
public void enable(boolean  cond);
public String getLabel();
public boolean isEnabled();
public void setLabel(String label);
```

A menu item that is *disabled* is grayed, but remains visible. You cannot select it. You can also change the name of menu items using the *setLabel()* method.

Creating Submenus

To add menu items that expand to the right into more menu items, we just add instances of the *Menu* class, rather than of the

MenuItem class, and add the *MenuItems* to them. There is no logical limit to the depth you can extend menus, but extending them more than one level makes them hard to use and understand.

So to complete the example we began above, we write the following menu code:

```
//Setup menu is Setup->    Appearance,
//                         Preferences->Colors
//                         Filetypes
//                         Sound

Appearance = new MenuItem("Appearance");
Setup.add(Appearance);

Preferences = new Menu("Preferences");    //extends
Setup.add(Preferences);    //add menu here for sub menus
  Colors = new MenuItem("Colors");
  Preferences.add(Colors);

  Filetypes = new MenuItem("Filetypes");
  Preferences.add(Filetypes);
Sound = new MenuItem("Sound");
Setup.add("Sound");
```

The resulting extended menu is shown in Figure 15-3. The program is MenuFrame.java on the Companion CD-ROM.

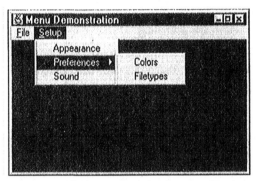

Figure 15-3: The Setup menu, showing second level menus.

Other Menu Features

In addition to the usual click and drop-down behavior of menus, there are a few other features you probably will find useful.

Disabling MenuItems

If you construct a fairly elaborate menu structure, there may be times when you don't wish for a user to select a given menu item. For example, if the user had not yet selected a data file to operate on, then calling a math function is inappropriate. You can make sure that this can't happen by disabling those menu functions using the usual *disable()* method:

```
mathItem.disable();
```

You can enable that item later when the file has been read in:

```
mathItem.enable();
```

Tearoff Menus

When you create a menu, you can use the alternate constructor:

```
mnu = new Menu(String title, boolean tearoff);
```

The *tearoff* argument is supposed to determine whether the menu is a "tearoff menu." Such a menu is supposed to stay down after you raise your finger from the mouse button. This, of course, is the normal behavior under Windows 95. As far as we can determine, this behavior has only been implemented on the Solaris platform. The boolean argument is otherwise ignored at present.

Checkbox Menus

The *CheckboxMenuItem* is a special type of menu item that can be checked or unchecked using the mouse or using the *setState(boolean)* method. You can also find out whether it is checked using the *getState()* method. This object behaves as an ordinary menu item in all implementations of Java 1.0.

Receiving Menu Commands

Clicking on a menu item generates an *action* event. As with other *action* events, you check which control caused the event and call the relevant routine:

```
public boolean action(Event evt, Object arg)
{
if (evt.target == Exit)     //Exit menu selected
  {
  clickedExit();            //call exit routine
  return true;
  }
}
```

Dialogs

A dialog is a temporary window that comes up to obtain information from the user or to warn the user of some impending condition, usually an error. We have already seen the *FileDialog* in Chapter 12. Let's see how we would implement it in this simple menu program.

The FileDialog

The *FileDialog* is a class that brings up that operating system's File I Open or File I Save dialog. You can set which mode it comes up in as part of the constructor:

```
FileDialog fdlg =
    new FileDialog(this, "Open file", FileDialog.OPEN);
```
or
```
FileDialog fdlg =
    new FileDialog(this, "Open file", FileDialog.SAVE);
```

Once you have created an instance of the file dialog, you can use the *setDirectory()* and *setFile()* methods to specify where it should start and what the default filename should be. The dialog doesn't actually appear until its *show()* method is called. The FileDialog object is always a *modal* dialog, meaning that:

❧ Input to other windows is blocked while it is displayed.

❧ No code is executed in the calling thread after the *show()* method is called until the FileDialog object is dismissed by selecting OK or Cancel.

To call a dialog from our Open menu item, we simply insert the following in the *action* routine:

```
if (evt.target == Open)
    {
    FileDialog fdlg = new FileDialog(this,
            "Open",FileDialog.LOAD);
    fdlg.show();                //start dialog display
```

```
//display selected file name
filelabel.setText(fdlg.getFile());
return true;
}
```

The *FileDialog* will remain in control until it is closed with either OK or Cancel, as shown in Figure 15-4, and then control will return to the statement following the *show()* method call. You can then obtain the selected filename using the *getFile()* method. In the example above, we display that filename in a label in the main window. The complete program for launching the *FileDialog* from the File | Open menu is MenuFrame.java in the \chapter15 directory of the Companion CD-ROM.

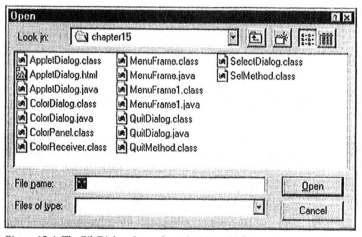

Figure 15-4: The FileDialog shown from the MenuDialog program.

How Dialogs Are Used

A dialog is a window that is meant to be displayed temporarily to obtain or import information. You usually use a dialog to ask for information, such as a name or password. You can also pop up dialogs as warnings if the user is about to exit or delete something. In addition, you can use dialogs to select filenames, colors, fonts, or other system-like parameters.

In Java, the *Dialog* class is a window that can be created normally, or more usually, as a modal window. The default layout for a dialog window is the BorderLayout.

To create a modal dialog, you invoke the constructor:

```
public Dialog(Frame p, String title, boolean modal);
```

You could invoke this constructor directly by calling:

```
Dialog qdialog = new Dialog(this, "Quit Yet?", true);
```

However, it is more common to extend the *Dialog* class and put all of the control and layout information inside the derived class:

```
class QuitDialog extends Dialog
{
boolean exitflag;          //set if OK clicked
Button OK, Cancel;         //two buttons
//-------------------------------------------
 public QuitDialog(Frame fr)
 {
//create modal dialog with title bar
 super(fr, "Ready to Quit?", true);
 Panel p1 = new Panel();
 OK = new Button("OK");
 Cancel = new Button("No");
 add("South", p1);
 p1.add(OK);                //put buttons in panel
 p1.add(Cancel);
 resize(200,100);           //size the dialog
 exitflag = false;
 }
//-------------------------------------------
```

```
public boolean action(Event evt, Object arg)
 {
 if (evt.target == OK)      //OK button clicked
   {
   exitflag = true;         //set exit flag
  hide();
   return true;
   }
 else
 if (evt.target == Cancel) //Cancel button clicked
  {
  exitflag = false;         //unset exit flag
  hide();
  return true;
  }
else
  return super.action(evt, arg);
  }
//-----------------------------------------
public boolean getExitflag()
{
return exitflag;            //return state of flag
}
```

Then we create an instance of this new class in response to the File | Exit menu item selection:

```
private void clickedExit()
{
 QuitDialog qdlg = new QuitDialog(this);
 qdlg.show();
```

Like the *FileDialog*, members of the *Dialog* class are invisible when created and appear as modal windows when their *show()* method is called.

However, in Java 1.0x, dialogs are modal, *but* they do not block execution of the calling thread. So, while you might at first think you could check the state of the exit flag when the dialog closes like this:

```
QuitDialog qdlg = new QuitDialog(this);

qdlg.show();
System.out.println("Dialog passed");
if (qdlg.getExitflag())
   System.exit(0);        //exit if ok clicked
```

this will not work in Java 1.0x. Instead, the code continues executing even though the dialog is being displayed. So the *if* statement testing the exit flag is executed immediately and the flag is thus always *false*. To prove this, run the MenuDialog on the Companion CD-ROM program and select File I Exit. As soon as the dialog appears, the message "Dialog passed" will be printed on the screen.

Since dialogs do not block the calling thread, we have to go to some lengths to communicate between the dialog box class and the parent class. Basically, the dialog box needs to pass information back to the calling program by calling a predefined public method. Since any program ought to be able to use our *QuitDialog*, we don't want the method to only be part of a single class. Instead, we will make use of an *interface* to specify the method that the calling class must provide:

```
interface QuitMethod
{
 public void setQuit();
}
```

Remember, all an interface means is that you promise that you will provide methods having the calling arguments you specify. Then we have our calling class implement that interface by:

```
class MenuFrame1 extends Frame implements QuitMethod
```

and we then write a *setQuit* method:

```
public void setQuit()
{
 System.exit(0);    //exit when this method is called
}
```

Now our revised *QuitDialog* must be provided with a reference to our calling class as part of the constructor as well as a reference to the parent frame:

```
public QuitDialog(Frame fr, QuitMethod qm)
```

We need the frame reference to create a dialog:

```
super(fr, "Ready to Quit?", true);
```

and the parent reference to call the parent's *setQuit* method:

```
Quitm.setQuit();    //call parent's quit method
```

The code for this class is given on the Companion CD-ROM as MenuFrame1.java and QuitDialog.java and is shown below:

```
class QuitDialog extends Dialog
{
Button OK, Cancel;
QuitMethod Quitm;
Frame frm;
//-------------------------------------------
 public QuitDialog(Frame fr, QuitMethod qm)
 {
 super(fr, "Ready to Quit?", true);
 Quitm = qm;                      //ref to calling class
 frm = fr;                        //ref to parent frame
 Panel p1 = new Panel();
 OK = new Button("OK");           //create buttons
 Cancel = new Button("No");
 add("South", p1);
 p1.add(OK);                      //add to panel
 p1.add(Cancel);
 setBackground(Color.white);
 }
//-------------------------------------------
public void show()
{
 super.show();
 Point pt = frm.location();       //position above
 reshape(pt.x, pt.y, 200,100);    //the parent
 }
//-------------------------------------------
```

```
public boolean action(Event evt, Object arg)
{
if (evt.target == OK)
  {
  Quitm.setQuit();        //call parent's quit method
  dispose();              //and exit
  return true;
  }
else
if (evt.target == Cancel)
  {
  dispose();              //otherwise just leave
  return true;
  }
else
  return super.action(evt, arg);
  }
}
```

Then to call the dialog, we pass it the frame argument and the *QuitMethod* argument:

```
//start up quit dialog
QuitDialog qdlg = new QuitDialog(this,this);
qdlg.show();            //show the dialog
```

Note that both of them are the *this* reference, since the current class is both the parent frame and an instance of a class implementing the QuitMethod interface.

Calling Dialogs From Applets

Since dialogs require a frame as a parent, you might think that you can't pop up a dialog box from an applet. However, there is nothing to stop you from creating an invisible frame and using it as the parent of a dialog window.

Consider the following code from the example program AppletDialog on your Companion CD-ROM. This applet displays a single push button labeled "Colors" and a label which is initially set to "no color." When we press this button, a dialog comes up as shown in Figure 15-5. Here we can select one of three colors and click on OK to pass that color choice back to the main applet. This requires an interface:

```
interface SelMethod
{
  public void setColorName(String s);
}
```

that the dialog can call to pass the color name to the calling program.

Figure 15-5: The color dialog produced by the AppletDialog program.

We need to create a frame and pass the dialog an instance of the *SelectMethod* class:

```
Frame fr = new Frame();   //create invisible frame
SelectDialog sdlg = new SelectDialog(fr, this);
sdlg.show();
```

Note that here the frame argument is distinct from the parent argument. The frame is the invisible one just created, and the *this* reference refers to the applet.

We then create a dialog with the OK and Cancel buttons in the southern border and put a panel in the middle to hold the three option buttons:

```
class SelectDialog extends Dialog
{
```

```
Button OK, Cancel;
CheckboxGroup cbg;
Checkbox red, green, blue;
SelMethod selm;
//-------------------------------------------
 public SelectDialog(Frame fr, SelMethod sm)
 {
 super(fr, "Select Color", true);
 selm = sm;                        //save reference to parent
 Panel p1 = new Panel();           //panel in south
 OK = new Button("OK");            //create buttons
 Cancel = new Button("No");
 add("South", p1);
 p1.add(OK);                       //put the buttons in the
panel
 p1.add(Cancel);
 cbg = new CheckboxGroup();        //create 3 radio buttons
 red = new Checkbox("red", cbg, true);
 green = new Checkbox("green", cbg, false);
 blue = new Checkbox("blue", cbg, false);
 Panel p2 = new Panel();
 add("Center", p2);
 p2.add(red);                      //add radio buttons to center
 p2.add(green);
 p2.add(blue);
 resize(200,100);
 }
```

Then, when the OK button is clicked, we send the color name back to the calling applet:

```
private void clickedOK()
{
String colorname="none";
if (red.getState()) colorname="red";
if (green.getState()) colorname="green";
if (blue.getState()) colorname="blue";
selm.setColorName(colorname);
}
```

A Real Color Dialog Box

Rather than just selecting colors by name, why not select them by color? Here we'll build a dialog containing 16 color squares that you can select with your mouse and send back to the main program using the same interface technique we used above. The interface is as follows:

```
interface ColorReceiver
{
 public void setColorOption(Color c);
}
```

The dialog is shown in Figure 15-6.

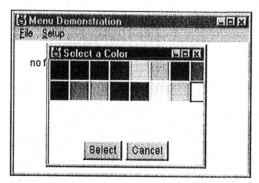

Figure 15-6: The ColorDialog displayed by the ColorDialog.java class.

We will use this same MenuFrame1 program we developed above in the previous section, now implementing another of the menu commands, to select Color preferences. Now our main class implements *two* interfaces as well as being derived from the *Frame* class:

```
class MenuFrame1 extends Frame
implements QuitMethod, ColorReceiver
```

Our *setColorOption* method changes the background of the frame, saves that color in a private variable, and repaints the screen:

```
public void setColorOption(Color c)
{
background = c;     //save the color
setBackground(c);   //change the background
repaint();          //repaint window
}
```

To construct the dialog, we put the OK and Cancel buttons in the south border, put a panel with a null layout in the center, and place the 16 color panels in two rows. Our color panels are derived from the *Panel* class and can receive *mouseDown* events. We will received them at the dialog level, however, so that we can highlight the one we click on and unhighlight whichever one was previously selected.

Building the Color Panels

Java defines 12 different colors by name. We can define the rest using convenient RGB combinations. Each instance of our *ColorPanel* class consists of a color and the coordinates where the colored box will be placed:

```
class ColorPanel extends Panel
{
Color color;
boolean highlighted;
//-----------------------------------------------------
public void setHighlight(boolean flag)
{
highlighted = flag;
repaint();
}
//-----------------------------------------------------
  public ColorPanel(int x, int y, Color c)
  {
  color = c;
  highlighted = false;
```

```
reshape(x, y, 25, 25);
  }
}
```

So in our main *Dialog* class, we create 16 instances of this box and place them in two rows:

```
public class ColorDialog extends Dialog
{
Button OK, Cancel;                  //buttons at bottom
ColorReceiver colrecvr;             //parent
Color color      ;                  //current color & default
color
ColorPanel selectedPanel;           //currently selected color
panel
//----------------------------------------------------
public ColorDialog(Frame fr, ColorReceiver colr, Color
defaultColor)
  {
  super(fr, "Select a Color", true);
  setBackground(Color.white);
  colrecvr = colr;                  //parent
  color = defaultColor;             //color at outset
  Panel p1 = new Panel();
  OK = new Button("Select");        //create two buttons
  Cancel = new Button("Cancel");    //at bottom
  add("South", p1);
  p1.add(OK);
  p1.add(Cancel);
  Panel pc = new Panel();           //panel for color blocks
  add("Center", pc);
  pc.setLayout(null);               // no layout manager
  //create a 2 x 8 array of 16 color squares in panels
  pc.add(new ColorPanel(0,0, Color.black ));
//dark blue
  pc.add(new ColorPanel(25,0,new Color(0,0,0x80)));
  //dark green
  pc.add(new ColorPanel(50,0,new Color(0,0x80,0)));
//dark cyan
  pc.add(new ColorPanel(75,0,new Color(0,0x80,0x80)));
```

```
pc.add(new ColorPanel(100,0, Color.pink));
pc.add(new ColorPanel(125,0, Color.orange));
pc.add(new ColorPanel(150,0, Color.darkGray));
pc.add(new ColorPanel(175,0, Color.gray));
pc.add(new ColorPanel( 0,25,Color.blue));
pc.add(new ColorPanel(25, 25, Color.green));
pc.add(new ColorPanel(50,25,Color.cyan));
pc.add(new ColorPanel(75,25, Color.red));
pc.add(new ColorPanel(100,25, Color.magenta));
pc.add(new ColorPanel(125,25, Color.yellow));
pc.add(new ColorPanel(150,25, Color.lightGray));
pc.add(new ColorPanel(175,25, Color.white));
```

Highlighting the Color Blocks

At any given time, one of these colors is the "current" color, and we should highlight it on entry to the dialog. Then, when we click on a color, we should highlight that color and unhighlight the previously selected color. We highlight a color by setting its *highlight* property to *true*. In the *paint* method, we redraw the color with a double-line gray border if it is selected:

```
public void paint(Graphics g)
   {
//fill block with this blocks color
  g.setColor(color);
  Dimension d = size();              //get current size
  g.fillRect(0,0, d.width-1, d.height-1);
//draw line around color box which is either
  g.setColor(Color.white);           //white
  if (highlighted)
     {
     g.setColor(Color.darkGray);     //or gray
     g.drawRect(1,1,d.width-3, d.height-3);
     }
//draw outer line in white or gray
  g.drawRect(0,0,d.width-1, d.height-1);
   }
```

Highlighting the Default Color

When we enter the dialog box, the calling class (in this case, MenuFrame1) already has some color. We pass this default color into the *ColorDialog* class and would like that color to be highlighted when the dialog box is first shown. So far, we have created 16 boxes, but we have not done anything to tell the dialog which is the current color. This colors is passed in, but we need to compare it against each of the 16 colors's boxes we are displaying.

We do this by iterating through all of the color boxes contained in the *p2 Panel* control, and if one matches, we highlight it:

```
int count = pc.countComponents(); //number of blockas
  for (int i=0; i< count; i++)      //move thry them
    {
    ColorPanel cp = (ColorPanel)pc.getComponent(i);
    if (cp.getColor() == color)    //if one matches
      {
      cp.setHighlight(true);       //highlight it
      selectedPanel = cp;          //and remember it
      }
    }
```

Highlighting in Response to Click

When we click on a block, we want to highlight it and unhighlight the previously selected color block. Now, the only place we can remember the last selected color is at the dialog box level. So we intercept the *mouseDown* event and change the state of the two colors:

```
public boolean mouseDown(Event evt, int x, int y)
{
if (evt.target instanceof ColorPanel)
 {
 if (selectedPanel != null)
   //unhighlight previously selected color
   selectedPanel.setHighlight(false);
 //highlight new color
```

```
selectedPanel = (ColorPanel)evt.target;
//save new selected color
color = selectedPanel.getColor();
//and highlight it
selectedPanel.setHighlight(true);
return true;
}
return super.handleEvent(evt);
}
```

Feedback for Mouse Down & Up

Users of this class like to see some indication that their mouse clicks
have been received. While clicking on a block, we would prefer that
something happen when the mouse button is down and something else happen when the mouse button is raised. So, inside the
ColorPanel class, we intercept *mouseDown* and *mouseUp*, but return
false from *mouseDown* so it passes the event on to the *ColorDialog*
class, where we can remember which color was selected:

```
private void outline(color)
{
//draw box around selected color block
Graphics g =getGraphics();
Dimension d = size();
g.setColor(color);  // in specified color
g.drawRect(0,0, d.width-1, d.height-1);
}
//------------------------------------------------
public boolean mouseDown(Event evt, int x, int y)
{
outline(Color.black);     //draw box in black
return false;             //but pass event on to parent
}
//------------------------------------------------
public boolean mouseUp(Event evt, int x, int y)
{
outline(Color.white);     //draw box in white
```

```
    return true;        //do not pass event further
    }
```

Using Thread Blocking for Modal Dialog

Niemeyer and Peck [7] have described another way to make dialogs modal in Java 1.0, so that the *calling* method does not proceed
until the dialog completes. In this approach, you override the
dialog's *show()* method with one that is synchronized and use the
wait() method to block the thread:

```
public synchronized void show()
{
super.show();               //call real show method
wait();                     //block here until notified
}
```

Then, to exit from the dialog, when an OK or Cancel button is
pressed, you call the *notifyAll()* method:

```
public synchronized boolean handleEvent(Event evt)
{
  if (evt.target == OK)
   {
   dispose();
   notifyAll();
   return true;
   }
else
  return super.handleEvent(evt);
}
```

Moving On

In this chapter, we've learned how to build menus and respond to menu item clicks. We've also learned how to display dialogs in both applications and applets and how to write interfaces that allow calling programs to be accessed by the results of the dialog.

In the next chapters, we'll begin considering how to build actual, useful classes of the kind we might use in real programs.

16

Classes & Binary Files in Java

Wе've seen a lot of the classes that Java provides, and we've built some simple classes as part of our discussion of files and images. We now need to understand a little more about how classes hierarchies are designed.

When you design classes, you should always try to arrange them to represent the physical reality they are modeling. Programming using objects is more natural than your old ways, because you tend to think of everyday life in terms of objects all the time: send the customer the quote, get the price from the vendor, get the documents from the server, send a letter to your child, and so on.

In general, you want to design simple objects representing fundamental components of your computing problem and then design more complex derived classes, which represent the actual interactions your program is intended to solve.

Viewing a Customer File

Now we are going to write a program to read in a list of customers from a file and allow the user to view and modify each customer. The minimum logical unit in such a program is a single customer, who will have attributes like name, address, and phone number.

Then we will have to build some sort of container to hold the entire array of customers. This could be a data file structure, a database, or an in-memory array, and we shouldn't have to know how it manages this storage. So, in keeping with the style introduced in Visual Basic 4.0, we will call this container a Customers object.

In addition, we will need a *visual interface* class to display the customer list and another *details* class to display the details of a single customer. We can represent these classes schematically as shown in Figure 16-1.

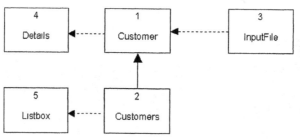

Figure 16-1: The class structure of a simple program to view customer files.

The Customer Class

The basic *Customer* class is shown below. The constructor starts with the first and last name. You can then set the remaining fields with the *set...* accessor methods and can read out any of the fields using the *get...* accessor methods. For compactness in displaying essentially repetitive code, we have not put the braces on separate lines in this code display:

```
class Customer
{
//this class represents the data on
//one customer
private String first_name;
private String last_name;
private String address;
```

```java
private String town;
private String state;
private String zip;
private String phone;
//-------------------------------------------
public Customer(String frname, String lname)
 {first_name = frname;
 last_name = lname;}
//-------------------------------------------
public String getFrname()
 { return first_name;}
//-------------------------------------------
public void setFrname(String s)
 {first_name = s;}
//-------------------------------------------
public String getLname()
 {return last_name;}
//-------------------------------------------
public void setLname(String s)
 {last_name = s;}
//-------------------------------------------
public String getAddress()
 { return address;}
//-------------------------------------------
public void setAddress(String s)
 {address = s;}
//-------------------------------------------
public String getTown()
 { return town;}
//-------------------------------------------
public void setTown(String s)
 {town = s;}
//-------------------------------------------
public String getState()
 { return state;}
//-------------------------------------------
public void setState(String s)
 {state = s;}
//-------------------------------------------
```

```
public String getZip()
  { return zip;}
//---------------------------------------
public void setZip(String s)
  {zip = s;}
//---------------------------------------
public String getPhone()
  { return phone;}
//---------------------------------------
public void setPhone(String s)
  {phone = s;}
}
```

While the accessor functions here are fairly bare bones, you could easily imagine having these functions check each field's validity, strip off excess spaces, and even control name capitalization.

The Customers Class

The *Customers* class is a container of some sort for instances of the *Customer* class where the list of customers is stored. It is at this level that we will deal with how the data are stored on disk and read in, as well as how they are stored in memory.

We'll read out customer data from a simple comma-delimited file in the form:

```
frname1, lastname1, address1, town1, state1, zipcode1, phone1
frname2, lastname2, address2, town2, state2, zipcode2, phone2
etc.
```

We can do this easily using the *read* method from the *InputFile* class we developed in Chapter 12. A fragment of the constructor from the *Customers* class is shown below:

```
public Customers(String filename)
{
InputFile f = new InputFile(filename);
String frname="", lname;
while (frname != null)
```

```
   {
   frname = f.read();        //read one field from file
```

Once we have read in the fields, we can create an instance of the Customer object and add it to the collection inside the *Customers* class. As we have done previously, we will use the *Vector* class to store an array of these objects. We illustrate the complete constructor below. Note that we keep reading new customer records until the *read* method returns a null:

```
class Customers
{
//this class serves as a container for all
//of the customers. On invocation, it reads them
//from a data file and keeps them in a vector
//of Customer objects
Vector cust;
//------------------------------------------------
public Customers(String filename)
{
InputFile f = new InputFile(filename);    //open file
cust = new Vector();                       //create vector
String frname="", lname;
while (frname != null)
   {
   frname = f.read();              //read first name
   if(frname != null)              //and proceed if not null
   {
   lname = f.read();               //get last name
   //create a Customer object
   Customer customer = new Customer(frname, lname);
   customer.setAddress(f.read()); //read remaining
   customer.setTown(f.read());    //fields
   customer.setState(f.read());
   customer.setZip(f.read());
   customer.setPhone(f.read());
   cust.addElement(customer);     //add to vector
   } //endif
   } //end while
}
```

The remainder of our *Customers* class simply allows us to determine the size of the vector and get and store elements into the vector:

```java
public int getCount()
{
 return cust.size();        //number in vector
}
//-------------------------------------
public void setCust(Customer c, int i)
{
cust.setElementAt(c, i);   //change object
}
//-------------------------------------
public Customer getCust(int i)
{
//get a customer object from the vector
if ((i >= 0) && (i <cust.size()))
   return (Customer)cust.elementAt(i);
else
   return null;
}
```

Displaying the Customer List

Now that we know how to read the customer file into a vector of customer objects, we've learned most of the hard stuff. It's relatively simple to instantiate the *Customers* class and add its elements to the list box:

```java
public custread()
{
super("Customer list");         //create frame
setLayout(new BorderLayout());
Panel psouth = new Panel();
add("South", psouth);           //put buttons along bottom
```

```
view = new Button("View");
psouth.add(view);
view.disable();                    //disabled until list clicked
close = new Button("Close");
psouth.add(close);

// read the file and create customer container
custs = new Customers("people.add");
custlist = new List(10, false); //insert list box
add("Center", custlist);
//add first and last names to list box
for (int i = 0; i < custs.getCount(); i++)
  {
  Customer c = custs.getCust(i);
  custlist.addItem(c.getFrname() +" "+c.getLname());
  }
reshape(100,100,250,150);
show();                            //show the frame window
  }
```

This brings up a display of the customer names in a list box with buttons labeled View and Close along the bottom, as illustrated in Figure 16-2. The program custread.java is in the \chapter16 directory on the Companion CD-ROM.

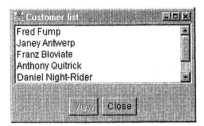

Figure 16-2: The list box view shown by the custread.java program.

Showing Customer Details

Now we'd like to display the details of whichever customer we selected. We've arranged the program so that View is disabled until you click on one of the customer names:

```
public boolean handleEvent(Event evt)
{
//enable View button once a line in the list box
//has been selected
if((evt.target == custlist)&&
      (evt.id == Event.LIST_SELECT))
   {
   view.enable();          //enable view button
   return true;
   }
return super.handleEvent(evt);
}
```

Then, when we click on View, we respond by selecting the customer based on the line in the list box, which is selected, and launching the Viewer dialog:

```
public void clickedView()
{
int i = custlist.getSelectedIndex();
if (i >=0)
 {
//display view box with selected customer
Customer c = custs.getCust(i); //get selected customer
Viewer vw = new Viewer(this, this, c);
vw.show();
}//end if
}
```

We want to bring up a dialog box showing each of the customer fields, as we illustrate in Figure 16-3.

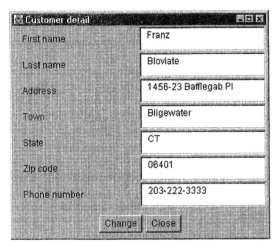

Figure 16-3: The custread customer details dialog.

Our *Customer* class contains seven data elements for us to display. We can quickly put together a modal dialog where the center is a 7 X 2 cell grid of labels and TextFields, and a bottom row in the southern border containing Change and Close buttons. As we create the seven text fields, we load them with strings from that customer's data. Since this is a dialog that must return data to the calling class, we also pass a reference to the parent class that implements a SendCustomer interface:

```
class Viewer extends Dialog
{
TextField fname, lname, address;
TextField town, state, zip, phone;
Button OK, Cancel;
SendCustomer fsc;
Customer thisCust;

//display customer selected in list box
public Viewer(Frame fr, SendCustomer fc, Customer c)
{
super(fr, "Customer detail", true);      //create window
```

```
fsc = fc;    //save reference to parent
thisCust = c;
Panel sp = new Panel();    //panel for buttons
add("South", sp);
OK = new Button("Change");
Cancel = new Button("Close");
sp.add(OK);
sp.add(Cancel);
Panel p = new Panel();
add("Center", p);

p.setLayout(new GridLayout(7,2)); //grid for center

//load text fields with info on customer
p.add(new Label("First name"));
fname = new TextField(c.getFrname());
p.add(fname);

p.add(new Label("Last name"));
lname = new TextField(c.getLname());
p.add(lname);

p.add(new Label("Address"));
address = new TextField(c.getAddress());
p.add(address);

p.add(new Label("Town"));
town = new TextField(c.getTown());
p.add(town);

p.add(new Label("State"));
state = new TextField(c.getState());
p.add(state);

p.add(new Label("Zip code"));
zip = new TextField(c.getZip());
p.add(zip);

p.add(new Label("Phone number"));
```

```
phone = new TextField(c.getPhone());
p.add(phone);
reshape(100,100,350,300);
}
```

Now each of these customer fields is editable, and we ought to be able to both view the current values and store changed values if the user clicks on Save:

```
private void clickedOK()
{
//load customer object with info from text fields
 thisCust.setFrname(fname.getText());
 thisCust.setLname(lname.getText());
 thisCust.setAddress(address.getText());
 thisCust.setTown(town.getText());
 thisCust.setState(state.getText());
 thisCust.setZip(zip.getText());
 thisCust.setPhone(phone.getText());
 fsc.setCustomer(thisCust);
 }
```

After copying them back into the thisCust customer object, we use the interface call setCustomer to put the data back into the parent:

```
public void setCustomer(Customer c)
{
//changes customer data for currently selected customer
//used by.dialog box to call back
int i = custlist.getSelectedIndex();
if (i >=0)
 {
 custs.setCust(c, i);
custlist.replaceItem(c.getFrname() + " " +
                     c.getLname(), i);
 }//end if
 }
```

This replaces the old element in the vector with the object containing the revised values and replaces the corresponding line in the list box with the new customer name.

Handling Binary Files

In the previous example, we read in our information from a comma-delimited file: one line per customer. While reading such a file is quite simple, if some information changes, there is no simple way to replace a line in such a file without rewriting the entire file. A more common format for storing data is a binary file with fixed length records, so that customer number *n* is found at the byte position *n x record_length* in the file. Then we can read and write each record independently of the others.

First, we'll build a *BinaryFile* class, which allows us to read and write binary data while containing the exceptions within the class.

Let's suppose our data are stored in a binary file described in Visual Basic by:

```
Type customer
  frname As String * 20
  lname As String * 20
  address As String * 30
  town As String * 20
  state As String * 2
  zip As String * 5
  phone As String * 15
End Type
```

The Visual Basic program makebinary.vbp on the Companion CD-ROM uses this record description to produce the binary file customer.rec, which is also on your example disk.

We can read binary files using the *RandomAccessFile* class. We'll derive a new class *BinaryFile* from *RandomAccessFile* to allow reading and writing of records more easily and the concealment of the *try...catch* exception handling:

```
import java.io.*;
class BinaryFile
{
private RandomAccessFile f;      //contains Random.. file
boolean IOError = false;         //error flag
private int bytes_read;
//-----------------------------------------------
```

```java
public BinaryFile(String filename, String mode)
 {
  try
  {  f = new RandomAccessFile(filename, mode);  }
  catch (IOException e)
  {
   System.out.println("no such file");
   IOError = true;
  }
 }
//----------------------
public byte[] readBytes(int num_bytes)
{
//reads current record from file
byte b[] = new byte[num_bytes];          //create array
try
  { bytes_read = f.read(b); }    //read in bytes
catch (IOException e)
  {
  System.out.println("File read error");
  IOError = true;
  }
if (bytes_read < num_bytes)
   IOError = true;
return b;
}
//----------------------
public boolean writeBytes(byte b[])
{
//write bytes at current position
  try
  {  f.write(b);  }
  catch (IOException e)
  {
  System.out.println("File write error");
  IOError = true;
  }
return IOError;
 }
```

```
//-----------------------
public boolean writeBytes(byte b[], int n)
{
//write bytes at record position n
seek(b.length * n);
writeBytes(b);
return IOError;
}
//----------------------
private void seek(int n)
{
try
 { f.seek(n); }
catch(IOException e)
 {
 System.out.println("File seek error");
 IOError = true;
 }
}
//----------------------
public byte[] readBytes(int record_number,
                        int num_bytes)
{
//seeks to a particular record and reads it
seek(record_number * num_bytes);
return readBytes(num_bytes);
}
//----------------------
public boolean error()
{ return IOError; }
}
```

Then, we'll derive a new class *binaryCustomer* from *Customer* and *bCustomers* from *Customers,* which read data into the vector from the customer.rec binary file. Java doesn't have the concept of a structure or record, but we can easily build a class that reads data in the format we show above.

Our *bCustomer* class contains the binary file byte layout and uses the BinaryFile *readBytes* method to read each of the fields:

```
class bCustomer extends Customer
{
static final int f_name=20, sfname =0;
static final int l_name=20, slname=f_name;
static final int address=30, saddress = slname+l_name;
static final int town = 20, stown = saddress+address;
static final int state =2, sstate = stown+town;
static final int zip = 5, szip = sstate+state;
static final int phone =15, sphone = szip+zip;
public static final int RECLEN = sphone+phone;

    public bCustomer(byte b[])
    {
    super(new String(b, 0, sfname, f_name).trim(),
        new String(b, 0, slname, l_name).trim());
    setAddress(new String(b, 0, saddress,
        address).trim());
    setTown(new String(b, 0, stown, town).trim());
    setState(new String(b, 0, sstate, state).trim());
    setZip(new String(b, 0, szip, zip).trim());
    setPhone(new String(b, 0, sphone, phone).trim());
    }
}
```

Note that this is the entire class definition; all the other methods are inherited from the parent *Customer* class. Each instance of the *bCustomer* class extracts the bytes for each field from an input byte array that is always *bCustomer.RECLEN* bytes long.

The *binaryCustomers* class replaces the *Customers* class and actually reads the data from the binary file and stores it in a vector of bCustomer objects as before:

```
class binaryCustomers
{
//this class serves as a container for all
//of the customers. On invocation, it reads them
```

```
//from a data file and keeps them in a vector
//of Customer objects
Vector cust;
BinaryFile f;
public binaryCustomers(String filename)
{
f = new BinaryFile(filename, "rw");
cust = new Vector();
while (! f.error())
  {
  byte b[] = f.readBytes(bCustomer.RECLEN);
  if(! f.error())
   {
   bCustomer customer = new bCustomer(b);
   cust.addElement(customer);
   } //endif
  } //end while
}
//-------------------------------------
public int getCount()
{
 return cust.size();
}
//-------------------------------------
public void setCust(bCustomer c, int i)
{
cust.setElementAt(c, i);   //change in vector
f.writeBytes(c.getBytes(), i); //change in file
}
//-------------------------------------
public bCustomer getCust(int i)
{
if ((i>=0) && (i <cust.size()))
  return (bCustomer)cust.elementAt(i);
else
  return null;
}
}
```

This class also writes the changed data back to the correct record in the file. But to do this, it needs a class that provides methods for pulling the data out of byte arrays and putting them into strings and pulling byte arrays back out of strings to reconstruct the byte records array. This is the *bCustomer* class, which is derived from the *Customer* class:

```java
class bCustomer extends Customer
{
static final int f_name=20, sfname =0;
static final int l_name=20, slname=f_name;
static final int address=30, saddress = slname + l_name;
static final int town = 20, stown = saddress+address;
static final int state =2, sstate = stown+town;
static final int zip = 5, szip = sstate+state;
static final int phone =15, sphone = szip+zip;
public static final int RECLEN = sphone+phone;

public bCustomer(byte b[])
{
super(new String(b, 0, sfname, f_name).trim(),
    new String(b, 0, slname, l_name).trim());
setAddress(new String(b, 0, saddress,
    address).trim());
setTown(new String(b, 0, stown, town).trim());
setState(new String(b, 0, sstate, state).trim());
setZip(new String(b, 0, szip, zip).trim());
setPhone(new String(b, 0, sphone, phone).trim());
}
//-------------------------------------------
private void put_bytes(byte[] b, String s, int offset)
{
///puts bytes from string into byte array
s.getBytes(0, s.length(), b, offset);
}
//-------------------------------------------
public byte[] getBytes()
{
byte b[] = new byte[RECLEN];        //create byte record
put_bytes(b, getFrname(), sfname);
```

```
put_bytes(b, getLname(), slname);
put_bytes(b, getAddress(), saddress);
put_bytes(b, getTown(), stown);
put_bytes(b, getState(), sstate);
put_bytes(b, getZip(), szip);
put_bytes(b, getPhone(), sphone);
return b;
}
}
```

This *bCustomer* class makes use of the *String* methods to convert between arrays of 8-bit bytes and 16-bit string characters. This allows us to continue to use the underlying *Customer* class where each field is stored as a String.

Review of Class Construction

In building these classes, we've now seen how we start with the concept of a *Customer* class, irrespective of the data representation on disk, and construct our classes using the customer unit. As we moved to a binary file format, we derived a *bCustomer* class, which converted byte arrays into Strings and vice-versa, but without changing our base customer class in any way.

We also had to revise the *Customers* collection class to make a *binaryCustomers* class that handled the actual reading and writing of the binary file. However, since it had only two methods with different return types and a different constructor, we simply replaced it.

Moving On

In this chapter, we've reviewed how to handle simple class design and written a simple program to read in and display data from a customer list. Then we extended those simple classes to handle reading and writing data from binary files as well.

In the following chapters, we'll look a little more at how to use the keyboard and mouse and then discuss building our own controls from scratch.

17

Keyboard Input in Java

So far, we have used the keyboard to enter data only when we used TextFields on forms to type in data. However, you can use the keyboard to enter data even if you are not using the *awt* classes to produce a windowing interface. In addition, you can use various special keys in user interfaces to make your entry screens more flexible and easier to use. In this chapter, we'll discuss how you can intercept single keystrokes and how you can read and process keyboard input.

Direct Keyboard Input

If you look at the *System* class, you will find that it contains the static *in* and *out* classes:

```
public static InputStream in;
public static PrintStream out;
```

We have been using the *System.out* class copiously throughout this book as a simple printing and debugging tool. It is sometimes convenient to be able to type in a few characters from the keyboard to start a test program as you begin to develop classes.

We'll illustrate how to use *System.in* by writing a program that allows us to enter a string followed by a return and then prints that string back out immediately afterward. Now the *InputStream* class itself only allows input of single bytes and would be fairly cumbersome to use directly. Instead, we'll use the *DataInputStream* class, which contains the convenient *readLine()* method. It also allows you to read bytes, chars, floats, doubles, ints, and longs directly.

The constructor for the *DataInputStream* class is:

```
public DataInputStream(InputStream in);
```

This leads to the following conceptually simple (although incomplete) program:

```
import java.io.*;
public class Sysin1
{
public static void main(String argv[])
{
//create input stream
DataInputStream Keybd = new DataInputStream(System.in);
String s = Keybd.readLine();        //read a line of text
System.out.println(s);              //print it out
System.exit(0);                     //and exit
}
}
```

This program (Sysin1.java on the Companion CD-ROM) will not compile without error because the *readLine()* method throws an exception, which you must catch. Our second try, with the exception caught, is:

```
import java.io.*;
public class Sysin2
{
public static void main(String argv[])
{
DataInputStream Keybd = new DataInputStream(System.in);
try
  {String s = Keybd.readLine(); }
catch(IOException e)
```

```
{System.out.println("keyboard error");}
System.out.println(s);
System.exit(0);
 }
}
```

This version also will not compile without errors, because the String s is created inside the *try* block and has no existence in the main program. Remember that you can declare variables within any block, and they vanish once you leave that block (or variable *scope*). This version (Sysin2.java) gives the error:

```
Sysin2.java(11): Undefined variable s
```

Clearly we need to declare the String s outside the *try* block. So we again rewrite the program as:

```
import java.io.*;
public class Sysin
{
public static void main(String argv[])
{
String s;
DataInputStream Keybd = new DataInputStream(System.in);
try
 {s = Keybd.readLine(); }
catch (IOException e)
  {System.out.println("Keyboard error");}
System.out.println(s);
System.exit(0);
 }
}
```

This version (Sysin3.java) gives the compiler error:

```
Sysin3.java(12):
Variable s may not have been initialized
```

The error is generated because a value is assigned to *s* only inside the *try* block. If an exception is thrown by the *readLine* method, *s* will never have a value. We can easily correct this sort of error by assigning *s* some value such as *null* or " " before executing the *try* block:

```
import java.io.*;
public class Sysin
{
public static void main(String argv[])
{
String s = null;
DataInputStream Keybd = new DataInputStream(System.in);
try
  {s = Keybd.readLine(); }
catch (IOException e)
  {System.out.println("Keyboard error");}
System.out.println(s);
System.exit(0);
  }
}
```

Finally we have a version that compiles and executes without error, Sysin4.java.

Prompting for Input

If we execute Sysin4.java, the Java Virtual Machine program prints out loading information and then nothing happens. We have to know that it is now time to type in a value. So we might consider putting in a *print* statement to indicate that input will now be accepted. In our little test program (Sysin5.java), we print out a > character:

```
import java.io.*;
public class Sysin5
{
 public static void main(String argv[])
 {
String s = null;
DataInputStream Kbd = new DataInputStream(System.in);
try
{System.out.print(">");          //print prompt
```

```
s = Kbd.readLine(); }
catch (IOException e)
 {System.out.println("Keyboard error");}
System.out.println(s);
System.exit(0);
 }
}
```

However, if we execute this program, we find that the > character is not printed at once. Instead, it is printed along with the output from:

```
System.out.println(s);
```

This is because output to the output stream *out* is *buffered* and is not usually printed until a newline character is placed in the stream. You can modify this behavior, however, by simply flushing all the characters from the output stream using the *flush()* method:

```
try
 {System.out.print(">");   //print prompt
  System.out.flush();      //force output before newline
 s = Keybd.readLine(); }
 catch (IOException e)
 { System.out.println("Keyboard error");}
 System.out.println(s);
```

This final version with the prompt character is in the program file Sysin.java on the Companion CD-ROM.

Processing Input Arguments

All stand-alone programs start with:

```
public static void main(String argv[])
```

The argument *argv[]* represents an array of strings built up from the space-separated command-line arguments to your Java program. Unlike C, the program name is not one of the command-line arguments. Using the following program Sysarg.java:

```
import java.io.*;
public class Sysarg
{
```

```
public static void main(String argv[])
{
for (int i = 0; i< argv.length; i++)
 System.out.println(argv[i]);
System.exit(0);
 }
 }
```

if you type:

```
java Sysarg abc -d e f
```

the program will print out:

```
abc
-d
e
f
```

You can parse these arguments to control the flow of your program. Such methods are useful when writing server programs, which often do not have GUI interfaces, or in writing small development test programs.

Default & Cancel Buttons

In Visual Basic dialogs, one of the buttons can be designated the default button and another designated the Cancel button. The default button is executed when the Enter key is pressed, no matter which control has the input focus, and the Cancel button is executed when the Escape key is pressed, usually causing the window to close.

In Java, we can give buttons these functions by trapping keystrokes at the form level, rather than within a particular control, and taking the appropriate action.

To illustrate how to do this, we'll write a simple program with a label control and a button labeled Change, as shown in Figure 17-1. When you click on Change, it brings up a dialog where the text of that label field is shown in a TextField you can edit, along with an OK button and a Cancel button, as shown in Figure 17-2. If you click on OK, any changes in the text field are sent back to the original, and if you click on Cancel, the dialog is dismissed without any changes being made.

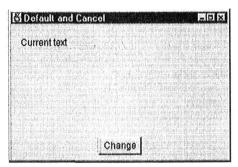

Figure 17-1: The simple DefCancel.java main window.

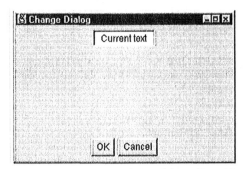

Figure 17-2: The Change dialog of the DefCancel.java program.

The *DefCancel* window is created in the usual way using a BorderLayout:

```
public class DefCancel extends Frame implements LbText
{
Label datastring;
Button dialog;
//-------------------------------------------
public DefCancel()
  {
  super("Default and Cancel");
  setLayout(new BorderLayout());
  datastring = new Label("Current text");
  Panel p0 = new Panel();
```

```
p0.setLayout(new GridLayout(3,1));
add("Center", p0);
p0.add(datastring);      //to upper third
Panel p1 = new Panel();  //centers button
add("South", p1);
dialog = new Button("Change");
p1.add(dialog);
reshape(100,100,300,200);
show();
}
```

Clicking on Change launches the ChangeDialog window in the usual way:

```
public boolean action(Event evt, Object arg)
 {
 if(evt.target == dialog)
   {
   ChangeDialog CDlg =
    new ChangeDialog(this, this, datastring.getText());
   CDlg.show();
   return true;
   }
 return super.action(evt, arg);
 }
```

The ChangeDialog window communicates back to the main window using the interface LbText:

```
interface LbText
{
 public void setLbText(String s);
}
```

where the *local* method simply copies the specified string into the label text:

```
public void setLbText(String s)
{
datastring.setText(s);
}
```

The *ChangeDialog* class is derived from *Dialog* in the usual way and has the default border layout, with two buttons along the bottom and the text field in the center:

```
class ChangeDialog extends Dialog
 {
 TextField labeltext;
 Button OK, Cancel;
 LbText lbtext;
//-----------------------------------------
 public ChangeDialog(Frame fr, LbText lbt, String s)
 {
 super(fr, "Change Dialog", true);     //create dlg
 labeltext = new TextField(s);
 lbtext = lbt;                         //save interface ref
 Panel p0 = new Panel();
 add("Center", p0);
 p0.add(labeltext);                    //text field in middle
 Panel p1 = new Panel();
 add("South", p1);
 OK = new Button("OK");                //OK and Cancel at bottom
 p1.add(OK);
 Cancel = new Button("Cancel");
 p1.add(Cancel);
<Compu reshape(100,100,300,200);
 }
```

Finally, the buttons are detected in an *action* routine as usual, calling little *clicked...* routines as we have done before:

```
private void clickedOK()
{
lbtext.setLbText(labeltext.getText());
dispose();
}
//-----------------------------------------
private void clickedCancel()
{
dispose();
}
//-----------------------------------------
public boolean action (Event evt, Object arg)
{
if (evt.target == OK)
  {
```

```
    clickedOK();
    return true;
    }
if (evt.target == Cancel)
    {
    clickedCancel();
    return true;
    }
 return super.action(evt, arg);
    }
```

The new and critical part of the *dialog* routine is the addition of a *handleEvent* method that traps keystrokes. The value of keystrokes is kept in the *key* field of the Event object, and we need only compare them to the Enter (newline) character and the Escape character. Java defines the newline character using the escape sequence '\n' but does not provide a way to represent the Escape character. It has the ASCII value 27, however, and since the *Event.key* field is of type int, we can define a named constant Escape, as we illustrate below:

```
//-------------------------------------------
public boolean handleEvent(Event evt)
{
final int Escape = 27;      //keyboard value
if(evt.key == '\n')
  {
  clickedOK();              //newline clicks OK
  return true;
  }
if (evt.key == Escape)
  {
  clickedCancel();          //Escape clicks Cancel
  return true;
  }
return super.handleEvent(evt);
}
```

This illustrates why putting the code you execute on a button click into a little private method is so valuable; we now call them from two places in the dialog.

Indicating the Default Button

In Visual Basic and Windows programs in general, the default button is usually indicated by a thicker line drawn around the button. The buttons provided in the awt don't have methods to indicate this, but you can easily add a line around the button in the *paint* routine.

It is not necessary to add the controls using a null layout for you to know where to draw the box around the button. Instead, you simply ask the button for its location and size and draw an appropriate rectangle. Since the button is added to a Panel container, we need to obtain that container's graphics object to draw in the proper coordinate system. The following *paint* routine shows how the default box can be drawn around the button:

```
public void paint (Graphics g)
{
Point pt = OK.location();      //find where it is
Dimension sz = OK.size();      //and get its size
Graphics g1 = p1.getGraphics();//panel's graphics
//draw rectangle around the OK button
g1.drawRect(pt.x-1, pt.y-1, sz.width+1, sz.height+1);
}
```

The result of this default rectangle drawing is shown in Figure 17-3, and the code for this program is in the DefCancelo.java file in \chapter17 or the Companion CD-ROM.

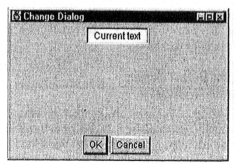

Figure 17-3: Showing a default button by drawing a rectangle around it.

Setting the Focus in a Dialog

When there are several controls in a dialog, and especially when there are several text fields, you will make your dialog more usable if you can type data into the default field and press Enter to save the data and close the dialog.

While the *requestFocus* method can be used to set the focus to the text field in this example, this method works only after the dialog is shown. Thus, in order to set the focus, we override the *show()* method as follows:

```
public void show()
{
super.show();              //show the dialog
labeltext.requestFocus(); //and set the focus
}
```

Other Function Keys

You can handle most of the function keys in the same way. They have been defined as named constants as part of the *Event* class:

```
public final static int DOWN;
public final static int END;
public final static int F1;
```

```
public final static int F2;
public final static int F3;
public final static int F4;
public final static int F5;
public final static int F6;
public final static int F7;
public final static int F8;
public final static int F9;
public final static int F10;
public final static int F11;
public final static int F12;
public final static int HOME;
public final static int LEFT;
public final static int PGDN;
public final static int PGUP;
public final static int RIGHT;
public final static int UP;
```

You can test for any of them in your *handleEvent* or *keyDown* methods. In fact, all of these keys cause a special KEY_ACTION event you can specifically test for as well. This gives you the opportunity to use these function keys for shortcuts wherever you might be able to simplify your program.

Tabbing Between Fields in a Dialog

The Java 1.0 awt for Windows 95 provides no way for you to move between fields on a form using tabs or arrow keys. As with the default and Cancel keys, you can program this behavior yourself fairly easily. First let's create a window with three text fields, two radio buttons, and OK and Cancel buttons, as shown in Figure 17-4.

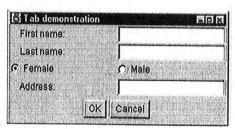

Figure 17-4: The Tabbit window.

As we create these form elements and add them to the frame, we'll also put those we wish to tab between into a vector that we can move through when we tab between fields. Of course, we won't include the label fields, but we will include the radio buttons and the command buttons. We create those fields as follows:

```java
import java.awt.*;
import java.util.*;

public class Tabbit extends Frame
{
private TextField frname, lname;
private CheckboxGroup cbg;
private Checkbox Male, Female;
private TextField Address;
private Button OK, Cancel;
private Vector TabList;          //list of controls
private int tab_index;
final int Escape = 27;           //Escape key
//----------------------------------------------
public Tabbit()
{
super ("Tab demonstration");     //create frame
setLayout(new BorderLayout());
TabList = new Vector();          //create tab vector

Panel p0 = new Panel();
add("Center", p0);
p0.setLayout(new GridLayout(4,2));
```

```
//Now add lines for name, sex, address, etc.
p0.add(new Label("First name:"));
frname = new TextField(15);
p0.add(frname);
TabList.addElement(frname);    //add control to list
p0.add(new Label("Last name:"));

lname = new TextField(20);
p0.add(lname);
TabList.addElement(lname);      //add control to list

cbg = new CheckboxGroup();
Female = new Checkbox("Female",cbg, true);
Male = new Checkbox("Male", cbg, false);
p0.add(Female);
p0.add(Male);
TabList.addElement(Female);     //add control to list
TabList.addElement(Male);       //add control to list

p0.add(new Label("Address:"));
Address = new TextField(20);
p0.add(Address);
TabList.addElement(Address);    //add control to list

Panel p1 = new Panel();
add("South", p1);               //flow layout
OK = new Button("OK");
Cancel = new Button("Cancel");
p1.add(OK);
TabList.addElement(OK);         //add control to list
p1.add(Cancel);
TabList.addElement(Cancel);     //add control to list

reshape(100,100, 300,150);
show();
setTab(0);                      //set focus to first tab
}
```

We then create a *setTab* method that sets the focus to whichever control in that list we select. We also provide for wrap around; if the index is too large, we reset to the first control, and if the index is less than zero, we reset to the last control:

```
private void setTab(int tb)
{
//sets the focus to the next tab
if (tb >= TabList.size())
  tb = 0;                          //reset if at end
if (tb <0 )
  tb = TabList.size()-1;           //set to end if < 0
tab_index = tb;

//set the focus to the next control
((Component)(TabList.elementAt(tab_index)))
    .requestFocus();
}
```

As with other vectors we have used, we recognize that it returns elements of type Object. We can then cast them to whatever type they actually are. Since all visual controls are derived from the Component type, we cast them all to that base class, which has the requisite *requestFocus()* method.

ENUMERATING COMPONENTS IN ANY CONTAINER WINDOW

You can also ask any container, such as a Frame, Window, or Panel, for the number of components it contains:

```
int count = fr.countComponents();
```

You can then move through the list of components by simply asking for a reference to each component by index:

```
(fr.getComponent(i)).setFocus();
```

However, this presumes that there are no components (such as labels) that you wish to skip and that all of the components are in a single panel. Since we usually use several panels to control the layout, this is seldom the case.

Intercepting Tab Keystrokes

Now we can intercept three different keystrokes: the newline, the Escape, and the tab key. Since our primary purpose is to catch keystrokes, let's use the *keyDown* method rather than the general *handleEvent* method:

```java
public boolean keyDown(Event evt, int key)
{
switch (key)
 {
 case '\t':                 //tab key
   setTab(tab_index +1);
    return true;
 case '\n':                 //Enter key
   clickedOK();
    return true;
 case Escape:               //Escape key
   clickedCancel();
    return true;
 }
return super.keyDown(evt, key);
}
```

Note that since we return directly from within each case of the *switch* statement, we don't need *break* statements to end each case. This program, called Tabbit.java, is on the Companion CD-ROM.

Catching the Backtab Character

The backward tab character indicated on the tab key as |← would appear to be generated by holding down the Shift key and pressing the Tab key. Actually, this still generates the same forward tab character as pressing the Tab key by itself. However, the Event object has a number of public fields that allow us to detect the fact that the Shift key has also been depressed. These fields are:

```java
public Object arg;
public int clickCount;
public Event evt;
public int id;
```

```
public int key;
public int modifiers;
public Object target;
public long when;
public int x;
public int y;
```

In particular the *modifiers* field can be ANDed with one of several masks:

```
// possible masks for the modifiers field
public final static int ALT_MASK
public final static int CTRL_MASK;
public final static int META_MASK;
public final static int SHIFT_MASK;
```

In this case, we simply need to AND the modifiers field with the SHIFT_MASK to determine if the Shift key has been pressed along with the tab key. If it has, we decrement the tab list pointer, and if it hasn't, we increment the tab list pointer. The final version of our *keyDown* routine is as follows:

```
public boolean keyDown(Event evt, int key)
{
switch (key)
 {
 case '\t':                    //tab or backtab
   if ((evt.modifiers & Event.SHIFT_MASK) != 0)
     setTab(tab_index -1);   //back tab
   else
     setTab(tab_index +1);   //tab
   return true;
 case '\n':
   clickedOK();              //Enter
   return true;
 case Escape:
   clickedCancel();         //Escape
   return true;
 }
return super.keyDown(evt, key);
 }
```

In a similar manner, we can determine if the Alt, Ctrl, or Shift
keys are depressed. While the Shift key will capitalize alphabetic
characters, you can only detect Shift/function keys by checking
the modifiers field using the Shift mask.

Highlighting TextFields

When the most likely change you will make is to replace a text
field completely with new text, it is annoying to have to laboriously erase the previous contents. To highlight the entire text field,
press Shift+End. Then, the next character you type will replace the
entire text string.

An even better way is for the highlighting to take place automatically when you tab into these fields. One possible approach (which
doesn't work) would be to derive a new version of the *TextField* class
that always highlights its contents whenever it receives a *gotFocus()*
event. However, in Java 1.0 under Windows 95, the *requestFocus()*
method does not cause the *gotFocus()* method to be called.

Instead, we'll just check to see whether the control is an instance
of the *TextField* class and, if so, call its *selectAll()* method directly:

```
private void setTab(int tb)
{
//sets the focus to the next tab
if (tb >= TabList.size())
   tb = 0;                          //reset if at end
if (tb <0 )
   tb = TabList.size()-1;           //set to end if < 0
tab_index = tb;

//set the focus to the next control
Component c =(Component)(TabList.elementAt(tab_index));
c.requestFocus();
if (c instanceof TextField)       //if a textfield
   {
   TextField t = (TextField)c;    //cast to this type
   t.selectAll();                 //and select all
                                  //characters
   }
}
```

Moving On

In this chapter, we've dissected the details of keyboard use in Java from the *System.in* stream to how to make default and Cancel buttons and how to tab through a list of controls. In the next chapter, we'll take a closer look at the mouse.

18

Using the Mouse in Java

We have used the mouse for a number of things in earlier chapters. However, since the mouse is an integral part of the graphical environment, we show you all of its capabilities in detail in this chapter so you can appreciate how it can be used.

As you will see, we can detect mouse up and down button changes, mouse movement, and when the mouse enters or leaves a window. You can also detect which button was clicked by looking at the modifier flag. In addition, you can control the shape of the mouse cursor.

Mouse Methods

The basic graphic *Component* class contains the following convenience *mouse* methods taken from the more general *handleEvent* method:

```
public boolean mouseDown(Event  evt, int  x, int  y);
public boolean mouseDrag(Event  evt, int  x, int  y);
public boolean mouseEnter(Event  evt, int  x, int  y);
public boolean mouseExit(Event  evt, int  x, int  y);
public boolean mouseMove(Event  evt, int  x, int  y);
public boolean mouseUp(Event  evt, int  x, int  y);
```

Further, the *Frame* class allows you to change the cursor to any of 14 different shapes named:

```
public final static int CROSSHAIR_CURSOR;
public final static int DEFAULT_CURSOR;
public final static int E_RESIZE_CURSOR;
public final static int HAND_CURSOR;
public final static int MOVE_CURSOR;
public final static int N_RESIZE_CURSOR;
public final static int NE_RESIZE_CURSOR;
public final static int NW_RESIZE_CURSOR;
public final static int S_RESIZE_CURSOR;
public final static int SE_RESIZE_CURSOR;
public final static int SW_RESIZE_CURSOR;
public final static int TEXT_CURSOR;
public final static int W_RESIZE_CURSOR;
public final static int WAIT_CURSOR;
```

In Windows 95, several of these are identical, such as N_RESIZE and S_RESIZE. The *setCursor* method, which allows you to change the cursor appearance, is a method only of the *Frame* class. It does not apply to Windows, Containers, or Applets. So in effect, applets cannot change the mouse cursor unless they create separate frame windows.

Changing the Mouse Cursor Type

If you change the cursor as the mouse moves over a form or window, it can be a valuable clue to the user that different activities will take place at different positions on the screen. To illustrate how this is done, the Curses.java program on the Companion CD-ROM creates an array of 14 panels in a 2 X 7 GridLayout and assigns a different cursor index to each of them. Since the numerical values that correspond to each of the cursor types vary between 0 and 13, we use these index values as the actual cursor types:

```
import java.awt.*;
//--------------------------------
public class Curses extends Frame
//illustrates the 14 different cursor types
```

```
{
//----------------------------------
 public Curses()
 {
 super ("Cursor Demo");
 //layy out a 7 x 2 grid
 setLayout(new GridLayout(7,2));
 //Create 14 panels, each with a different index
 for (int i =0; i<14; i++)
    {
    cPanel p = new cPanel(this, i);
    add(p);
    }
 reshape(100,100, 300,150);
 show();
 }
//----------------------------------
public boolean handleEvent(Event evt)
{
if (evt.id == Event.WINDOW_DESTROY)
  System.exit(0);
return super.handleEvent(evt);
}
//----------------------------------
 static public void main(String argv[])
 {
 new Curses();
 }
//----------------------------------
}
//==================================
class cPanel extends Panel
{
int index;              //cursor index
Frame frm;
//----------------------------------
public cPanel(Frame fr, int i)
{
super();
index = i;      //Save the index of this cursor
frm = fr;       //remember the parent frame
```

```
}
//--------------------------------
public void paint(Graphics g)
{
Dimension sz = size();
g.setColor(Color.gray);
//draw a gray frame around each panel
g.drawRect(0,0, sz.width-1, sz.height-1);
//write the cursor name in black inside the panel
g.setColor(Color.black);
g.drawString(cursor_name(index), 1,12);
}
//--------------------------------
public boolean mouseEnter(Event evt, int x, int y)
{
//as the mouse enters the panel
//set the cursor to this panels type
frm.setCursor(index);
return true;
}
//--------------------------------
private String cursor_name(int i)
{
//returns the name of each cursor
//from its index
String s="";
switch(i)
 {
 case 0:
   s="Default";    break;
 case 1:
   s="crosshair";  break;
 case 2:
   s="text";       break;
 case 3:
   s="wait";       break;
 case 4:
   s="sw_resize";  break;
 case 5:
   s="se_resize";  break;
```

```
case 6:
  s="nw_resize";  break;
case 7:
  s="ne_resize";  break;
case 8:
  s="n_resize";   break;
case 9:
  s="s_resize";   break;
case 10:
  s="w_resize";   break;
case 11:
  s="e_resize";   break;
case 12:
  s="hand";       break;
case 13:
  s="move";       break;
}
return s;
}
//---------------------------------
}
```

This program works by creating 14 instances of the *cPanel* class, derived from *Panel*. When we create each instance, we pass in a reference to the parent Frame so we can execute its *setCursor* method. We also pass in the index of the particular cursor we want to display. Then when the *mouseEnter* method for that panel is executed by a passing mouse pointer, we change the shape of the pointer using:

```
public boolean mouseEnter(Event evt, int x, int y)
{
//as the mouse enters the panel
//set the cursor to this panels type
frm.setCursor(index);
return true;
}
```

to call the parent frame's *setCursor* method. The resulting program display is shown in Figure 18-1.

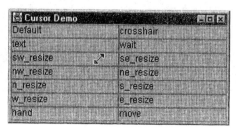

Figure 18-1: The display of the Curses.java program, listing the 14 possible cursor types.

Changing the Cursor in Separated Controls

The only reason that the Curses program cursor always produces the right cursor is that the cPanel containers are laid out next to each other with no separation. If there is a background frame where the cursor is to take on another shape, you must specifically program this case. Figure 18-2 shows the display of the Mouse1.java program where there are three colored panels separated on the Frame background.

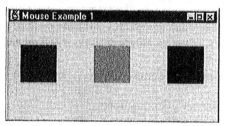

Figure 18-2: The Mouse1.java program display.

We create the panels in the usual way:

```
public class Mouse1 extends Frame
{
sqPanel Red, Green, Blue;
 public Mouse1()
 {
 super("Mouse Example 1");              //Frame caption
 setLayout(null);
 Red = new sqPanel(this, Color.red);    //3 panels
 Green = new sqPanel(this, Color.green);
 Blue = new sqPanel(this, Color.blue);
 add(Red);                              //add them to
 add(Green);                            //the layout
 add(Blue);
 Red.reshape(20,50,50,50);              //and position them
 Green.reshape(120,50,50,50);
 Blue.reshape(220,50,50,50);
 reshape(100,100,290,150);
 show();
 }
```

Our *sqPanel* class simply fills the background and upon receiving a *mouseEnter* event, saves the current cursor and sets the cursor to the crosshair type:

```
class sqPanel extends Panel
 {
 Color color;          //save the color
 Frame frame;          //and the parent frame
 int cursor_type;
  public sqPanel(Frame fr, Color c)
  {
  color = c;
  frame = fr;
  }
//----------------------------
public boolean mouseEnter(Event evt, int x, int y)
{
//on entry save the previous cursor
cursor_type = frame.getCursorType();
```

```
//and set it to crosshair type
frame.setCursor(Frame.CROSSHAIR_CURSOR);
return true;
}
//-----------------------------
public boolean mouseExit(Event evt, int x, int y)
{
frame.setCursor(cursor_type);
return true;
}
//-----------------------------
public void paint(Graphics g)
{
Dimension sz = size();
g.setColor(color);
g.fillRect(0, 0, sz.width-1, sz.height-1);
}
}
```

Then on *mouseExit*, it sets the cursor back to the saved cursor type
we had on entry:

```
frame.setCursor(cursor_type);
```

This should guarantee that the cursor returns to whatever state
it had before it entered the colored square. But this is not always
the case, illustrating the subtlety of this set of methods. If you
move your mouse very quickly from one square to another, the
mouseEnter event may "beat" the *mouseExit* event to the event
queue, and the entry and exits will get out of synch. In this case,
the mouse cursor will stay as a crosshair even while moving on
the frame background. You can see this happen in the
Mouse1b.java program, where the *enter* and *exit* methods print out
a message as they are called, and you can observe their getting out
of synch. This program is on the Companion CD-ROM.

The solution to this dilemma is implemented in the original Mouse1.java program: put a *mouseEnter* method in the *Frame* class to reset the mouse cursor to the default whenever the mouse leaves one of the panels and again moves over the background:

```
public boolean mouseEnter(Event evt, int x, int y)
{
setCursor(Frame.DEFAULT_CURSOR);
return true;
}
```

Capturing Mouse Clicks

The *mouseDown* and *mouseUp* methods can be received by any child of Component, which is to say by any visual control. If you want to take some action when the user clicks on a control, you can simply subclass the *mouseDown* event for that control.

It is advisable, however, to give the user some feedback to indicate that he has clicked on the control. In the Mouse2.java program, whose display is shown in Figure 18-3, the program draws an outline square around the control when the mouse is down, and draws the control without the outline when the mouse is up.

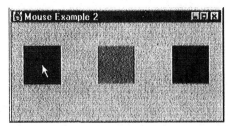

Figure 18-3: The display of the Mouse2.java program, showing how we outline a square when we click the mouse on it.

To produce this outline, we set a flag when the *mouseDown* event is received and clear it when the *mouseUp* event occurs:

```
//-------------------------------
public boolean mouseDown(Event evt, int x, int y)
{
isFrame = true;              //set frame outline flag
repaint();                   //and redraw
return true;
}
//-------------------------------
public boolean mouseUp(Event evt, int x, int y)
{
isFrame = false;            //clear frame outline flag
repaint();                  //and redraw
return true;
}
```

Then we force the panel to redraw itself by calling the *repaint* method, which in turn calls the *paint* method. In this *paint* method, we draw the outline square only if the isFrame flag is true:

```
public void paint(Graphics g)
{
Dimension sz = size();
g.setColor(color);  //fill with spec'd color
g.fillRect(0, 0, sz.width-1, sz.height-1);
if (isFrame)
  { //draw outline if flag is set
  g.setColor(Color.black);
  g.drawRect(0, 0, sz.width-1, sz.height-1);
  }
}
```

Double-clicking

There is no specific event for a double-click of a mouse button. However, one of the Event fields contains the number of consecutive *mouseDown* events, and you can use it to detect a double-click:

```
public boolean mouseDown(Event evt, int x, int y)
{
if (evt.clickCount >1 )              //assume double click
  isFrame = true;
else                                 //otherwise single click
  isFrame = false;
repaint();
return true;
}
```

This is illustrated in the Mouse5.java program on the Companion CD-ROM.

Double-clicking in List Boxes

In the case of list boxes, the LIST_SELECT event occurs if a mouse is clicked on a line of the list box. The ACTION event occurs if you double-click on a line. In this case, the Object argument of the *action* method contains the string for that line. The same *action* event also occurs if you press the Enter key after selecting a line in a list box.

Dragging With the Mouse

One powerful, but less-used, feature is the ability to drag controls around using the mouse. You might do this to rearrange controls for your own purposes at run time, or you might do it to establish communication between two controls.

The *mouseDrag* method is executed whenever the mouse button is depressed inside a control and then moved with the mouse button held down. It does not occur if the button is already down when the mouse enters the control boundary; instead this is treated as an attempt to drag the background. *Mouse enter* and *exit* methods are not called during a drag; all mouse movements are received by the control where the mouse was first depressed, even if it moves outside the control.

The mouse movements a control receives during *mouseDrag* contain the mouse's current X-Y coordinates *relative to that control.* Thus, if you want a control to actually move when you are dragging the mouse over it, you must compute the mouse's position in the containing frame and move the mouse in that coordinate space.

For example, in the Mouse3.java program, we put up the same three colored panels, but allow them to be moved about by dragging them with the mouse. Our revised *sqPanel* class saves the position of the *mouseDown* event in two private variables:

```
class sqPanel3 extends Panel
  {
  Color color;              //saved color
  Frame frame;              //and frame reference
  boolean isFrame;          //whether outlined
  int xpos, ypos;           //mouse click location
//----------------------------
  public sqPanel3(Frame fr, Color c)
    {
    color = c;              //save color
    frame = fr;             //and frame reference
    isFrame = false;
    }
//----------------------------
public boolean mouseDown(Event evt, int x, int y)
{
isFrame = true;
xpos = x; ypos = y;       //remember where mouse clicked
repaint();
return true;
}
```

Then whenever the mouse is dragged, we compute where to move the control by:

1. Getting the current mouse position.

2. Computing the delta from where the mouse was originally clicked.

3. Getting the current control position in the parent frame.

4. Moving the control by adding the delta to the parent position.

We do this as follows:

```
public boolean mouseDrag(Event evt, int x, int y)
{
Point pt = location();   //find out where panel is
int dx = x - xpos;       //figure how much mouse moved
int dy = y - ypos;
move(pt.x + dx, pt.y + dy);       //move mouse by delta
return true;
}
```

Limitations on Dragging

In Java, while the dragged component in a frame can be moved anywhere you like, it cannot be moved "on top" of a component that was added to the frame later. We added the three instances to the frame in the order:

```
add(Red);                //add them to
add(Green);              //the layout
add(Blue);
```

Thus, while we can drag the red square over the green or blue one and the green over the blue, we cannot drag the blue one over either the red or the green. This is illustrated in Figure 18-4, showing the overlapping panels.

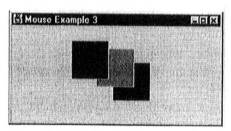

Figure 18-4: The Mouse3.java program, showing that you cannot drag compo-nents on top of each other in a different order than you initially added them to the frame or container.

Dragging has another major limitation—if you have placed controls inside a panel for purposes of layout, you cannot drag them outside that panel at all. Dragging only occurs within a single container, whether a frame, a panel, or a window. We'll see a way to get around this later in the chapter.

Right & Center Button Mouse Clicks

There is no specific method in Java for receiving mouse clicks from more than one mouse button, because not all platforms Java runs on support multibutton mice. Instead, you can check the *modifiers* field of the event to see if the META _MASK bit is set. If it is, you can choose to take a different action. Similarly, if you click the middle button of a three-button mouse, the ALT_MASK bit is set.

In our Mouse4.java example program, we are going to pop up a tip Window that displays some text. In our simple example, we'll display the name of the color of the window.

Remember that a Window is a container like a Frame, but with-out a title bar. It does have an independent existence, however, and is not dependent on the positions of controls inside other panels or frames.

To pop up our tip Window, we modify the *mouseDown* method as follows:

```
public boolean mouseDown(Event evt, int x, int y)
{
 if ((evt.modifiers & Event.META_MASK)!=0)
   {
   //If right button, create tip window
   tip = new TipWindow(frame, color);
   tip.show();
   }
   else
   {
   //otherwise just set the outline flag
    isFrame = true;
    repaint();
   }
 return true;
 }
```

To create a Window, you need to make it the child of a Frame. This is simple in the case of applications, but if you want a tip Window in an applet, you must first create an invisible parent frame. Our *TipWindow* class is as follows:

```
class TipWindow extends Window
{
Color color;               //color of panel
String label;              //name to display
Frame frame;               //parent frame
 public TipWindow(Frame fr, Color c)
 {
 super (fr);                //create window
 frame = fr;                //save frame and color
 color = c;
 setBackground(Color.yellow);   //yellow bkgnd
 if (color == Color.red)        //compute name
     label="Red";
 if (color == Color.blue)
     label="Blue";
 if (color == Color.green)
```

```
    label="Green";
 }
//-------------------------------
public void show()
 {
super.show();
//locate parent frame
 Point pt = frame.location();
//and position window at (50,50) over it
 reshape(pt.x + 50, pt.y + 50, 25, 12);
 }
//-------------------------------
public void paint (Graphics g)
 {
g.drawString(label,0,12); //draw label
Dimension sz = size();
//and outline the window with a black border
 g.drawRect(0,0,sz.width-1, sz.height-1);
 }
 }
```

Finally, we want to make sure our "tip" disappears when we raise the right mouse button. We don't have to check which button was raised; if the reference to the tip Window is not *null*, we'll dispose of the window:

```
public boolean mouseUp(Event evt, int x, int y)
 {
if (tip != null)    //If there is a tip window…
  {
  tip.dispose();    //dispose of popup window
  tip = null;       //set reference to null
  }
  isFrame = false;
  repaint();
return true;
 }
```

Figure 18-5 shows a tip Window popped up over our Mouse4 frame.

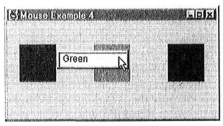

Figure 18-5: The tip Window in the Mouse4.java example program.

Drag & Drop in Java

Drag and drop is a feature of several operating system platforms, but it has not yet been abstracted into Java. However, it is not entirely impossible to carry out drag-and-drop operations using a separate top level window to contain the object you want to drag. In the example we develop here, we will work with a customer list of names and two drop targets representing Delete and View, as shown in Figure 18-6.

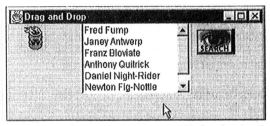

Figure 18-6: The DragonDrop program display showing the two drop targets and the list of customers.

The DragonDrop program we discuss here shows a list of customers in the middle of the window. We'll drag the selected customer either to the View target, which will bring up a detail view of that customer, or to the Delete target, which will delete the customer from the list.

Now the problem, as we've noted above, is that even if we made each customer in the central list an independently moveable visual object, we could not necessarily drag these objects over the drop targets if the targets were added to the frame later than the list objects were, because they would move behind them in the Frame. Further, if we grouped the objects using panels, we wouldn't be able to move the object outside that panel.

To solve this problem, we will adopt the strategy of creating a new window containing a single customer whenever we click on one customer in the list box. Since this window is completely separate from the frame, we can move it anywhere above the frame we want to by dragging it with the mouse. Then we have only the problem of how to tell the underlying drop target that we have dropped an object on it.

First, we'll create a list box as a child of the *List* class that can create a window when it receives a *click* event:

```
class dList extends List
{
//list box to show customers
//keeps list of references to array to send to
//drag window as well
Vector customers;        //list of customers
DragonDrop frm;          //parent form
DragWindow dragwin;      //window to pop up
//-------------------------------------
public dList(DragonDrop fr, int numlines)
  {
  super(numlines, false);     //create list
  frm= fr;                    //save frame
  customers = new Vector();   //create vector
  }
//-------------------------------------
public void clear()
```

```java
  {
//clears both list and vector
customers = new Vector();
delItems(0, countItems()-1);    //java bug work-around
  }
//------------------------------------
 public void addItem(Customer c)
  {
 //adds a customer to the vector and the list box
 String s = c.getFrname()+" "+c.getLname();
 super.addItem(s);
 customers.addElement(c);
  }
//------------------------------------
public void clickedList()
{
//if list is clicked on, pop up drag window
  int index = getSelectedIndex();
  Customer customer =
      (Customer)customers.elementAt(index);
  //create drag window
  dragwin = new DragWindow(frm, customer, index);
  Point pt = frm.location();
  dragwin.reshape(pt.x,  pt.y, 25, 12);
  dragwin.show();
  dragwin.toFront();  //keep it on top
}
//------------------------------------
public boolean handleEvent(Event evt)
{
 if (evt.id == Event.LIST_SELECT)
  {
 clickedList();
 return true;
  }
 return super.handleEvent(evt);
  }
  }
```

The important code in this *listbox* class is the *clickedList* method, which creates an instance of the *DragWindow* class. This class is derived from *Window* as we'll see below. It positions this window over the list item you clicked on and displays it.

The DragWindow Class

The *DragWindow* class is really central to our drag-and-drop program. It contains a reference to the customer object we are dragging around and draws the first name of the customer on the screen during the *paint* method.

We want to be able to drag it anywhere on the screen and then release the mouse button there, "dropping" it onto the target control underneath. Clearly, dragging the window is quite easy. As before, we record the location of the *mouseDown* event and move the window based on the change in mouse position during dragging.

In addition, when the mouse is down and we are dragging the window about, we change the border from a single black line to a black line with a blue rectangle just inside it to emphasize that an action is taking place:

```java
class DragWindow extends Window
{
//borderless window to drag over
//drop targets
DragonDrop frame;        //parent
String caption;
int x0, y0;              //where clicked on
int index;               //position in list
boolean outline = false;
Customer customer;
//-------------------------------------
 public DragWindow(DragonDrop fr, Customer c,int i)
 {
 super(fr);
 frame= fr;
 customer =c;
 caption = c.getFrname();        //First name as caption
 index = i;
 }
```

```
//--------------------------------------
public void show()
{
super.show();
//get parent frame location on desktop
Point pt = frame.location();
//compute where to appear from index and parent
move(pt.x+100, pt.y + 20 + index*15);
}
//--------------------------------------
 public void paint(Graphics g)
 {
 g.drawString(caption, 0,15);    //draw caption
 Dimension sz =size();
 g.drawRect(0,0, sz.width-1, sz.height-1);
 if (outline)                     //draw thicker border
  {
  g.setColor(Color.blue);
  g.drawRect(1,1, sz.width-3, sz.height-3);
  }
 }
//-------------------
public boolean mouseDown(Event evt, int x, int y)
{
x0 = x;                          //remember where mouse
y0 = y;                          //is clicked
outline = true;                  //draw thicker outline
repaint();
return true;
}
//-------------------
 public boolean mouseDrag(Event evt, int x, int y)
 {
 int dx = x - x0;                //find mouse delta
 int dy = y - y0;
 Point pt = location();
 move(pt.x + dx, pt.y + dy);    //move window
 return true;
 }
 }
```

How to Perform a Drop

When we "drop" a control onto another one, we need to tell the underlying control about the event. One way would be to define a *custom* event that we send to the other control. However, Java does not currently allow for *custom* events or for a *Drop* event, so we will use an interface instead.

Any control that we want to receive a *drop* action must implement the DropIn interface:

```
//------ interface for dropping in------------
interface DropIn
{
  public void dropIn(Object c);
}
```

Then we need only for the DragWindow to call the *dropIn* method of the underlying control to pass the object to it and have it execute the drop. Note that in no way do we specify *what* the *dropIn* method is to do. Each control object will implement its own version of this method, depending on what it accomplishes.

The other thing our DragWindow must do is find out what object it is on top of. This does, of course, presume that we wrote the underlying drop window and that it, too, is a Java program. We simply ask the underlying window for a list of its components, what their coordinates are, and whether our mouse is above any of them. Then we ask whether the component we are over is of type *DropIn*, or in other words, whether it implements that interface. If it does, we can execute the *dropIn* method, and if not, we simply dismiss the window without executing a drop. All of this takes place in the *mouseUp* and *executeDrop* methods of the DragWindow:

```
private void executeDrop(int x, int y)
{
Component c = null;
Point pt1 = location(); //get window location
x += pt1.x;              //compute absolute mouse location
y += pt1.y;

int count = frame.countComponents();
```

```
boolean found = false;
int i = 0;
//scan through components looking for one which we
//are above and which is a drop target
while ( (i < count) && (! found))
   {
   c = frame.getComponent(i);      //get each component
   Point pt = c.location(); //find its location
   pt1 = c.getParent().location(); //and the frames locn
   int thisx = pt.x + pt1.x;      //absolute
   int thisy = pt.y + pt1.y;      //component locn
   Dimension sz = c.size();
   if ((thisx <= x) && (x <= thisx+sz.width) &&
         (thisy <= y) &&(y  <=thisy+sz.height))
     found = true;                //is overhead
   //is it also a drop target?
   found = found && (c instanceof DropIn);
   if (! found) i++;
   }
if (found)      //execute drop only if legal
   {
   ((DropIn)c).dropIn(customer); //call drop method
   }
}
//--------------------------------------
  public boolean mouseUp(Event evt, int x, int y)
  {
  outline = false;      //undraw thick border
  repaint();
  executeDrop(x, y);    //execute the drop if legal
  dispose();            //close the window
  return true;
  }
```

One simplifying assumption we made in this code is that there are no panels containing further controls. There is nothing to prevent constructing such a screen, but the *executeDrop* method would then have to scan each panel's components, to see if any of them were drop targets as well, and compute their location by adding the component's coordinates to the panel's coordinates as well as to the Frame's coordinates.

The Drop Targets

When we created our window, we created two panels to hold images of type *ImagePanel* and *DeletePanel*. The *ImagePanel* simply draws the image as usual and provides a *dropIn* method to launch a viewer for the customer whose object is dropped into the target:

```
class ImagePanel extends Panel implements DropIn
{
//a drop panel to view and change a customer
Image img;
DragonDrop frm;
//----------------------------------------
 public ImagePanel(Image im, Frame fr)
 {
 super();
 img = im;         //remember image
 frm = (DragonDrop)fr;  //and parent
 }
//----------------------------------------
public void paint(Graphics g)
{
int w = img.getWidth(frm);
int h = img.getHeight(frm);
resize(w+1, h+1);
Dimension sz = size();

//draw image
g.drawImage(img, sz.width/2-w/2,0, w+1, h+1, frm);

//and border
g.setColor(Color.cyan);
g.drawRect(0,0,w,h);
}
//----------------------------------------
public void dropIn(Object c)
{
```

```
Viewer vw =
  new Viewer(frm, (SendCustomer)frm,(Customer) c);
  vw.show();
}
//---------------------------------------
}
```

Note that the *ImagePanel* implements the DropIn interface. Its *dropIn* method creates a new viewer and passes a reference to the parent frame and to the customer. The viewer, which is identical to that in earlier chapters, displays the customer data and allows you to change it. Since the Frame implements the same SendCustomer interface, the viewer can send the changed customer object back to the parent frame.

The Delete Target

In addition, we have a second window of type *DeletePanel*, which also implements the DropIn interface and deletes a customer from the list. We can simply derive it from the *ImagePanel*, but reimplement the *dropIn* method:

```
class DeletePanel extends ImagePanel
{
// a drop panel to delete a customer
DragonDrop frm;
  public DeletePanel(Image im, Frame fr)
  {
  super(im, fr);
  frm = (DragonDrop)fr;   //remember parent
  }
//---------------------------------------
public void dropIn(Object c)
{
//interface from drag object
//deletes specified customer
  frm.deleteCustomer((Customer)c);
  }
  }
```

The Parent Frame

Now that we have looked at all of the pieces, let's finish up by looking at how we create the master frame window. To simplify our scan for a drop target, we'll implement this window using the *null* layout, and simply place the two panels and the list box by absolute pixel position:

```
public class DragonDrop extends Frame implements SendCustomer
{
Customers custs;          //container class for list
Image viewer, trash;      //two images for drop targets
ImagePanel vw;            //panels for images
DeletePanel tr;
MediaTracker itrk;        //track image read-in
dList custlist;           //customer list
//-------------------------------------------
public DragonDrop()
{
super("Drag and Drop");             //create frame
// read the file and create customer container
custs = new Customers("people.add");
setLayout(null);
//read in the two images
itrk = new MediaTracker(this);
trash = getToolkit().getImage("trash.gif");
viewer = getToolkit().getImage("view.gif");
itrk.addImage(trash, 0);
itrk.addImage(viewer, 1);
wait_for_images(itrk);              //wait for them to be read in
tr = new DeletePanel(trash, this);  //create one panel
vw = new ImagePanel(viewer,this);   //and the other
add(tr);
add(vw);
tr.reshape(20,25,trash.getWidth(this)+2,
trash.getHeight(this)+2);
vw.reshape(250,25,viewer.getWidth(this)+2,
viewer.getHeight(this)+2);
//add first and last names to list box
custlist = new dList(this, 8);
add(custlist);
```

```
load_list();           //adds names to list box
reshape(100,100,350,150);
show();                //show the frame window
custlist.reshape(100, 20, 150, 100);
tr.repaint();          //refresh images
vw.repaint();
}
//-----------------------------------------------
private void load_list()
{
//adds the names to the list box
for (int i = 0; i < custs.getCount(); i++)
  {
  Customer c = custs.getCust(i);
  custlist.addItem(c);
  }
}
//-----------------------------------------------
private void wait_for_images(MediaTracker track)
{
//check to see if they are done loading
 for (int i = 0; i < 2; i++)
   {
   try
     {
     track.waitForID(i);
     }
   catch (InterruptedException e) {};
   if(track.isErrorID(i))
     System.out.println("Error loading image: " + i);
   }
  if(track.isErrorAny())
    System.out.println("loading error");
}
//-----------------------------------------------
public void setCustomer(Customer c)
{
//changes customer data for currently selected customer
//used by dialog box to call back
int i = custlist.getSelectedIndex();
if (i >=0)
```

```
    {
    custs.setCust(c, i);
    load_list();
    }//end if
    }
    //-----------------------------------------------
    public boolean handleEvent(Event evt)
    {
    if (evt.id == Event.WINDOW_DESTROY)
      System.exit(0);
    return super.handleEvent(evt);
    }
    //-----------------------------------------------
    public void deleteCustomer(Customer c)
    {
    custs.deleteCust(c);    //delete from collection
    custlist.clear();       //clear and
    load_list();            //reload list box
    }
    //-----------------------------------------------
    static public void main(String argv[])
    {
    new DragonDrop();
    }
    }
```

The final program code is given on the Companion CD-ROM as DragonDrop.java, and an example of dragging a window onto a target is shown in Figure 18-7.

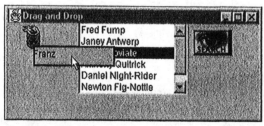

Figure 18-7: Dragging a window over a control in DragonDrop.java.

Moving On

In this chapter, we've looked in great detail at how to use the mouse. We've seen how to receive clicks, double-clicks, drags, right-clicks, and even implement drag-and-drop. In the process, we've extended a number of common controls to make them more useful. Now let's take a look at how to build our own controls from scratch.

19

Building Custom Controls

We have already been making small modifications in the standard Java controls by deriving new controls with different mouse behavior or a different outline. In this chapter, we'll look at how to build several such controls using the *Panel* and *Canvas* classes.

A Frame Panel

The Visual Basic Frame control is simply a box on the form into which you can insert controls that you want to group together, such as radio buttons. It also serves an important purpose in grouping together controls that have a similar purpose, even if they are not radio buttons.

In Java, the Panel container allows you to group controls together primarily for layout purposes. Panels are not visible and have no direct effect on CheckboxGroups, which cause radio buttons to group together. Creating a panel that has these features is quite simple, however, and we'll make this our first custom control in this chapter.

In this example, we are going to use the GridBagLayout to create the data entry screen shown in Figure 19-1. The label, the text field, and the two command buttons are handled normally. The two panel frames are designed to take up two vertical grid positions, and each instance of the *outlinePanel* contains its own CheckboxGroup, so you don't need to specify one yourself.

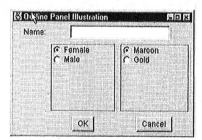

Figure 19-1: The screen layout of the outPanel.java program.

The code for setting up this control layout is shown below. If you don't remember how the GridBagLayout works, review Chapter 9. In essence, we use the *add_component* method to specify the *x* and *y* grid position and the number of grid cells each component is to occupy:

```java
class outPanel extends Frame
{
Label lbname;              //name label
TextField tfname;          //entry field
outlinePanel psex;         //two outlined panels
outlinePanel pteam;
CheckboxGroup cbsex, cbteam;
Checkbox Male, Female, Maroon, Gold;     //4 radios
Button OK, Cancel;                    //two pushbuttons
GridBagConstraints gbc;
GridBagLayout gbl;
//--------------------------------------
public outPanel()
{
super("Outline Panel Illustration");
```

```
setBackground(Color.lightGray);
gbl =new GridBagLayout();
gbc = new GridBagConstraints();
setLayout(gbl);
 gbc.ipadx = 5;         //make buttons wider
 gbc.ipady = 3;         //make buttons higher
 gbc.insets.left =4;
 gbc.insets.right =4;
 gbc.insets.bottom =4;
 gbc.insets.top =4;
 gbc.weightx =1;
 gbc.weighty =1;

 lbname = new Label("Name:");  //label
 add_component(lbname, 0,0,1,1);
 tfname = new TextField(20);   //text entry field
 add_component(tfname, 1,0,3,1);
 //panel with two buttons for sex
 psex = new outlinePanel();    //first panel
 add_component(psex, 1,1,1,2); //insert in layout

 //put two radio buttons in panel
 Female = psex.addCheckbox("Female", true);
 Male = psex.addCheckbox("Male",  false);
 psex.resize(78,45);

 //second panel with 2 radio buttons
 pteam = new outlinePanel();
 add_component(pteam, 2,1,1,2);
 Maroon = pteam.addCheckbox("Maroon", true);
 Gold = pteam.addCheckbox("Gold", false);
 pteam.resize(78, 43);

 //add two command buttons to bottom
 OK = new Button("OK");              //buttons at bottom
 Cancel = new Button("Cancel");
 add_component(OK, 1,4,1,1);
 add_component(Cancel, 2, 4,1,1);
 reshape(100,100, 300,200);
 show();
```

```
    }
//----------------------------------------
    private void add_component(Component c, int x, int y,
                    int w, int h)
    {
    gbc.gridx = x;
    gbc.gridy = y;
    gbc.gridwidth = w;
    gbc.gridheight =h;
    add(c);
    gbl.setConstraints(c, gbc);
    }
}
```

The Visual Basic frame is outlined in two colors: a gray box with white interior lines on the top and left and white exterior lines on the right and bottom. We duplicate that style in this *outlinePanel* class shown below. In addition, our class allows you to add check boxes to an automatically created CheckboxGroup and arranges them in vertical order:

```
class outlinePanel extends Panel
{
CheckboxGroup cbg;
int yposn;
Vector cblist;
//--------------------------------------
public outlinePanel()
{
super();
cbg = new CheckboxGroup();      //for radio buttons
setLayout(null);
yposn = 3;
cblist = new Vector();
}
//--------------------------------------
public void reshape(int x, int y, int w, int h)
{
super.reshape(x,y,w,h);
for (int i=0; i< cblist.size(); i++)
```

```
        {
        Component c = (Component)cblist.elementAt(i);
        c.reshape(c.location().x, c.location().y, w-6,
                  c.size().height);
        }
    }
//---------------------------------------
public Checkbox addCheckbox(String s, boolean checked)
{
Checkbox cb = new Checkbox(s, cbg, checked);
add(cb);
cblist.addElement(cb);
cb.reshape(3, yposn, 50, 12);
yposn += 15;
return cb;
}
//---------------------------------------
public void paint(Graphics g)
{
Dimension sz = size();
Point pt = location();
g.setColor(Color.darkGray);    // graw rectangle
g.drawRect(0, 0, sz.width-2, sz.height-2);

//outline gray rectangle with 2 white inner lines
g.setColor(Color.white);
g.drawLine(1, 1, sz.width-3, 1);
g.drawLine(1, 1, 1, sz.height-3);

//and two white outer lines
g.drawLine(0,sz.height-1,sz.width-1,sz.height-1);
g.drawLine(sz.width-1, 0, sz.width-1, sz.height-1);
}
//---------------------------------------
}
```

You should note carefully that the *outlinePanel* class has a null
layout. If any other layout manager is specified, it will attempt to
stretch the radio button components to fill the panel, and the

frame lines will be obscured. This precludes using the GridLayout, for example, to align the radio buttons automatically.

Creating an Image Button

A picture button is a button that contains one or more images as well as a caption. In some designs, you don't need a caption as the icon makes the button's purpose completely clear.

We will build our picture button out of the Canvas component, which is specifically designed to be subclassed for such purposes. The Canvas receives all the usual mouse events, but it does not define an *action* event since these would vary with the type of control. Instead, we will intercept the *mouseUp* event and use it to represent a button click action.

Several things happen when you click on a button. First, the shading around the button changes to represent a "down" state instead of an "up" state, and second, the button caption or picture moves one pixel down and one pixel to the right to simulate the button's being depressed.

In their up state, Java buttons are outlined by one white line on the top and left and two black lines on the right and bottom. In their down state, this reverses, with two black lines on the top and left and one white line on the right and bottom. While buttons in Visual Basic usually become the default button when you click on them and are then outlined with a single black line as well, this is not usual in Java, although it is simple to implement.

Designing the Example

We will start by designing the *ImgButnExample* class, which will, in turn, call the *ImageButton* class. We will simply construct a frame that contains an image button and a label that changes when we click it:

```
class ImgButnExample extends Frame
{
Label state; //label to show if button pressed
```

```
ImageButton ibutn;  //image button
//------------------------------------
public ImgButnExample()
  {
  super("Image Button Example");          //create frame
  setLayout(new BorderLayout());
  setBackground(Color.gray);
  state = new Label("unimpressed");       //create label
  add("Center", state);
//read in image for button
  Image upmail = getToolkit().getImage("mail02a.gif");
//create image button
  ibutn = new ImageButton("Mail", upmail);
  Panel p1 = new Panel();
  add("South", p1);
  p1.add(ibutn);               //add button to south border
  ibutn.resize(75, 50);        //say what shape you want
  reshape(100,100,300,200);
  show();                      //and show the frame
  }
```

Acting on a Button Click

Since the Canvas does not generate an *action* event, we will intercept the *mouseUp* event as the *click* event and use it to change the
label text:

```
public boolean mouseUp(Event evt, int x, int y)
  {
  if (evt.target == ibutn)
    {
    state.setText("You have mail");
    return true;
    }
  return super.mouseUp(evt, x, y);
  }
```

This is the complete example program, and we now can define the
events and methods we'll need for our image button.

The ImageButton Methods

From the previous example, we see that we need a constructor that passes in an image and a label string for the button. We show a simplified version of that constructor below. We'll add the other images later.

```
public class ImageButton extends Canvas
{
int xpos, ypos;              //place to draw the button
int xwidth, yheight;
int d1 = 1, d2 = 2;         //posn of double lines
boolean down;               //true if button down
Image upImage= null;        //always need one of these
int Image_x, Image_w;       //image locn on the button
int Image_y, Image_h;
int textw, textx, texth;    //caption location
String caption;             //button caption
boolean enabled;
boolean focus;              //draw rectangle inside if true
//---------------------------------------------------
public ImageButton(String captn, Image img)
{
super();
xwidth = yheight = 0;
upImage = img;     //will always be at least one image
Image_x = (xwidth - upImage.getWidth(this))/2;
caption = captn;
setFont(new Font("Helvetica",Font.PLAIN,12));
enabled = true;
}
```

The Mouse Click Events

Within our image button, we need to respond to both the *mouseDown* and *mouseUp* events. In this class, we simply set or clear the down flag and repaint the control accordingly:

```
public boolean mouseDown(Event evt, int x, int y)
{
down = true;        //set down and focus flags
focus = true;
repaint();
return false;       //but pass event on
}
//------------------------------------------------------------
public boolean mouseUp(Event evt, int x, int y)
{
down = false;       //clear down flag
repaint();
return false;       //pass event on
}
```

The Simplified paint Routine

Now, we need to discuss how to draw the button. We draw lines around it depending on whether the mouse is down or up and draw the image at (x,y) or (x+1, y+1):

```
private void draw_uplines()
{
 g.setColor(Color.white);      //draw white lines
 g.drawLine(0, 0, xwidth-d1, 0);
 g.drawLine(0, 0, 0, yheight-1);

 g.setColor(Color.black);      //draw black lines
 g.drawLine(xwidth-1, 0, xwidth-1, yheight-1);
 g.drawLine(xwidth-2, 0, xwidth-2, yheight-2);
 g.drawLine(1, yheight-d2, xwidth-d2, yheight-d2);
 g.drawLine(0, yheight-d1, xwidth-d1, yheight-d1);
}
//----------------------------------------------
private void draw_downlines()
{
// draw black lines
g.setColor(Color.black);
```

```
        g.drawLine(0, 0, 0, yheight);
        g.drawLine(1, 1, 1, yheight-1);
        g.drawLine(0, 0, xwidth, 0);
        g.drawLine(1, 1, xwidth-1, 1);
        // draw white lines
        g.setColor(Color.white);
        g.drawLine(d1, yheight-d1, xwidth- d1, yheight-d1);
        g.drawLine(xwidth-d1, yheight-d1, xwidth- d1, d1);
        }
//------------------------------
public void paint (Graphics g)
 {
 textw = g.getFontMetrics().stringWidth(caption);
 texth = g.getFontMetrics().getHeight();
 textx=(xwidth - textw)/2;
 Image_w = upImage.getWidth(this);
 Image_h = upImage.getHeight(this);
 Image_y = upImage.getHeight(this);
 Image_x = (xwidth - Image_w)/2;

 dImage = upImage;      //regular up Image if enabled
 if (! down)
  {
  //draw up-image in button------------
   if (UpImage != null)     //only draw if image loaded
    {
    g.drawImage(dImage, Image_x, 2,
          Color.lightGray, this);
    g.drawString(caption, textx, yheight-5);
    }
   draw_uplines();
 }
// Draw image and lines for button------------
else
  {
   g.drawImage(upImage, Image_x+1, 3,
          Color.lightGray, this);
   g.drawString(caption, textx+1, yheight-4);
   }
```

```
    draw_downlines();
    }
```

With this simple introduction, we can now execute our first example program, as shown in Figure 19-2. The code is in the ImgButnExample1.java file on the Companion CD-ROM.

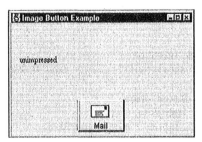

Figure 19-2: The ImgButnExample1 program, showing the image button.

Up & Down Images

In the simple example in the last section, we drew a single image on the button and moved it over one pixel when the button was in the down position. You can produce a more entertaining and reinforcing button by using two images: one up and one down. To do this, we simply need a method to tell the class about a second image:

```
public void setDownImage(Image img)
    {
    downImage  = img; //save image for button down
    }
```

This is illustrated in our revised *paint* routine below and in the example program ImgButnExample2.java on the Companion CD-ROM.

```
public void paint (Graphics g)
    {
    textw = g.getFontMetrics().stringWidth(caption);
    texth = g.getFontMetrics().getHeight();
```

```
        textx=(xwidth - textw)/2;
        Image_w = upImage.getWidth(this);
        Image_h = upImage.getHeight(this);
        Image_y = upImage.getHeight(this);
        Image_x = (xwidth - Image_w)/2;

    Image dImage;
    dImage = upImage;       //regular up Image if enabled
    if (! down)
     {
     //draw up-image in button------------
       if (! upImage.equals(null)) //only draw if loaded
       {
       g.drawImage(dImage, Image_x, 2,
             Color.lightGray, this);
       g.drawString(caption, textx, yheight-5);
       }
       draw_uplines();
       }
    // Draw image and lines for button down----------------
    else
     {
     if (downImage == null &&  upImage!=null)
       {
       //draw shifted one pixel
       g.drawImage(upImage, Image_x+1, 3,
             Color.lightGray, this);
       g.drawString(caption, textx+1, yheight-4);
       }
     if ( downImage != null)
       {
       //draw alternate image
       g.drawImage(downImage, Image_x, 2,
             Color.lightGray, this);
       g.drawString(caption, textx+1, yheight-4);
       }
     draw_downlines();
     }
    }
```

Figure 19-3 illustrates the down image of this program as well as how the lines around the button change in the down position.

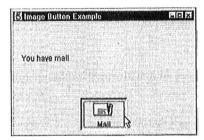

Figure 19-3: The down image display of the ImgButnExample2 program.

Constructing a Grayed-Out Image

When your image button is disabled, it means that clicking on it has no effect; it will not depress, and it will not receive mouse messages. The underlying *Canvas* class will take care of this disabling of the button, but there will be no visual cue that the button is disabled.

The most common way to show this is to "gray out" the image and text on the button. David Flanagan[3] has succinctly illustrated how to make a separate gray image using the *RBGImageFilter* class. Basically, you average every color at every pixel with white to make a grayed-out image:

```
class GrayFilter extends RGBImageFilter
//from O'Flanagan - Nutshell
{
  public GrayFilter()
  {
  canFilterIndexColorModel = true;
  }
//-------------------------------------------
  public int filterRGB(int x, int y, int rgb)
  {
  //average each color with white
```

```
int a = rgb & 0xff000000; //alpha transparency bits
int r = ((rgb & 0xff0000) + 0xff0000)/2;
int g = ((rgb & 0x00ff00) + 0x00ff00)/2;
int b = ((rgb & 0x0000ff) + 0x0000ff)/2;
return a | r | g | b;
 }
 }
```

Then we create a gray image during the initialization of the class:

```
Image grayImage = null;                    //if disabled

ImageFilter f = new GrayFilter();          //from Flanagan
ImageProducer pr =
    new FilteredImageSource(upImage.getSource(), f);
grayImage = this.createImage(pr);
Image_x = (xwidth - upImage.getWidth(this))/2;
```

and use it in our *paint* routine instead of the *upImage* if the control is disabled:

```
Image dImage;
if (! enabled)
  dImage = grayImage;    //gray image if disabled
else
  dImage = upImage;      //regular up Image if enabled
```

The program ImgButnExample3.java illustrates disabling an image button. The disabled image is shown in Figure 19-4.

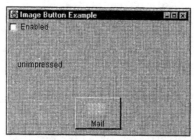

Figure 19-4: The ImgButnExample3 program, showing the disabled image button.

Setting the Focus

A component has the input *focus*, if it is the current component, and will receive keyboard messages as well as mouse messages. In Java, a button having the input focus shows a rounded rectangle drawn with dotted lines inside the button area. Java, however, does not provide a direct way to draw a dotted-line rectangle, so rather than drawing it a line segment at a time, we'll just draw a rounded, dark gray rectangle, 5 pixels in from the outside of the button and with a 5-pixel rounding at each corner:

```
if (focus)     //if focus draw rounded rectangle
   {
   g.setColor(Color.darkGray);
   g.drawRoundRect(5, 5, xwidth-10, yheight-10, 5, 5);
   }
```

We also need a method for responding to focus events, so we extend the *gotFocus* method to set the focus flag:

```
public boolean gotFocus(Event evt,  Object arg)
{
 focus = true;
 repaint();
 return true;
}
//-----------------------------------------------
public boolean lostFocus(Event evt,  Object arg)
{
 focus = false;
 repaint();
 return true;
}
```

We set the focus on the *mouseDown* event as you might expect:

```
public boolean mouseDown(Event evt, int x, int y)
{
down = true; //button is now down
focus = true;      //and has the focus
repaint();         //redraw
```

```
return false;        //and allow children to recv mesgs
}
```

The ImgButnExample4.java program allows you to tab back
and forth between a text field and the image button as shown in
Figure 19-5.

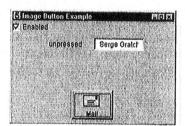

*Figure 19-5: The ImgButnExample4.java program, showing the focus on the
image button.*

In this program, we make an array of controls as before and detect the Tab key to move the focus between the controls:

```
private void setTab(int tb)
  {
  if (tb >= tab_list.size())
    tb=0;
  if (tb < 0)
    tb = tab_list.size()-1;
  tabindex = tb;
  Component c = ( (Component)tab_list.elementAt(tabindex));
  c.requestFocus();
  }
//-------------------------------------------
public boolean keyDown(Event evt, int key)
{
switch (key)
  {
  case '\t':
    if ((evt.modifiers & Event.SHIFT_MASK) != 0)
      setTab(tabindex -1);
```

```
        else
          setTab(tabindex +1);
        return true;
      }
    return super.keyDown(evt, key);
    }
```

Controlling the Size of a Custom Control

In our example code, we specifically set the size of the image button:

```
    ibutn.resize(75, 50);      //say what shape you want
```

but as we have seen, we seldom set a specific size for a button when the layout is controlled by a layout manager. Instead, the layout is determined by the layout manager asking each control for its *preferredSize*. Thus, in order for our custom control to work with layout managers, we have to implement this method.

Normally, the *preferredSize* method checks to see if the control is a native control for that platform, and if so, passes the request to that "peer" control. If it is not, it simply returns the last values set by *resize* or *reshape* methods. Since our homegrown controls do not have peers, we have to handle this ourselves. If a *reshape* or *resize* method is called, we save the size to return from this method, and if it has not been called, we calculate the size based on the size of the image and the text:

```
    public Dimension preferredSize()

    {
    if (xwidth == 0)          //if no size has been spec'd
    {
    int w = 40, h = 40;       //default image size
    Graphics g = getGraphics();
    if (upImage != null)
      {
      w = upImage.getWidth(this) + 8;
      h = upImage.getHeight(this) + 8;
      }
```

```
if (caption.length() >0 )
  {
  texth = g.getFontMetrics().getHeight();
  h += texth ;
  int textw = g.getFontMetrics().stringWidth(caption);
  if (textw > w)
    w = textw + 8; //if text is wider than image
  }
 return new Dimension(w, h);
}
else
 //otherwise return last specified size
  return new Dimension(xwidth, yheight);
}
```

Figure 19-6 shows the same image button sized according to the preferred size.

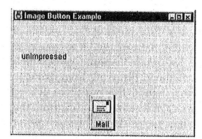

Figure 19-6: The image button sized according to its preferred size routine.

A Custom List Box

The Java list box control is a pretty plain-vanilla control. It has only a vertical scroll bar, has no way to mix fonts or colors, and does not support right-mouse clicking. However, much as we drew an image and the lines for a button, we can derive our own list box from the *Canvas* class by simply drawing the lines of the visible list elements on the screen:

```
class b_List extends Canvas
{
  Vector Items;          //array of all elements in list
  int xpos, ypos, xwidth, yheight;
  int texth;
  int h;
  DisplayItem MarkedItem; //element currently marked
  int marked;            //index of element marked
  int list_max;          //maximum number of lines
  Scrollbar scroll;      //defined in outer class
  int top_line;          //index of top line
  int master_width=0;
//---------------------------------------------
public b_List(Scrollbar scroll_bar)
  {
     scroll = scroll_bar;   //passed in from parent panel
     Items = new Vector(10);
     setFont(new Font("Helvetica",Font.PLAIN,12));
     top_line = 0;
     texth = 14;
     scroll.hide();        //only visible if more lines
  }
```

The only difficult part of this control is drawing a scroll bar that appears only when there are more elements in the list box than can be shown at once. We'll accomplish this by putting the Canvas and the scroll bar inside a Panel and showing and hiding the scroll bar depending on the number of lines in the list:

```
public class bList extends Panel
{
//This is a wrapper class for the bList class
//so that the scroll bar and canvas can exist
//in the same Panel
//It extends panel and CONTAINS an instance
//of our list box
//and an instance of a scroll bar
b_List lb;             //our own list box
```

```
Scrollbar scroll;         //a vertical scroll bar
int x, y, w , h;
//-------------------------------------------------
 public bList()
 {
   setLayout(null);
   //create scroll bar
   scroll = new Scrollbar(Scrollbar.VERTICAL);
   add(scroll);
   lb = new b_List(scroll);     //create Listbox
   add(lb);
   setBackground(Color.white);
   lb.show();
 }
```

To highlight the selected line in the list box, we simply draw a colored rectangle and then draw the text in a light color over the rectangle. The advantage of this approach is that we can pick any colors we want and make them selectable.

The DisplayItem Class

No matter how we have scrolled the list box, we need to know which of the elements is currently selected to be highlighted. We can keep track of this using a simple *DisplayItem* class where each item knows whether or not it is marked:

```
class DisplayItem
{
boolean marked;      //whether marked
String label;        //text to display
//-------------------------------------------
public DisplayItem(String s)
{label = s;}
//-------------------------------------------
public boolean isMarked()
{return marked;}
//-------------------------------------------
public String getName()
```

```
{return label;}
//-----------------------------------------
public void setMarked(boolean b)
{marked =b;}
//-----------------------------------------
}
```

While in this example we only allow a single-selection list box, we can clearly extend this to multiselect list boxes quite easily.

Drawing the Text in the List Box

Central to the display of the items in the list box is the *drawNodes* method, which calls the *drawNode* method for each line, and decides whether or not to highlight it:

```
private void drawNode(int i, Graphics g, int h)
   {
   // draws one line of List
   DisplayItem di = (DisplayItem)(Items.elementAt(i));
   int leftside = 0;

     if (di.isMarked()) //display with bar if marked
       {
         g.setColor(Color.blue );
         g.fillRect(leftside, h-4, xwidth-2, texth+1);
         g.setColor(Color.yellow);
       }
     else
       {
     //display black on white if not
         g.setColor(Color.white);
         g.fillRect(leftside, h-4, xwidth-2, texth+1);
         g.setColor(Color.black );
       }
     g.drawString(di.getName(), leftside , h + texth-5);
   }
//-----------------------------------------
   private void drawNodes(Graphics g)
```

```
{
//draws all current lines of list
// from DisplayedItems list
int leftside;
h = 2;
int dsize = Items.size();
int lastline = top_line + list_max;
if (lastline > dsize)
  lastline = dsize;
for (int i = top_line; i < lastline; i++)
  {
  drawNode(i, g, h);
  h += texth;
  }
}
```

Note that we start drawing at *top_line* rather than at line zero. This allows for scrolling of the list with the scroll bar.

The mouseDown Event

The other important part of a list box function is deciding where the mouse click occurred so that you can determine which line to highlight. You do this by simply dividing the mouse position by the font height. Then you decide whether any line is already marked, and if so, unmark it. Finally, you mark the current line and save a reference to that object:

```
public boolean mouseDown(Event evt, int x, int y)
{
// intercepts mouse down event
 DisplayItem di;
 int leftside;
 int h;
//if you click on an unselected item, the old selected
//item is deselected and the new one selected.
//if you click a the selected item it is deselected
  Graphics g = getGraphics();
  int i = (y-2)/texth + top_line;
```

```
//make sure actual item selected
  if ((i < Items.size()) && (i >= 0))
    {
    di = (DisplayItem)Items.elementAt(i);
      if (MarkedItem != null)
        {
        //unmark previously marked item
       MarkedItem.setMarked(false);
         h =  (marked-top_line) *texth +2;
    //draw un-highlighted node
         drawNode(marked, g, h);
         }
      if (di == MarkedItem)
        {
         if ((evt.modifiers & Event.META_MASK) ==0)
          {
          MarkedItem = null;
          }
         }
      else
        {
        di.setMarked(true);
        MarkedItem = di;
        marked = i;
      //distance from top of screen, not list
        h =  (i-top_line) *texth +2;
        drawNode(i, g, h);     //draw highlighted node
        }
    }
  return super.mouseDown(evt, x, y);
}
```

Passing Events to the Parent Classes

Now, since we have created a class, *b_list*, that is contained in a class, *bList*, if we get mouse messages from the subsidiary and private *b_list* class, a statement like:

```
if ((evt.target == blist) &&(evt.id==Event.MOUSE_DOWN))
   {
```

would fail, since *evt.target* is actually the *private b_List* class. We solve this by *posting* an event to the *parent* or calling class from the *bList* class:

```
public boolean mouseDown(Event evt, int x, int y)
{
Container p = getParent();
p.postEvent(new Event(this, Event.MOUSE_DOWN, ""));
return super.mouseDown(evt, x, y);
}
```

This gives us the opportunity to receive the *mouseDown* event in the parent program ourList.java on the Companion CD-ROM and display a tip window when the list is right-clicked:

```
public boolean mouseDown(Event evt, int x, int y)
  {
//here we intercept a right mouse click
  if (((evt.modifiers & Event.META_MASK)!= 0)
    && (evt.target  == bList))
    {
    tip = new Tipwindow(this, lb.getText());
    Graphics g = getGraphics();
    int w =
    g.getFontMetrics().stringWidth(lb.getText());
    int h = g.getFontMetrics().getHeight();
    tip.reshape(x, y, w, h);
    tip.show();
    lb.setText("right mouse");
    }
  return super.mouseDown(evt, x, y);
  }
```

The List Box Events

Since this is not a "real" list box, it doesn't produce the usual LIST_SELECT and LIST_DESELECT events we might like to receive. However, using this same *postEvent* method, it is not difficult to create them by adding some code to the *mouseDown* method. Note that we use the parent as the source of the message as well as the place to post it:

```
if ((i < Items.size()) && (i >= 0))
    {
    getParent().postEvent(new Event(getParent(),
      Event.MOUSE_DOWN, ""));
    di = (DisplayItem)Items.elementAt(i);
      if (MarkedItem != null)
        {
      MarkedItem.setMarked(false);    //unmark
        h = (marked-top_line) *texth +2;
        drawNode(marked, g, h);         //draw
        }
      if (di == MarkedItem)
        {
        if ((evt.modifiers & Event.META_MASK) ==0)
        {
        getParent().postEvent(new Event(getParent(),
      Event.LIST_DESELECT,
      new String(getSelectedItem()))));
        MarkedItem = null;
        }
      }
      else
        {
      di.setMarked(true);
      MarkedItem = di;
      marked = i;
      h = (i-top_line) *texth +2;      //distance
```

```
        drawNode(i, g, h);                    //draw
        getParent().postEvent(new Event(getParent(),
      Event.LIST_SELECT, new
      String(getSelectedItem())));
        }
  }
```

The final list box is shown in Figure 19-7, and the driver program
is called ourList.java. The list class is *bList.java*.

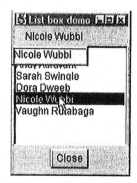

Figure 19-7: Our own list box shown in the ourList.java program.

Building a TreeList Control

As we have just seen, you can easily write your own list box. A
tree list where you can expand categories is shown in Figure 19-8.

Figure 19-8: A TreeList control.

The *TreeList.java* class on the Companion CD-ROM and its accompanying example program, TreeLister.java, show how to extend the *bList* class by making the *DisplayNode* class one that contains references to subitems. The drawing of the tree list includes drawing little file folders in open or closed positions and indenting the subcategories appropriately. The *mouseDown* event detects whether you have clicked on a line or on the file folder icon and decides whether to expand a tree or just highlight a line.

Moving On

In this chapter, we've looked at how to make three custom controls. As you can imagine, it's simple to create more as you need them. You can make toolbars out of little picture buttons and add images to list boxes to make image lists.

In the next two chapters, we'll look at how to make, debug, and package applications and applets.

20

Using Packages

The Java package provides a convenient way to group classes in separate name spaces. This makes it possible to have classes with the same name in each package. This could occur whenever a group of programmers is working on a project, or when a program you are writing uses some classes from a commercial package. To make use of classes within a given package, you need to either refer to them by a name that includes the package name:

```
pkg.class.method();
```

or use the *import* statement to indicate that you will be using files from a given package:

```
import pkg;

class.method();
```

We've already seen examples of this, of course, in using the Java package classes. We could write:

```
lb = new java.awt.Label("label");
```

or we more conventionally write:

```
import java.awt.*;
lb = new Label("label");
```

The Java Packages

The *Java* classes are divided into several packages, as we have seen:

```
java.lang
java.awt
java.io
java.net
java.util
java.applet
java.awt.image
```

You can import an entire package, as we have been doing, by:

```
import java.awt.*;
```

or just import the classes you will be using:

```
import java.awt.Label;
```

There is no difference between these two approaches in the size of the executables or their speed, but the compilation speed may be somewhat faster if you only import the classes from a package that you will be using. Considering how fast Java compilers have become, this is of much less import than it was a few months earlier.

While Java compilers in general require that you specifically import any packages you use, all compilers automatically import the *java.lang.** class, since all of the basic language elements are defined in this class.

The Default Package

So far, we have not been using any *package* statements and have not written any programs that are part of a named package. All classes without a *package* statement are automatically made part of the default package.

The CLASSPATH Variable

The environment variable CLASSPATH must be set to point to the directory that is one level *above* the directory where packages will be found. There can be any number of such packages, separated (in Windows) by semicolons:

```
set CLASSPATH = c:\café\java\lib;c:\JFactory11;
```

You can set them by putting the a statement similar to the above into your autoexec.bat file or by typing it on the keyboard. If you want to add the path c:\testlib, you can type:

```
set CLASSPATH = c:\testlib;%CLASSPATH%
```

to append the testlib directory to the front of the CLASSPATH. If you now type:

```
echo %CLASSPATH%
```

at a DOS prompt, Windows 95 will print out:

```
c:\testlib;c:\café\java\lib;c:\JFactory11;
```

If you are using the *Roguewave JFactory* classes, they are found in the directory:

```
c:\Jfactory11\com\roguewave\widgets
```

By putting c:\JFactory11 in the CLASSPATH, the following *import* statement allows the compiler to find the classes:

```
import com.roguewave.widgets.*;
```

and this is the statement that is inserted by Rogue Wave's JFactory system.

Classes.zip Files

The Java file classes.zip in the c:\java\lib directory or the c:\Café\java\lib directory is not a zip file in the usual sense: the files are not compressed. Instead, the zip file classes.zip is used as a repository of classes that include a directory structure within the zip file.

The usual CLASSPATH statement to include the *Java* classes is:

```
set CLASSPATH = c:\java\lib;
```

or:

```
set CLASSPATH = c:\java\lib\classes.zip;
```

In either case, the compiler finds a file that contains a subdirectory structure of Java and Sun classes. Figure 20-1 shows the WinZip display of the contents of this file. Note that it is not compressed and that the directory structure is clearly preserved. This is not a file that you unpack; it serves as a kind of library structure.

WinZip - classes.zip						
File Actions Options Help						
Name	Date	Time	Size	Ratio	Packed	Path
TextFieldPeer.class	08/27/96	01:17	337	0%	337	java\awt\peer\
WindowPeer.class	08/27/96	01:17	262	0%	262	java\awt\peer\
Point.class	08/27/96	01:17	1,031	0%	1,031	java\awt\
Polygon.class	08/27/96	01:17	1,903	0%	1,903	java\awt\
Rectangle.class	08/27/96	01:17	3,064	0%	3,064	java\awt\
Scrolbar.class	08/27/96	01:17	2,655	0%	2,655	java\awt\
TextArea.class	08/27/96	01:17	2,469	0%	2,469	java\awt\
TextComponent.class	08/27/96	01:17	2,143	0%	2,143	java\awt\
TextField.class	08/27/96	01:17	1,948	0%	1,948	java\awt\
Toolkit.class	08/27/96	01:17	3,178	0%	3,178	java\awt\
Window.class	08/27/96	01:17	3,025	0%	3,025	java\awt\
BufferedInputStream.class	08/27/96	01:12	1,913	0%	1,913	java\io\
BufferedOutputStream.class	08/27/96	01:12	1,028	0%	1,028	java\io\
ByteArrayInputStream.class	08/27/96	01:12	1,088	0%	1,088	java\io\
Selected 0 files, 0 bytes			Total 595 files, 1,362KB			

Figure 20-1: A WinZip display of the directory structure of part of the Java classes.zip.

Now, while the CLASSPATH environment variable points to the directory above the actual classes when they are unzipped, the variable points directly to the directory that contains the zip file.

Creating Your Own Package

Let's suppose we want to create our own package, named vbjava. We start by creating a directory structure:

```
c:\testlib\vbjava
```

We add to the CLASSPATH a pointer to the directory above; to the testlib directory:

```
set classpath=c:\testlib;%classpath%
```

Then we can put classes directly in the vbjava directory or in directories under it . If the classes are *in* that directory, we add an *import* statement pointing to that it:

```
import vbjava.*;
```

Despite the asterisk, indicating all the classes it finds, this *import* statement only includes reference to classes in the vbjava directory. It does not include directories under it.

If you want to create additional classes in directories under that directory, you need to import the additional directories specifically as well:

```
import vbjava.bList.*;
```

where this implies that the classes to be imported are in the

```
c:\testlib\vbjava\bList
```

directory. Note that the *import* statement is case sensitive and must accurately reflect the case of the directories.

The Package Statement

To put classes in this package, you must include a *package* statement in each class file that reflects its directory position. The *package* statement must be the first noncomment line in each source file and must include the directory structure of the package.

If the class is in the vbjava directory, each file must start with the statement:

```
package vbjava;
```

If the classes are in subsidiary directories, they must start with, for example:

```
package vbjava.blist;
```

You are not restricted to a single class in any directory, but all of them must include the *package* statement to be recognized during compilation of any programs that import them.

An Example Package

On your Companion CD-ROM, you will find the directory testlib containing the directory vbjava. In the vbjava directory is a version of our *ImageButton* class that contains the *package* statement:

```
package vbjava;
```

In the \chapter20 directory of your Companion CD-ROM is the program Img.java, which contains the statement:

```
import vbjava.*;
```

If you add the directory path to testlib to your CLASSPATH:

```
set classpath=d:\testlib;%classpath%
```

you should be able to compile the program Img.java without error.

Compiling With Symantec Compilers

The Symantec Café compiler sj and the Café development system do not use the CLASSPATH environment variable. Instead, if you are using the integrated development environment, the Project I Options menu allows you to specify the path of any additional packages you want to include.

If you want to include additional packages in your program while compiling from the command line, you can add the additional paths to the CLASSPATH variable in the sc.ini file in the Café\bin directory, or you can include all of the classes from the command line:

```
sj -classpath c:\Cafe\Java\Lib\classes.zip; _
    c:\projects\javabook\testlib; Img.java
```

Class Visibility Within Packages

Packages provide an additional level of visibility of methods between classes within the class. Any method or variable that is declared as *public* is, of course, visible to any other class. And as before, any method or variable declared as *private* is, as usual, only visible within the class. However, any variable or method that is neither declared as public or private is said to have *package visibility*. Any other class in the package has access to these variables and methods as if they were public.

Making Your Own Classes.zip File

Combining a set of class files into a classes.zip file can be more efficient. The total space they occupy is the same; disk file overhead in reading from a single zip file during compilation and the runtime loading of classes over the Internet will certainly be less. More to the point, you don't have to require the user of your program to copy a set of classes into a directory structure on his computer to use your program. Instead, he need only copy one zip file to any place specified in his CLASSPATH.

You can combine any group of classes into a single zip file using zip programs such as WinZip. You must combine the files:

◈ Without compression (-e0).

◈ Preserving their directory structure (-rp).

◈ Preserving long filenames.

The PKZIP program does not support long filenames and cannot be used. WinZip32 version 6.2 or later, which is available as shareware from Nico-Mak Computing (www.winzip.com) and on the Companion CD-ROM, can be used from the command line to make such files.

Let's suppose we want to put the bList.class and b_List.class files into a classes.zip file. Our command line for doing so would be:

```
wpath\winzip32 -a -r -e0 path\classes.zip path\b*.class
```

However, since WinZip is usually installed in the c:\Program Files\winzip directory and not in our path, we can add it to our path by:

```
set path=c:\"Program Files\winzip";%path%
```

Then we can type the program name from the command line. However, you must type the complete path for both the source and the destination zip file:

```
winzip32 -a -r -e0 zpath\classes.zip cpath\b*.class
```

where -a means add, -e0 means do not compress, and -r means to include subdirectories. You can see the results of this file combination in the WinZip viewer window shown in Figure 20-2.

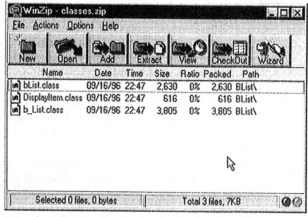

Figure 20-2: The WinZip display of our simple classes.zip file.

While you must include the complete path name, for both the source file and the zip file, you can also run WinZip first, set it to the directories you will be using, and then exit. WinZip will then remember these settings in its winzip32.ini file, which is stored in the Windows directory.

Putting a Package in a Zip File

To put the compiled classes of a package into a zip file, you must declare them as package members when compiling them as you usually do. Then, they must be stored in a directory that has the same name as the package. For example, we take the *bList* class from Chapter 19 and make it and its supporting classes part of a package called *BList*. We put these classes in the directory testlib\src\BList, and from the testlib\src directory, we run WinZip so that the path in the zip file is BList\:

```
winzip32 -a -r -e0 \testlib\classes.zip \testlib\src\*.class
```

The contents of this packaged zip file are shown in Figure 20-3.

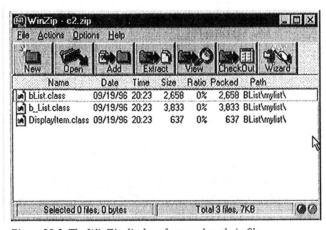

Figure 20-3: The WinZip display of our packaged zip file.

Then we set the CLASSPATH to specifically include this classes.zip file:

```
set CLASSPATH=\testlib\classes.zip;%CLASSPATH%
```

The example program listdisp.java imports this class from the:

```
import BList.bList; //import from our library
import java.awt.*;

public class listdisp extends Frame
{
bList list;                     //custom list box type
//---------------------------------------------------
 public listdisp()
 {
 super("List demo");
 list = new bList();        //create custom list box
 list.addItem("fooie");    //add a line to it
 reshape(100, 100, 300,200);
 show();
 }
//---------------------------------------------------
 static public void main(String argv[])
 {
 new listdisp();
 }
 }
```

Moving On

In this chapter, we've looked at how packages and zipped library files are constructed. We've seen that packages allow us to subdivide the name space as well as group useful functions. We'll go on now to see how to build real, useful Web pages containing Java applets.

21

Building Web Pages

One of the most common reasons for writing Java programs is to enhance the look and functionality of World Wide Web pages. For you to appreciate how a Java applet and the Web page can interact, we'll take a few pages here to review the basics of Web page construction. If you already know how to construct Web pages, you can skip right on to Chapter 22, where we'll begin discussing how applets interact with Web pages.

HTML Documents

A World Wide Web page consists of formatted text, laid out in various ways, along with images and, perhaps, Java applets. Throughout the page, there are underlined terms called *links*. When you click on a link, the browser loads the new page that the link refers to. The new page can be an additional page on the same topic and within the same Web site, or it can be a link to a page anywhere on the network, hence the name "World Wide" Web.

Every Web page is a text file with formatting tags enclosed in angle brackets (<tag>) that describe how that text is to be drawn. The tags comprise the HyperText Markup Language, or HTML. To indicate that text is to appear in a particular format, you enclose it between a start tag and an end tag. The start tag consists of one or more characters inside the angle brackets, and the end tag contains the same characters preceded by a forward slash. For example, to indicate the text that is to appear as a #1 head, you write:

```
<h1>This is the header</h1>
```

Web browsers such as Netscape Navigator and Microsoft Internet Explorer read in the HTML text file, interpret the tags, and format and display the text accordingly. Spaces and carriage returns are ignored in HTML. The formatting is controlled exclusively by the tags themselves. The tags may be in upper, lower, or mixed case, since case is ignored by the browsers.

There are any number of tools for building noninteractive Web pages; most of the popular word processors allow you to export any document into an HTML file. However, since tools for building interactive pages containing frames, forms, and applets have not yet emerged, you need to understand the rudiments of HTML syntax so that you can edit these files to produce the exact layout you have in mind.

TEMPLATES & TOOLS FOR MAKING WEB PAGES

While many people create their Web pages from scratch as we do in this chapter, you can also start using templates from a number of sources. The Netscape Web site (home.netscape.com) provides a dozen or so Web page templates as well as a number of useful images. In addition, the complete specifications for all of the HTML tags are available at the Netscape site.

There are also any number of programs for constructing Web pages, such as Microsoft FrontPage, Lotus InterNotes, and others.

Creating a Web Page With a Word Processor

Even if you plan to edit the Web page later to contain more complex elements, you can often get started by typing the basic text into a word processor and saving it as an HTML file. For example, if you are using Microsoft Word, you can select File I New and select the HTML.dot template. Then you can type in the rudiments of your Web page:

Then, if you save this text as an HTML file, you will find that the file is a text file, containing the following tags and text:

```
<HTML>
<HEAD>
<META NAME="GENERATOR" CONTENT="Internet Assistant">
<TITLE>Untitled</TITLE>
</HEAD>
<BODY>
<H1>Our Swim Team</H1>
<P>
The best in the state!
<UL>
<LI>We'd like you to join us.
<LI>See our address below.
</UL>
<HR>
<P>
Our address
</BODY>
</HTML>
```

Now let's see what these tags mean and how we can improve on them by editing this text.

The Structure of an HTML Page

Every HTML page must start with the <html> tag and should end with the </html> tag. Within a page, there are two regions: the head and the body. The head section contains the title that appears in the browser window's title bar, and may include *meta information* about which tools were used to produce the page. Note that our word processor–generated text above didn't fill in the <title> tag.

The body section consists of the text and all the tags that produce the visual layout, images, and tags that insert Java applets. The following is a very simple HTML Web page:

```
<html>
<head> <title>A Basic Web Page</title></head>
<body>
<H1>Our Swim Team</h1>
A description of the team
<p>
Some details on joining the team.
</body>
</html>
```

This page is given in the file basicpage.html on the Companion CD-ROM and is illustrated in Figure 21-1.

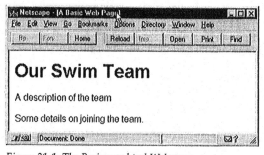

Figure 21-1: The Basicpage.html Web page.

Headers

The HTML language allows you to select headers at six different levels. Realistically, no one uses more than three or four, but you can see the effects of all six in the file headers.html. Note that we also use the <hr> tag to draw a horizontal line under the <h1> header:

```
<html>
<head> <title>Showing Headers</title></head>
<body>
<H1>Our Swim Team</h1>
<hr>
A description of the team
<h2>Joining the Team</h2>
Some details on joining the team.
<h3>Third level info</h3>
<h4>Fourth level info</h4>
<h5>Fifth level info</h5>
<h6>Sixth level info</h6>
</body></html>
```

These headers are displayed in Figure 21-2.

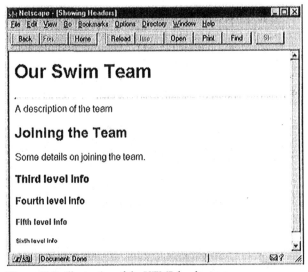

Figure 21-2: Illustration of the HTML header tags

Line Breaks

There are two ways to start a new line on the screen:

```
<p>The paragraph tag, and
<br>the line break tag.
```

These two tags differ in that a paragraph tag causes a line break and skips a blank line, while the <br> tag simply starts a new line. Neither <br> nor <p> require a corresponding end tag </br> or </p>, and these end tags are ignored by browsers.

A line break is also created automatically by using the <center> tag to center text that follows. If you want to center several lines, you need to specify breaks between them:

```
<center>
Our Team<br>
123 Aqua St. <br>
Anytown, IA<br>
</center>
```

Comments in HTML

Sometimes it is useful to add comments to your HTML, just as you do to Java programs, in order to explain what you are doing. You can also use comments to remove part of a Web page temporarily. The command tag begins with a left angle bracket, an exclamation point, and two hyphens:

```
<!-- This starts an HTML comment.
```

It can go on for several lines, but must end with two hyphens and a right angle bracket:

```
The end of the comment -->
```

Lists in HTML

HTML supports two kinds of lists: ordered (or numbered) and unordered (or bullet) lists. Numbered lists automatically increment the item number for each successive element, and bulleted lists are indented and prefixed with a bullet. You can nest and intermingle these to any level.

Ordered lists start with the <ol> tag and unordered lists with the <ul> tag. Each list line is introduced with an <li> tag and may end with an </li> end tag. A list line is also terminated by a new <li> tag or by the end of the list </ol> or </ul>.

For example, the following is a numbered list with two levels of bullet lists as sublists:

```
<html>
<head> <title>List Elements</title></head>
<body>
<ol>
<li>Our team is the strongest in the state.
   <ul>
   <li>We've won 5 state championships
   <li>We sent a swimmer to the Olympics
      <ul>
      <li>Silver medal in Seoul in 1988
      </ul>
   <li>We all lift weights
   </ul>
<li>Our coaches are the handsomest in the state
<li>Our parents are the most fecund.
   <ul>
   <li>Most families have 3 or more kids on the team.
   </ul>
</ol>
</body>
<html>
```

The indenting in the HTML source above is for readability; it has no effect on the alignment of the displayed text. The resulting Web page is shown in Figure 21-3.

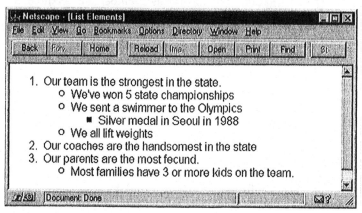

Figure 21-3: Illustration of nested ordered and unordered lists.

Fonts & Colors

You can change the font size and emphasis using the bold, italic, and underline tags:

```
Begin <b>boldface</b> plain text <i>italics</i> and
the following is <u>underlined</u>.
```

This produces the displayed text:

Begin **boldface** plain text *italics* and the following is <u>underlined</u>.

You can also nest the tags, creating bold plus italic; for example:

```
<b>Bold <i>bold and italic</i> only bold</b> plain.
```

which displays on a Web page as:

Bold *bold and italic* only bold plain.

A font can appear in one of seven sizes, which you can specify by the <Font size= *n*> tag where *n* is a number between 1 and 7. You can also increase or decrease the font size by preceding the number with a plus or minus sign:

```
<Font size=-1>
```

To revert to the previous font size, simply terminate that font with the

```
</Font>
```

tag.

In the same fashion, you can change the color of a font with the <Font color=*name*> tag, where the color can be one of the common color names: red, green, orange, yellow, blue, magenta, pink, cyan, silver, gray, or (believe it or not) teal. You can also specify any color you can describe in terms of its *rgb* value by enclosing that hexadecimal number in quotes. For example, the statement:

```
<Font color ="#8000ff">
```

produces a medium purple font color. Some browsers require that you precede the six-digit hexadecimal value with the # sign, and others will work even if you omit it.

These colors are less hard to predict if you aren't really experienced in color mixing, so some common ones are shown in Table 21-1.

Hexadecimal value	Color
000000	black
ff0000	red
00ff00	green
0000ff	blue
ffff00	yellow
40e0d0	turquoise
00ffff	cyan
ff0080	pink
ffd700	gold
ff8000	orange
60e000	mint green
add8e6	powder blue
e00080	purple mist
7fff00	chartreuse
228b22	racing green
a0522d	sienna
006400	dark green
ffa0c0	salmon
ff2020	radish
191970	midnight blue

Table 21-1: Hexadecimal values for common colors.

Some of the colors are named by Joe Burns, whose Web site at http://www.htmlgoodies.com/colors.html describes coloring your Web page. Of course, if your computer display is set to 16 or 256 colors, you won't see the differences among some of the more subtle shades above.

Background Colors

You can spruce up your Web page by specifying the background color as part of the <body> tag. As with the font color tag, you can specify the color either by name or by hexadecimal color value. The statement:

```
<body bgcolor = "#0000f0">
```

produces a medium blue background for your Web page.

Images

You can insert images in a Web page to illustrate your point. These images can be icons, drawings, cartoons, or even scanned photographs. Web page browsers support two standard image formats: GIF and JPEG. The GIF encoding scheme is more suitable for icons, cartoons, and line drawings, while the JPEG scheme does a better job on photographs. For the same image, a JPEG file will be a little smaller than a GIF, but may take longer for your browser to decompress.

To insert an image, you simply refer to its filename inside the <img> tag:

```
<img src="new.gif">
```

and your browser will insert it at that point on your Web page. For example, you might have a little "new" icon that you'd like to mark new parts of your Web page with when you change it. You can do this by simply adding the image to that line:

```
<ul>
  <li><img src="new.gif">How we did this year!
  <li>We've won 5 state championships
  <li>We sent a swimmer to the Olympics
</ul>
```

The Web page resulting from this image tag is shown in Figure 21-4 and is provided as an example file, img.html.

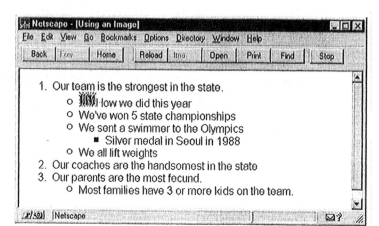

Figure 21-4: A list showing an image inserted in it.

Where to Get Images

There are huge numbers of images available on the World Wide Web. Search for "GIFs and Images." One popular source is IconBazaar. The Web address changes frequently, so use a search engine to locate it.

You can also make a copy of any image you see in your browser on any page from the Web by right-clicking on the image. A menu will pop up that allows you to save the image to a disk file. Of course you should be careful not to reuse copyrighted material or trademarks.

SEARCHING THE WEB

There are a number of free Web sites that provide tools for searching the Web. If you click on Search in Netscape Navigator, it allows you to choose from five of the most popular: Yahoo, AltaVista, Lycos, Magellan, and InfoSeek.

All of them are quite powerful, but they use different search and indexing methods, and if one does not find what you are looking for, try one of the others.

Putting Your Page on the Web

In order to give others access to your Web pages, you must put them "on the Web." This means that you must make some arrangement with an Internet Service Provider (ISP) who makes space available on his server for your Web page(s). This may or may not be the same provider that you use for your Internet access. For example, you might be dialing in to a provider such as Netcom or Worldnet to get your mail and access to the Internet, but using a different provider to host your Web pages.

The Web server provider will give you the filename and Internet address where you can put your Web page. Typically, your home page is named default.html and if the provider is named turkeynet.com, then your Web page address might be something like:

```
http://www.turkeynet.com/ourteam/
```

You can transfer the page to that address by signing on to your ISP and accessing the address they gave you using the ftp command or the ftp feature of your browser. For example, in Netscape Navigator, if you type in the address:

```
ftp://userid.password@ftp.turkeynet.com/ourteam
```

you can use the File | Upload menu item to transfer your Web page to the Web page server. This is illustrated in Figure 21-5.

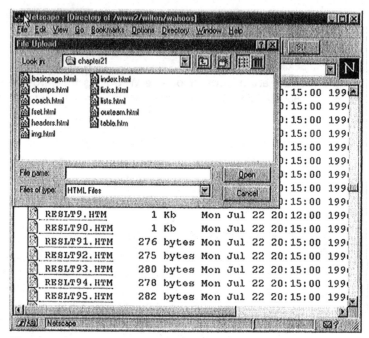

Figure 21-5: Using Netscape Navigator to upload your Web page.

Hyperlinks

So far, our little protoype Web page has been pretty boring. It's just a laundry list of little facts about "our team." These pages become more interesting if you provide links to related information. And now that we know how Web page addresses are specified, we can include some. To continue with our team example, let's assume it might be advantageous to include a link to the national swimming organization's Web page as well. To do so, we enclose the text that is to make up the link in an *anchor* tag, specifying the link as part of the beginning tag:

```
<li>Our team is a member of
<a href="http://www.usswim.org">
United States Swimming</a>
```

This produces a link, usually indicated by blue underlining, that allows you to jump to the U.S. Swimming home page by just clicking on it.

Links to More Pages of Your Own

In the same fashion, you could write more pages describing facets of your team and link them to your home Web page. Links to these local pages do not need to contain the complete Internet address, only the name of the file itself. This makes it easy to test the pages on your own computer using a browser and then move all of the pages to the Web server when they are completed.

For example, you might want to make another page, called champs.html, listing your team's accomplishments:

```
<html>
<head>
<title>State Championships</title>
</head>
<body bgcolor="00f0ff">
<h1>State Championships</h1>
<ul>
<li>1989 Girls Senior Champions
<li>1992 13-14 and 15-18 Boys Age Group Champion
<li>1994 Overall Age Group Girls Champion
<li>1995 Boys Senior Champions
<ul>
</body>
</html>
```

You can add this link to the line mentioning championships on the home page by simply referring to the file name; no Web address is needed, since you'll be uploading all of them to the same directory:

```
<li>We've won <a href="champs.html">
    5 state championships</a>
```

Links Within the Same Page

When your Web page is more than two or three screens long, it is not uncommon to insert a link from some spot near the top of the page to an area later in the page. The destination spot is tagged using an anchor tag with a *name* attribute rather than an *href* attribute:

```
<a name="address"><h2>Our address</h2></a>
```

The hyperlink reference within the same page must start with a # sign and is case sensitive:

```
<li>Our <a href="#address">team</a> is the strongest in the
state.
```

In the same fashion, if you want to refer to a particular spot in one page, you include a number sign (#) and the name tag in the hyperlink reference:

```
<a href="ourteam.html#address">See our address</a>
```

Mailto Links

You might want to include your team's e-mail address on your home page. You can make this a link to your actual address using the special *mailto* form of the anchor tag:

```
<a href="mailto:ourteam@turkeynet.com">Our Team</a><br>
```

When someone reading your page clicks on a mailto link, it will bring up the e-mail section of their browser and allow them to send e-mail to that address. The complete Web page is given on your Companion CD-ROM as ourteam.html and is shown in Figure 21-6.

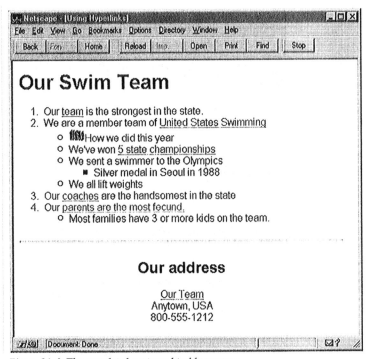

Figure 21-6: The completed ourteam.html home page.

Tables

Tables in HTML provide a convenient way to group text on a page so that the layout stays as you intended no matter what size or shape the page is displayed in your browser.

Tables are most easily generated using a word processor and saving the file as an HTML document. You can group HTML tags and text in table cells; the cells can either be outlined or hidden. The markup for tables is somewhat elaborate and we outline it in Table 21-2.

Tags	Description
<table> </table>	The entire table is surrounded by the table tags. This one has an invisible outline.
<table border=1></table>	This table has a border and outline for each cell that is one unit wide. Wider borders are possible but seldom used.
<td></td>	The text in each cell of the table is enclosed in the Table Data tags.
<tr></tr>	Each row is separated by the Table Row tag. The end tag is seldom used.
<caption></caption>	These tags surround a table caption that appears just above the table.
<th></th>	Highlights a table cell.
Attributes	**Description**
valign	Inside a <tr>, <td>, or <th> cell, it specifies how the text is aligned. The values can be *top*, *middle*, *bottom*, or *baseline*. The syntax is <td valign=middle>.
colspan	Specifies the number of columns a cell can span. The default, of course, is colspan=1.
Rowspan	Specifies the number of rows a cell can span. The default, of course, is rowspan=1.

Table 21-2: Table tags.

A simple table is shown in the file, table.html, which is given below:

```
<HTML>
<HEAD>
<META Name="Generator" Content="Lotus Word Pro">
<TITLE>Document Title</TITLE>
```

```
</HEAD>
<BODY>
<TABLE border=1 >
<caption>Our team is summarized below </caption >
<TD   valign=top>Four coaches
<TD   valign=top>Five squads
<TR>
<TD   valign=top>An active<br>
Parents club<br>
who help run swim meets.
<TD   valign=top><i>and a partridge in a pear tree</i>
</TABLE>
</BODY>
</HTML>
```

This table is shown in Figure 21-7.

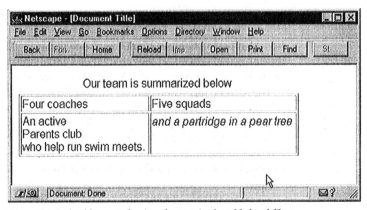

Figure 21-7: A table created using the tags in the table.html file.

Frames

Frames provide a mechanism to divide your browser page into sections where each section is displaying a separate Web page. Typically, we use frames to keep a fixed index along the side or bottom allowing us to change the main pane as the user clicks on the index frame.

A page consisting of frames is defined in a *frameset* document. Frameset documents have a <header> section, but have a <frameset> section instead of a <body> section. Such documents define the layout of the frames on the page and give the names of the HTML files that will initially occupy them.

The <frameset> tag has two possible attributes: ROWS and COLS. You can specify the size of the frames in pixels or in percentages:

```
<frameset cols=20%,80%>
<frameset cols = 50, *, 100>
```

In the first case, there are two frames; one will occupy 20 percent of the horizontal space and the other 80 percent. In the second case, the frames are 50 pixels wide, 100 pixels wide, and whatever is left.

The <frame tag> then defines the attributes of each of the frames in the order the frames are defined. The *src* attribute tells which file is to be displayed first in that frame and the *name* attribute names that frame so that links can specify which frame the referred-to document is to be displayed in. This is the content of the file, fset.html, a typical frameset document:

```
<html>
<head><title>Framed Document</title></head>
<frameset cols="30%,*" >
<frame src="index.html" name="index">
<frame src="ourteam.html" name="main">
</frameset>
</html>
```

The file, index.html, illustrates how this name attribute is used:

```
<html>
```

```
<body>
<a href="ourteam.html" target="main">Our team</a> <br>
<a href="champs.html" target="main">
Our winning record</a><br>
<a href="coach.html" target="main">Our coach</a>
</body>
</html>
```

The *target* attribute of the <href> tag in this index file says that when that link is selected, the contents of the "main" frame are replaced with the new document. The index frame remains unchanged. This is illustrated in Figure 21-8.

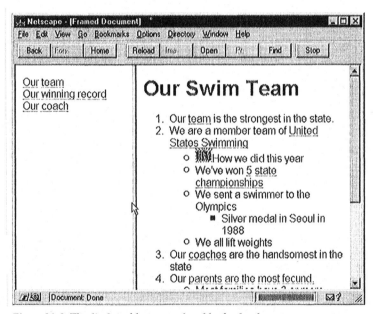

Figure 21-8: The display of frames produced by fset.html.

Moving On

In this chapter, we've reviewed how HTML Web pages are constructed. We've looked at the header, list, and font control tags, and how hypertext links are constructed. We also covered how tables and frames are constructed. Now that we've laid the groundwork for how Web pages work, we'll get back to Java and see how applets are integrated into more interesting Web pages.

22

Applets & Web Pages

One of the most useful applications of Java is in making more powerful Web pages. By combining Java with some of the HTML we've seen in the previous chapter, you can make highly interactive pages.

The Applet Tag

As we noted in Chapter 2, the <applet> tag is used to embed a Java applet in a Web page. If a given browser does not support Java applets, it will skip the tag and embed whatever text is between the applet tags:

```
<applet code="foo.class" width=300 height=200>
This browser does not support Java.
</applet>
```

The *width* and *height* attributes are required since Java does not control the space assigned on the Web page.

You can also pass any number of parameters from the Web page to the applet using the <param> tag, which must occur inside the applet tags. The <param> tag has two attributes, *name* and *value*.

You can pick any name you like for each parameter. Each value is a string. These are values passed from the Web page to the applet. Having these parameters makes it possible to make a more general Java class that carries out different operations depending on the settings of the arguments.

Displaying Pop-up Messages on a Web Page

Using the <param> tag, we can pass specific parameters to an applet and can even invoke an applet several times on a Web page, each with different parameters. In this example, we replace a specific word or phrase with an applet containing a button having that phrase on it. When you click on the button, more information on that word or phrase pops up.

Each instance of the applet contains two parameters: the caption and the extended *info*. The Web page code is given in InfoButton.html, which is shown below:

```
<html>
<head><title>Info Button Demo</title></head>
<body>
Our team has won many
<applet code="InfoButton.class" width=100 height = 25>
<param name="caption" value="championships">
<param name="info" value="1995 State Senior Champions">
</applet>
in the past 5 years.

<p>We want to thank our
<applet code="InfoButton.class" width=75 height = 25>
<param name="caption" value="parents">
<param name="info" value="Especially Freda, Sam and Ishtar">
</applet>
for their support.
</body>
</html>
```

The resulting applet display is shown in Figure 22-1. The code for this applet is given in the file, InfoButton.java. The primary class in that file is shown below. It obtains the values of the caption and info buttons, sets one as the button caption, and saves the other as the extended information to be popped up. Remember that the *init()* method is used rather than a constructor in starting up an applet:

```
public class InfoButton extends Applet
{
public void init()
{
iButton ib = new iButton(getParameter("caption"));
ib.setInfo(getParameter("info"));
add(ib);
}
}
```

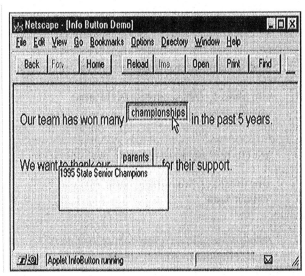

Figure 22-1: The InfoButton *class used on a Web page. A message pops up when you click on the button.*

The *iButton* class is derived from *Button* and pops up a window when the mouse is clicked:

```java
class iButton extends Button
{
String info;        //extended info
Frame fr;           //frame created
infoWindow win;     //to create Window from
 public iButton(String caption)
 {
  super(caption);   //pass caption to parent button class
  fr = new Frame(); //create invisible frame
 }
//-------------------------------------------
 public void setInfo(String s)
 {
 info = s;                          //save info string
 win = new infoWindow(fr, s);      //create window
 win.reshape(200,200,175, 50);
 win.setBackground(Color.yellow);
 }
//-------------------------------------------
 public boolean mouseDown(Event evt, int x, int y)
 {
 win.show(); //show window while donw
 return true;
 }
//-------------------------------------------
 public boolean mouseUp(Event evt, int x, int y)
 {
 win.hide(); //hide window when released
 return true;
 }
}
//====================================
class infoWindow extends Window
{
String info;
 public infoWindow(Frame fr, String s)
 {
 super(fr);
 info =s;    //save text
 }
```

```
//-------------------------------------------
public void paint(Graphics g)
{
// draw info string in window
g.drawString(info, 1,12);
}
}
```

When running over a network to a Web server, Java-enabled browsers will include the Unsigned Java Window banner along the bottom of the window. This message does not refer to the numerical sign, but to whether the applet producing the window has been authenticated or "signed." Several proposals for signing applets are under discussion among various vendors and standards bodies.

Tool Tip Pop-up Windows

Instead of popping up an instance of InfoWindow based on a button click, you can also use Java to insert in an HTML page ordinary text that causes a window to pop up when the mouse passes over it, much like the tool tip windows used in Windows 95. Rather than using a gray, clickable button, we'll simply insert the text in a label or canvas and have that control be the entire applet. Our HTML file is quite similar:

```
Our team has won many
<APPLET code="InfoCanvas.class" width=100 height = 25>
<PARAM name="caption" value="championships">
<PARAM name="info" value="1995 State Senior Champions">
</APPLET> in the past 5 years.

We want to thank our

<APPLET code="InfoCanvas.class" width=100 height = 25>
<PARAM name="caption" vaue="Especially Freda, Sam and
Ishtar">
</APPLET> for their support.
```

The program InfoCanvas creates an instance of the *iCanvas* class:

```
public class InfoCanvas extends Applet
{
```

```
//-----------------------------------------
 public void init()
 {
//get the caption for the canvas
 iCanvas ib =
    new iCanvas(this, getParameter("caption"));
//get the extended info to pop up
 ib.setInfo(getParameter("info"));
 ib.resize(100, 20);
 add(ib);
 }
 }
```

Then the *iCanvas* class draws the caption with a red border around it:

```
class iCanvas extends Canvas
{
String info, caption;
Frame fr;           //invisible frame
infoWindow win;     //window created to pop up
Applet app;         //calling applet
//-----------------------------------------
 public iCanvas(Applet applet, String capt)
 {
  super();
  caption = capt;   //save the caption
  app = applet;     //and the calling applet
  fr = new Frame(); //create invisible frame
 }
//-----------------------------------------
 public void setInfo(String s)
 {
 info = s;          //save info to pop up
 win = new infoWindow(fr, s);    //create window
 Graphics g =getGraphics();
 win.reshape(200, 150, 175, 50); //create hidden
 win.setBackground(Color.yellow);
 }
//-----------------------------------------
public void paint(Graphics g)
{
Dimension sz = size();
```

```
g.setColor(Color.red);      //draw red border
g.drawRect(0, 0, sz.width-1, sz.height-1);
g.setColor(Color.black);
g.drawString(caption, 1, 12);      //and black caption
}
```

Then, when you move the mouse over the canvas, the information pops up, and when the mouse moves out of the canvas, the window is hidden:

```
public boolean mouseEnter(Event evt, int x, int y)
{
win.show();         //show the window
return true;
}
//----------------------------------------
public boolean mouseExit(Event evt, int x, int y)
{
win.hide();         //hide the window
return true;
}
```

This is illustrated in Figure 22-2.

Figure 22-2: The InfoCanvas program, showing a window that pops up when the mouse is over a word.

Showing HTML Documents From Java

Java allows you to interact with the browser through the AppletContext interface, which every browser must support. This interface defines methods to load images and audio clips, and obtain a reference to one or all the applets on a page:

```
public  interface  java.applet.AppletContext
{
        // Methods
    public abstract Applet getApplet(String  name);
    public abstract Enumeration getApplets();
    public abstract AudioClip getAudioClip(URL  url);
    public abstract Image getImage(URL  url);
    public abstract void showDocument(URL  url);
    public abstract void
     showDocument(URL  url, String  target);
    public abstract void showStatus(String  status);
}
```

You can obtain the applet context from the applet using the *getAppletContext()* method. This gives us an easy way to use Java to tell the browser to load a new Web page.

Let's write a simple Web page with a button on it that causes another page to be loaded. We'll pass the applet the button caption and the filename of the Web page:

```
<html>
<head><title>Switch pages using Java</title></head>
<body>
<center><h1>Our Team</h1></center>
This web page describes how great Our Team is.
<p>
To find out about our practice schedule, click below.<br>
<applet code="htmlbutton.class" width=100 height=25>
<param name="caption" value="Schedule">
<param name="page" value="schedule.htm">
</applet>
<hr>
</body>
</html>
```

This page is given in the file showapp.html and displayed in
Figure 22-3.

Figure 22-3: The Web page showapp.html displayed.

The HTML Button Applet

This simple little applet just displays a button and causes the
applet to execute the *showDocument()* method on the document
you name in the page parameter. We start by getting the parameters as usual:

```
import java.awt.*;
import java.applet.*;
import java.net.*;

public class htmlbutton extends Applet
{
Button button;              //button to display
String HTMLaddress;         //page to display
//----------------------------------------
  public void init()
```

```
{
String caption = getParameter("caption");
HTMLaddress = getParameter("page");
button = new Button(caption);
add(button);
}
```

and then respond to the button click by converting the parameter string to a URL address and displaying it:

```
public void clickedButton()
{
URL url = null;          //null at first
try
  {
  url = new URL(getDocumentBase(), HTMLaddress);
  }
catch (MalformedURLException e)
  {System.out.println("bad url");}
getAppletContext().showDocument(url);
}
```

Creating a URL means that you use *getDocumentBase()* to get the base URL of the document or *getCodeBase()* to get the base URL of the applet and combine it with the filename of the page you want to display next. Note that the creation of a URL object always requires that you check for exceptions, since there is no guarantee that the address you pass in is valid. The Java program is called htmlbutton.java on the Companion CD-ROM.

Using Applets in Frames

A more typical example of using an applet to switch between pages is to put the applet in one frame on the page and switch between pages in another frame. We showed how to do this with two straight HTML pages and a frameset document in Chapter 21. However, if the descriptions of the page are long and may wrap around on lower resolution displays, using an ordinary list box might be preferable. An index frame is illustrated in Figure 22-4.

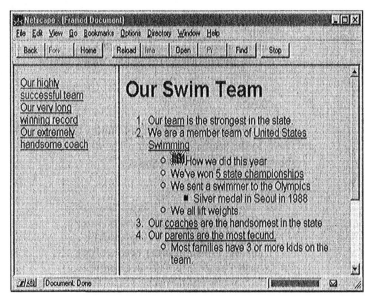

Figure 22-4: A framed HTML page where all of the index lines wrap into two lines.

Let's revise this page by putting a list box in the left-hand frame. We'll change the frameset document (now fset1.html) only slightly so that the left frame refers to a page containing the Java program jindex.class:

```
<html>
<head><title>Framed Document</title></head>
<frameset cols="30%,*" >
<frame src="jindex.html" name="index">
<frame src="ourteam.html" name="main">
</frameset>
</html>
```

The new document, which contains the class, is jindex.html and is simply:

```
<html>
<body>
<applet code="jindex.class" width=300 height=200>
<param name="indexfile" value="index.html">
</applet>
</body>
</html>
```

Now we have made the original index file a parameter that we pass to the jindex.class applet. The file index.html still contains references to three Web pages:

```
<html>
<body>
<a href="ourteam.html" target="main">
   Our highly successful team</a> <br>
<a href="champs.html" target="main">
   Our very long winning record</a><br>
<a href="coach.html" target="main">
   Our extremely handsome coach</a>
</body>
</html>
```

We'll write a program to read in and parse this file, which looks for the <href> tags to find the HTML files, and looks for the text between ">" and "<" to find the text for the list box.

Reading Files From the Web Server

We will be writing a program that gets the index filename, index.html, from an applet parameter, reads in the file, and parses it. It puts the text in a list box and the references to the HTML files into a Vector.

The important question is, how can we read files from the Web server? We accomplish this by opening a URL as usual and then using the URL class's *openStream* method to open an input data stream from:

```
import java.awt.*;
import java.applet.*;
```

```
import java.net.*;
import java.io.*;
import java.util.*;

public class jindex extends Applet
{
List list;   //listbox for data
URL url = null;     //URL we open
String address;     //name of html file
InputStream input; //file we open as input stream
DataInputStream f; //file we open
Vector Addresses;          //list of addresses
//------------------------------------------------
 public void init()
 {
 setLayout(new BorderLayout());
 list = new List(10, false);
 add("Center", list);
 Addresses = new Vector();         //space for url list
 address = getParameter("indexfile");
 try
  {
  //open the file on the server
  url = new URL(getCodeBase(), address);
  input = url.openStream();                 //get input stream
  }
 catch (MalformedURLException e)
  {System.out.println("bad url");}
 catch (IOException e)
  {System.out.println("error opening stream");}

//convert to DataInputStream class
 f = new DataInputStream(input);
 loadList(f);              //read in filenames and phrases
 }
```

Parsing the HTML Lines

Now that we have a way of reading lines from the *DataInputStream* class, we can parse out the <href> text and the phrase between the anchor tags using the following *parseLine()* method:

```
public void parseLine(String s)
{
//parses out url from href="blah"
//and tagged phrase from between > and <
int i = s.indexOf("href=");    //find start of url red
if (i >= 0)
  {
  i += 5;
  i = s.indexOf('\"', i);         //find first quote
  String address = s.substring(i + 1);
  i = address.indexOf('\"');      //find end quote
  address =address.substring(0, i); //here is the url
  Addresses.addElement(address);   //add to vector
  i = s.indexOf(">");
  String name = s.substring(i+1);
  i = name.indexOf("<");
  name = name.substring(0, i).trim();
  list.addItem(name);               //add to list box
  }
}
```

Viewing the Documents From the Java List

Now we have the text from the tagged phrases in the list box and the URLs they point to in a Vector table. When you click on a line in the list box, you want the display in the right-hand frame to change to the Web page it refers to. We use a form of the *showDocument()* method that allows you to refer to the frame's name:

```
private void clickedList()
{
int i = list.getSelectedIndex();
address = (String)Addresses.elementAt(i);
 try
   {
   url = new URL(getDocumentBase(), address);
   }
 catch (MalformedURLException e)
   {System.out.println("bad url");}
 getAppletContext().showDocument(url,  "main");
}
```

Here we are displaying the URL in the "main" frame on the Web page. The result is shown in Figure 22-5, and the program is given on the Companion CD-ROM as jindex.java.

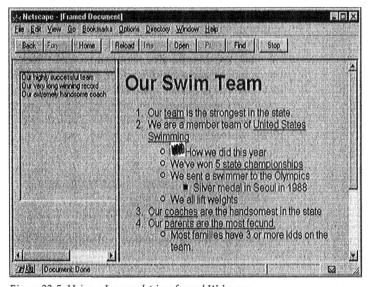

Figure 22-5: Using a Java applet in a framed Web page.

Playing Audio Clips in Applets

The Java *Applet* class contains methods that you can use to play audio clips on your Web pages. In Java 1.0, only the Sun .aufile format is supported. This is an 8-bit monaural format of limited (8 kHz) fidelity, but it produces relatively small data files for downloading. You can read about the format on the Web at www.ucsalf.ac.uk/cgibin/faq?audio-fmts/part2.

The audio formats that can be played are determined by the browser, and additional formats will eventually be supported by most browsers.

The two methods the *Applet* class supports are:

```
public void play(URL  url);
public void play(URL  url, String  name);
```

We'll consider the *play* method first. We'll write a simple applet, ding.java, to be played from ding.html, which contains a single button that causes the "ding.au" sound clip to be played.

Audio clips are separate files on your Web server, just as images are. They are downloaded when you request them, and as of Java 1.0, cannot be cached or tested for using the MediaTracker. Instead, the file is downloaded when you request that it begin playing. If the file does not exist, nothing happens and no error occurs.

To get an audio file as a URL, we do exactly what we did for the HTML file we read in the last section:

```
URL url = null;
 try
  {url = new URL(getCodeBase(), "ding.au");}
 catch(MalformedURLException e)
  {System.out.println("bad URL");}
```

Then, to play the file we just downloaded as a URL, we simply say:

```
play(url);            //play the clip
```

The complete program to play the audio file ding.au is shown below:

```
import java.awt.*;
import java.net.*;
import java.applet.*;

public class ding extends Applet
{
Button play;              //play a clip when clicked
//----------------------------------------------
public void init()
{
play = new Button("Ding");
add(play);                //put button on display
}
//----------------------------------------------
public boolean action(Event evt, Object arg)
{
if (evt.target==play)
 {
 playDing();              //play when clicked
 return true;
 }
return super.action(evt, arg);
}
//----------------------------------------------
private void playDing()
 {
 URL url = null;          //must be initialized
 //get the URL of the sound file
 try{
  url = new URL(getCodeBase(), "ding.au");}
 catch(MalformedURLException e)
 {System.out.println("bad URL");}
 play(url);               //and play it
 }
//----------------------------------------------
 }
```

The AudioClip Class

The *AudioClip* class provides a container for an audio file that gives you a little more control over the playing of the sound. You can obtain an AudioClip object using the *Applet* methods:

```
public AudioClip getAudioClip(URL  url);
public AudioClip getAudioClip(URL  url, String  name);
```

The *getAudioClip()* methods return immediately and the actual file is not downloaded until you play it.

The AudioClip objects then allow you to call the methods:

```
public abstract void loop();
public abstract void play();
public abstract void stop();
```

The *play()* method works exactly like the applet's *play* method, downloading and playing the file. However, if you choose to play the clip more than once, the browser recognizes that it has already been downloaded and plays it from its disk cache.

The *loop()* method plays the file continuously, and the *stop()* method stops playing the file. Since you can't tell how long downloading will take or even whether the file was downloaded at all, this remains a fairly primitive interface in Java 1.0.

In the example program dingding.java, we illustrate how you can use all of these functions. The *init()* method creates the AudioClip objects and the buttons to play one or both of the clips. It also includes a check box to indicate whether you want to loop continuously or not:

```
public class dingdong extends Applet
{
//allows you to play or loop on
//either or both sound clips
Button playDing, playDong, playBoth, stop;
AudioClip ding, dong;    //loaded here
Checkbox loop;           //loop id checked
//----------------------------------------
public void init()
{
```

```
setFont(new Font("Helvetica", Font.PLAIN, 12));
playDing = new Button("Ding");   //initialize
playDong = new Button("Dong");   //three
playBoth = new Button("Both");   //buttons
stop = new Button("Stop");
loop = new Checkbox("Loop");      //loop if on
add(playDing);                   //insert in display
add(playDong);
add(playBoth);
add(loop);
add(stop);
//convert two sound clip files to URLs
URL urlDing = makeURL("ding.au");
URL urlDong = makeURL("gong.au");
//make into AudioClip objects
ding = getAudioClip(urlDing);
dong = getAudioClip(urlDong);
}
```

The displayed window for the dingdong program is shown in Figure 22-6.

Figure 22-6: The dingdong.javaapplet for playing one or two sound files at once.

To play the clips once or in a loop, we write our own *play* method, which checks the state of the loop check box and plays or loops accordingly:

```
private void play(AudioClip clip)
 {
//play once or loop
//depending on check box state
if (loop.getState())
   clip.loop();
else
   clip.play();
 }
```

Making Audio Files

Since this .au file audio format is still unusual on PCs, you probably will need a conversion tool to convert the usual .wav files to .aufiles. The GoldWave shareware program:

```
www.cs.mun.ca/~chris3/goldwave
```

has a nice Windows 95 interface and supports a large number of audio formats. You can also use the SoX program:

```
www.info.unicaen.fr/~morise/dess/projet/formats/sox
```

for file conversion. This program is free and quite versatile, but does not have a friendly interface.

Audio in Applications

Nominally, Java only allows you to play audio clips from applets. However, nearly all platforms allow you to make use of the undocumented *sun.applet.AppletAudioClip* class, which can return an instance of an AudioClip within an application. The program appding.java, illustrated in Figure 22-7, shows how you can do this:

```
import java.awt.*;
import java.net.*;
```

```
import java.io.*;
import java.applet.*;
import sun.applet.AppletAudioClip;
//illustrates how to play an audio clip
//from an application
public class appding extends Frame
{
Button play;              //play a clip when clicked
//-----------------------------------------------
public appding()
{
super("Sound Application");
setLayout(new FlowLayout());
play = new Button("Ding");
add("Center", play);                //put button on display
reshape(100,100,100,100);
show();
}
//-----------------------------------------------
public boolean action(Event evt, Object arg)
{
if (evt.target == play)
 {
 playDing();              //play when clicked
 return true;
 }
return super.action(evt, arg);
}
//-----------------------------------------------
private void playDing()
 {
 URL url = null;          //must be initialized
 //get the URL of the sound file
 try
  {
  url = new URL("file|///ding.au");
  }
 catch(MalformedURLException e)
  {System.out.println("bad URL");}
```

```
//use sun class to get clip
AudioClip clip = new AppletAudioClip(url);
clip.play();              //and play it
}
//------------------------------------------------
static public void main(String argv[])
{
new appding();
}
//------------------------------------------------
}
```

The one disadvantage of this method is that you must still specify a URL to convert to an audio clip. This means that you have to convert a filename path to the peculiar URL syntax, which begins with "file | ///" and where drive colons are replaced with the pipe | symbol.

Figure 22-7: The appding application, illustrating how a sound can be played from an application rather than an applet.

Loading Zip Libraries

Once you have written an applet with a significant number of .class files, the downloading time over the Web can be extremely annoying. Each individual class file necessitates that your browser make a separate connection to the server to download it. In order to minimize the number of reconnections and individual downloads, you can combine all of your classes except the startup class into an archive zip file and put that file on the server instead of the individual class files. Downloading a single zip file is significantly faster than downloading the 10 or so component class files that it contains. However, loading classes from zip files once they are downloaded is somewhat slower than from unzipped files. In Java 1.1, the JAR file format will solve these problems. We discuss how to use WinZip to make these zip files in Chapter 20, "Using Packages."

To tell your browser to look for the classes in the archive file, use the <archive= tag> in your <applet> tag:

```
<applet code="dingaling.class" archive="c.zip"
  width=200 height=300>
```

Interapplet Communication

When you put more than one applet on a Web page, it is possible for these applets to communicate. Applets loaded and active on the same Web page (and in Navigator, fully visible on the screen) can share public variables and methods.

There are a couple of tricks to this interapplet communication scheme. First, you must name each applet using the <NAME> tag within the applet declaration on the Web page:

```
<applet code="app1.class"
  NAME="app1" width=100 height =100>
</applet>
<applet code="app2.class"
  NAME="app2" width=100 height =100>
</applet>
```

The <NAME> tag must be all uppercase, and, because of a bug in Navigator, the applet names *must* be all lower case.

Each applet can then refer to the other by these names. We'll write two applets: app1.java consists of a button and app2.java consists of a counter and a textfield where it is displayed. Our app2.java looks like this:

```
import java.awt.*;
import java.applet.*;
import java.util.*;
public class app2 extends Applet
{
```

```
public int Counter;
TextField tf;
public void init()
{
tf = new TextField("  0");
add(tf);
}
//--------------------------------
public int incr()
{
Counter++;
tf.setText(new Integer(Counter).toString());
repaint();
return Counter;
}
}
```

We have made the *incr* method public; therefore, it can be accessed from another applet on the same page. In order to access the other applet, we use the *getApplet* method of the AppletContext:

```
context = getAppletContext();
Applet applet = context.getApplet(appname);
```

Then we can access any public method or variable of the other applet(s) from this applet object. Note that in this brief example, we made the *Counter* variable public, so it could also be accessed directly if we chose. The complete applet app1 is given below and is illustrated in Figure 22-8:

```
public class app1 extends Applet
{
Button button;
String appname;
app2 app = null;
AppletContext context;
//--------------------------------
public void init()
{
button = new Button("Counter");
add(button);
appname="app2";
```

```
  }
//----------------------------------
  public boolean action(Event evt, Object arg)
  {
  if (evt.target == button)
   {
   context = getAppletContext();
   Applet applet = context.getApplet(appname);
   app = (app2)applet;
   int c = app.incr();
   return true;
   }
  return super.action(evt, arg);
  }
}
```

If there are a large number of applets running on a Web page,
you can use the *getApplets* method, which returns an Enumeration
object, from which you can obtain the names of each of the applets:

```
context = getAppletContext();
Enumeration e = context.getApplets();
while e.hasMoreElements()
 {
 System.out.println(e.nextElement());
 }
```

Figure 22-8: Two applets communicating while running on the same Web page.

Debugging Applets

If you have a single applet on a Web page, you can use the appletviewer program to test the program and place *System.out.println* statements to follow the code. If you are getting exceptions within the program, try running the appletviewer_g program, which will print out a trace of any program errors.

Finally, if you must run the program using a Web browser, Netscape Navigator provides a menu choice under Options: Show Java Console. This brings up a window that shows all of the output your Java program produces, both the *println* statements and any execution errors. This is illustrated in Figure 22-9.

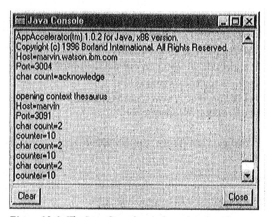

Figure 22-9: The Java Console window, showing the progress of an applet.

Moving On

In this chapter, we've seen some of the more sophisticated details of how Web pages and Java applets interact. We've learned about passing parameters to applets, pop-up windows, playing audio clips, and interapplet communication. Next, we'll look at Forms, CGI scripts, and briefly, at the JavaScript language.

23

Interacting With Web Page Forms

The basic HTML language provides some simple methods for adding interactive controls to Web pages inside <Form> tags. You can put text fields, check boxes, radio buttons, list boxes, and drop-down list boxes on the form for users to fill in. This approach is frequently used in today's Web pages to gather data, order merchandise, and add people to mailing lists. The disadvantage of the Web form approach is that the only way to process the filled-out HTML is to send it to the server, where a program you have written there processes the data. In this chapter, we'll look at the basic syntax of HTML forms and then discuss how you can use Java to process them on the server.

The HTML Form

All of the interactive elements on an HTML must be enclosed inside the <Form> tag. For example, the following simple form puts two text fields on the screen:

```
<html>
<head><title>Forms Example</title></head>
<body>
```

```
<form action="/cgi/getnames" method="post">
Please enter your name:<br>
First name:
<input type="text" size=20 maxlength=25 name="f_name">
Last name:
<input type="text" size=20 maxlength=25 name="l_name">
</form>
</body>
</html>
```

This is illustrated in Figure 23-1 and can be found on your Companion CD-ROM as form1.html.

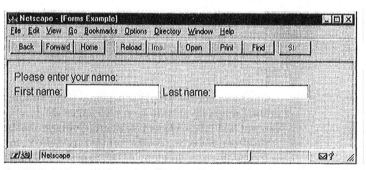

Figure 23-1: Two simple text entry fields on an HTML form.

Sending the Data to the Server

You can load the little Web page in the previous section into your browser and it will display the fields you see in Figure 23-1. However, they aren't very useful unless some program somewhere can act on them. This is what is specified in the <Form> tag. The keyword phrase:

```
action="/cgi/getnames"
```

indicates that a program called getnames in the /cgi directory is to be executed. We use UNIX-like forward slashes to separate the directory path even if the server is a PC. The other keywords:

```
method="post"
```

tell the form how to send the data. This is far and away the most common of two possible transmission methods. The other possible tag value is:

```
method="get"
```

but you will probably never need to use it.

OK, well enough; but how are the data sent? All of the data are sent when you click on the Submit button. This button may have any sort of label, but has the type "submit:"

```
<input type="submit" value="Send Data">
```

You can also include a Clear button, which clears all of the entry fields:

```
<input type="reset" value="Clear Data">
```

This packages up all the fields and sends them to the server, where the program /cgi/getnames is executed and fed that data. We'll look into the format of that data and what the server program does with it shortly.

The following example includes the two buttons. It is illustrated in Figure 23-2 and is form2.html on the Companion CD-ROM:

```
<html>
<head><title>Forms Example</title></head>
<body>
<form action="/cgi/getnames" method="post">
Please enter your name:<br>
First name:
<input type="text" size=20 maxlength=25 name="f_name">
Last name:
<input type="text" size=20 maxlength=25 name="l_name">
<center>
<input type="submit" value="Send Data">
<input type="reset" value="Clear Data">
</center>
</form>
</body>
</html>
```

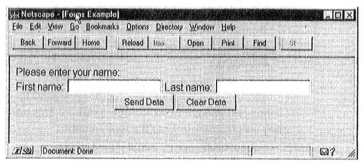

Figure 23-2: A simple HTML form with a submit (Send Data) and clear (Clear Data) button.

Form Fields

There are only six possible controls that you can place on a form, and they are summarized in Table 23-1.

Input Type=	Value=	Description
Text	Any text	A text entry field. You can use size= to specify the width of the field.
Textarea	Any text	A multiline text entry field. You can specify rows= and cols= to define its size.
Checkbox	Yesno	A single check box. The label is just text outside the check box input type.
Radio	AnyCHECKED	A radio button. The value may be any text, but you may include the CHECKED keyword on one of the buttons. The label for the button is just text outside the radio input type. The *names* of all the grouped radio buttons must be the same. To distinguish them, give them different *value* properties.

Input Type=	Value=	Description
Submit	Any text	The button that sends the form contents to the server.
Reset	Any text	The button that clears all the entry fields.

Table 23-1: The HTML Form controls.

Selection Lists

In addition to the simple inputs we show above, you can also include regular and drop-down list boxes, which are called Selection Lists. Since these lists can be of any length, they are bracketed with the <select> and </select> tags:

```
<Select name="fruits" size=5>
<option>Apples
<option>Avocados
<option>Cherries
<option>Pears
<option>Pomegranates
</select>
```

The *size* keyword indicates the number of lines to be displayed. There can be many more entries than lines.

You can also specify that one line is to be selected by default by adding the *Selected* keyword:

```
<option Selected>Pomegranates
```

If you want more than one list box element to be selected at once you can mark this list a multiselect by including the *multiple* keyword:

```
<select name="fruits" Multiple size=5>
```

Unfortunately, multiselect lists are not very easy to recognize or use. If you just click on a line, it will be selected by itself. To select more than one, you must do one of the following:

- ❧ Drag the mouse over the lines to be selected.

- ❧ Hold down Shift and select contiguous lines.

- ❧ Hold down Control and select noncontiguous lines.

You should probably use a series of check boxes instead if you want to allow multiple selection.

Drop-down Lists

The drop-down list is just a special case of the Selection list box, where you set size=1 or omit size altogether. In either case, a single-line list is displayed that drops down to reveal the list selections. While these drop-down lists can also be multiply selected, they aren't very easy to recognize or use, and a series of check boxes is again easier for your user to understand.

Making an Order Form

So now, let's use this form technology to order our evening meal. The simple HTML shown below will produce the order form shown in Figure 23-3. This file, order.html, is on your Companion CD-ROM:

```
<html>
<body>
<center>
<h1>Order your meal here</h1>
</center>
<form method="post" action="cgi/order.exe">

Name: <input type="text" width=25><br>
<input type="radio" name="wine">Red wine<br>
<input type="radio" name="wine">White wine<br>
<select name="meats" size=5>
<option>Roast chicken
<option>Steak bearnaise
<option>Duck ala orange
<option>Dull pasta salad
</select>
<p>
<input type="checkbox" name="soup">Soup<br>
<input type="checkbox" name="salad">Salad<br>
<p>
<center>
<input type="submit" name="Submit order">
```

```
<input type="reset" name="Clear entries">
</center>
</form>
</body>
</html>
```

Figure 23-3: A simple HTML form for ordering your dinner.

Now let's improve on this slightly by grouping these controls using a table. We'll put the name in one cell, the wine order in another, the meat order in a third, and the soup and salad in a fourth. The HTML that is given in the file, ordert.html, looks like this:

```
<HTML>
<HEAD>
<TITLE>Tabular meal order</TITLE>
</HEAD>
<BODY>
<h1>Order your meal here</h1>
```

```html
</center>
<form method="post" action="cgi/order.exe">

<!-- ----Group the order using a table----  -->
<TABLE>
<TR><TD WIDTH=295>
Name: <input type="text" width=25 name="Name"><br>
</TD>
<TD WIDTH=295>
<input type="radio" name="wine" value="redwine">
   Red wine<br>
<input type="radio" name="wine" value="whitewine">
   White wine<br>
</TD>
</TR>
<TR>
<TD WIDTH=295 align=center>
<select name="meats" size=5>
<option>Roast chicken
<option>Steak bearnaise
<option>Duck ala orange
<option>Dull pasta salad
</select>
</TD>
<TD WIDTH=295>
<input type="checkbox" name="soup">Soup<br>
<input type="checkbox" name="salad">Salad<br>
</TD>
</TR>
</TABLE>
<P>

<!-- Put submit centered outside table -->
<center>
<input type="submit" name="Submit order">
<input type="reset" name="Clear entries">
</center>
</form>

</BODY>
</HTML>
```

Note the use of the HTML comment, starting with <!— and ending with —>.The resulting order page is shown in Figure 23-4.

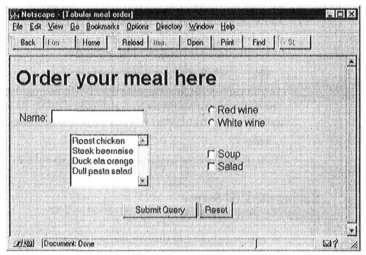

Figure 23-4: The HTML order form, grouped using table tags.

Submitting Your Form

Now that we've clicked on the Submit Query button, we need to understand what happens next. The submit operation sends a command string to the HTML server in a format called a CGI, or Common Gateway Interface, script. The data in this script launches the program you specify as part of the action tag and feeds the remainder of the script to its standard input. Standard input is the same path the data would take if you were typing it at the keyboard. The program then digests that data and usually constructs a new HTML page and sends it out its standard out channel. The output is then ingested by the Web server and sent back to your Web browser.

The format of the input to the program executed on the server is a single long line of text, with arguments separated by the ampersand (&) sign and spaces replaced by the plus (+) sign. In addition, special characters such as quotes, apostrophes, ampersands, and + signs are replaced by a percent (%) sign followed by their hexadecimal equivalent. Thus, if the diner's name is Fred O'Farkle, the CGI string would begin as:

```
name="Fred+O%27Farkle"&wine="redwine"&
```

As you can see, each control on the HTML form must have a name. The name is sent followed by a string containing its value. A field that has not been filled in will have a zero-length string sent:

```
name=""
```

We'll illustrate how to parse this in the next section.

Calling the CGI Server

Now we are going to discuss the actual calling and construction of the CGI server program. Traditionally, these servers have been written in the perl language, which is an unstructured C-like language popular with UNIX administrators. However, the servers can be written in any language and compiled for the platform the Web server is running on. We, of course, will consider writing the servers in Java.

In your action tag, you must specify the name of an actual file that exists in the directory you specify on your server. Thus, if you specify the form tag:

```
<form method="post" action="cgi/order.exe">
```

there must be a file called order.exe in the cgi subdirectory on your server. Sometimes server administration systems will redirect a cgi directory and have you put your files elsewhere, but they must exist. This is important because you cannot make an action string of the form:

```
action ="java cgiserver"
```

since it is not usual to install the java run-time system in your server's cgi directory. Instead, you must put a file there that launches the java interpreter for you. Thus, your *action* routine might contain:

```
action="myJava"
```

Then, if your Web server is on a UNIX platform, the myJava file might contain:

```
#!/bin/sh
java cgiserver
```

and if the server is on Windows NT or Windows 95, the myJava file would just contain:

```
java cgiserver
```

Writing a CGI Server in Java

The actual program that interprets the CGI string must accept the form string as a single long string through standard-input (keyboard) channel and must respond by creating a new Web page through standard-output. Of course, it probably also does something with the data it was sent, putting it into a table or database or sending an e-mail message somewhere.

We'll parse this CGI string using the cgiserver.java program on your Companion CD-ROM. We divide the various name-value pairs into single tokens by using the *StringTokenizer* class with the & character as the delimiter. Then, we replace the + signs with spaces. Third, we parse out the name as those characters to the left of the equals sign and the value as those characters within the quotation marks. Finally, we look for any hexadecimal character representations starting with the % sign and replace them with the actual character.

We will design the *cgiParse* class that does this parsing and adds each name-value pair to a table where we can retrieve it by name. The *Hashtable* class is ideal for this purpose since it provides a general storage mechanism for name-value pairs.

We add each name and value to the table and can retrieve them by name:

```
class cgiParse
{
String cgi;
Hashtable cgiNames;      //name-value pairs kept here
StringTokenizer tokens;
 //------------------------------------------
 public cgiParse(String s)
 {
cgi = s.replace('+', ' ');
makeTable();   //build table of name-value pairs
 }
 //-------------------------------------------------
 private void makeTable()
 {
int i;
cgiNames = new Hashtable();      //create table
//each name and value is delimited by "&"
tokens = new StringTokenizer(cgi, "&");
//loop until no more tokens in stream
while(tokens.hasMoreTokens())
   {
   String tok = tokens.nextToken();
   i = tok.indexOf("=");           //parse out name
   String name = tok.substring(0,i);
   name = replaceHex(name);
   //parse out value
   i = tok.indexOf("\"");          //remove quotes
   String value = tok.substring(i+1);
   i = value.indexOf("\"");      //up to last quote
   value = value.substring(0, i);
   value = replaceHex(value);
   Object ans = cgiNames.put(name, value);
   if (ans != null)      //error if one already exists
     System.out.println("Duplicate key:" + name);
   }
 }
 //-------------------------------------
public String getToken(String hashcode)
```

```
{
String s = (String)cgiNames.get(hashcode);
return(s);
}
//---------------------------------------
private String replaceHex(String tok)
{
//replace any hex characters with the actual character
int i = tok.indexOf("%");
while (i >= 0)
   {
   String left = tok.substring(0, i);      //save left
   tok = tok.substring(i+1);               //remove %-sign
   String hex = tok.substring(0,2);
   String right =tok.substring(2);
   byte value[] = new byte[1];
   //parse hex value into integer
   value[0] = (byte)Integer.parseInt(hex, 16);
   //convert to character
   String specChar = new String(value, 0);
   //recombine pieces
   tok = left + specChar + right;
   i = tok.indexOf("%");          //look for more %-signs
   }
return(tok);
}
}
```

The output Web page must start with the line:

```
Content-type: text/html
```

and be followed by a blank line. Then you begin with the tags of
the HTML page you wish to create in answer to this form. We can
now parse the entire input stream as shown in the cgiserver.java
program, whose main class is given below:

```
public class cgiserver
{
//----------------------------------------------
 public cgiserver()
 {
```

```java
cgiParse cgip;
String s ="";
// read in input command stream
DataInputStream inf= new DataInputStream(System.in);
try{s= inf.readLine();}
catch (IOException e)
  {System.out.println("input error");}
//prepare header
println("Content-type: html/text\n\n");
println("<html><title>Your order</title></head>\n");
println("<body>\n");
println("<h1>Thank you for your order</h1>\n");

//parse the cgi stream into name-value pairs
cgip = new cgiParse(s);
//get the person name and the main course choice
println("<b>Your name is:</b> " + cgip.getToken("name")
+"<p>");
println("<b>You ordered:</b> "+cgip.getToken("meat")
+"<p>");

//print out optional choices
println("<b>with:</b>");
if (cgip.getToken("wine").equals("redwine"))
  println("Red wine<br>");
if (cgip.getToken("wine").equals("whitewine"))
  println("White wine<br>");
if (cgip.getToken("soup").equals("on"))
  println("soup<br>");
if (cgip.getToken("salad").equals("on"))
  println("salad<br>");
println("</body></html>");
}
//-----------------------------------
public static void main(String argv[])
{
new cgiserver();
}
//-----------------------------------
```

```
private void println(String s)
{
System.out.println(s);
}
}
```

Testing a CGI Program

Once you have written and compiled your server program, you may realize that it can be a bit difficult to test except when running on a server. As a first test, simply create a text file containing a typical input stream, such as the answer.txt file on the Companion CD-ROM. Then you can create the output file by piping the answer.txt file into standard in and storing the output in text.html like this:

```
java cgiserver <answer.txt >test.html
```

Using the Alibaba Server to Test CGI

Another useful way to test CGI programs is by using a simple server running on your own machine. The Alibaba server is widely used for this purpose. You can find ordering information at

```
http://www.csm.co.at/csm
```

A 30-day trial version is provided on the Companion CD-ROM. After installing the Alibaba server, be sure that your system.ini file contains the lines:

```
[NonWindowsApp]
CommandEnvSize=8192
```

This value can be larger than 8192, but if it is missing, CGI programs will not work. Then you must define an alias directory for each "user" of your system. Alibaba acts as a server for the IP address 127.0.0.1 and has already defined a user:

```
http://127.0.0.1/alibaba
```

as equal to the \alibaba\htmldocs directory. You can add other usernames and define their directories.

Alibaba also automatically relocates any calls to the cgi-bin directory of the user account to the \alibaba\cgi-bin directory. You can then put your CGI server programs in this directory for execution. The result of this server program's interaction with the form ordert.html is shown in Figure 23-5.

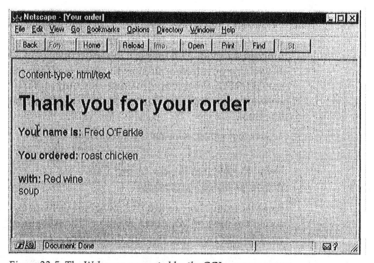

Figure 23-5: The Web page generated by the CGI server program.

Checking for Errors in CGI Data

You can usually construct a CGI form so that it is not possible to enter an inconsistent series of answers. The most common problem, however, is for users to omit an important answer, such as their name. In this case, the CGI string sent to your server program will have an empty string for that answer. You might choose to return an error page if this happens, to prompt the user to enter the data correctly:

```
cgip = cgiParse(s);
String name = cgip.getToken("name");
if (name.length()<= 0)
  {
  println("You forget to enter your name<p>");
   println("</body></html>");
  }
else
//  . . .
```

If there are a number of possible errors, you will need to test for all of them and return appropriate error pages.

Moving On

In this chapter, we've learned about forms on Web pages, how they send data to the server, and how to parse and respond to that data. We briefly mentioned error checking as part of your server program, and in the next chapter, we'll look at how to check these errors using JavaScript. Then in the following chapter, we'll look at how to use Java for the entire process.

24

What Is JavaScript?

Many people who are new to Web page programming confuse the Java language with the JavaScript language. They are actually the result of two separate development paths at two different companies: Sun and Netscape. JavaScript was originally named LiveScript and was designed to give a little more interactivity to Web pages. After Java became so popular, the language was renamed JavaScript and some attempts were made to give it a slightly object-oriented flavor and to allow it to communicate with Java applets. In fact, they are two different languages, with different purposes and widely different styles. In this chapter, we'll be giving JavaScript the once-over, so you can see how it is used and when you might use it.

Differences Between Java & JavaScript

JavaScript exists only within Web pages. It is not compiled: its statements are interpreted when the page is loaded, and you cannot write stand-alone JavaScript programs. Since it is not compiled, only a cursory syntax check is performed when the Web page is loaded by the browser, and errors can still occur when the program is executed that would be caught if the language were compiled. Thus, you need to test JavaScript programs very carefully before making them available on your Web pages.

JavaScript is primarily for computing strings and values; it does not itself have any GUI components, although you can refer to the basic Form controls within JavaScript. JavaScript has a close relationship to the browser and the Web page. You can determine the history of pages the user has visited and change links accordingly, and you can change such things as background color dynamically.

While JavaScript has a C- or Java-like syntax, using braces to set off blocks of code, it doesn't really allow you to create objects or to derive new objects from existing ones. The main purpose of JavaScript is to allow you to perform some computations affecting the appearance of your Web page and to validate input data before sending it off to a CGI server. Since JavaScript does allow you to check for the consistency of your input data, we will spend the rest of this brief chapter explaining what you can do with this useful little language.

Embedding JavaScript Programs

A JavaScript program is a part of an HTML document, just like a frame or a table is. It starts with the <script> tag and ends with the </script> tag:

```
<html>
<body>
<Script>
    //JavaScript statements go here
</script>
</body>
</html>
```

You can also optionally specify the language that you are embedding. This will become more important as other Web languages (such as VBScript) appear:

```
<script language="Javascript">
```

JavaScript programs can appear anywhere on a Web page, but if you write functions that are called from within those programs, the functions must appear in the <head> section of the Web page. This guarantees that the functions will have been loaded by the time the JavaScript main program is detected and interpreted later on the Web page:

```
<html>
<head>
<script>
 function square(x)
   {
   return x*x;
   }
</script>
</head>
```

In Navigator 3.0, you can also embed a JavaScript program from a separate file using the same <src=> tag we used to load images:

```
<script src="myscript.js">
```

For this feature to work properly, your Web server must map the ".js" extension to the type "application/x-javascript" and send this type information back in the HTML header.

JavaScript Variables

Variables in JavaScript are not typed and do not need to be declared in advance. You can just use them as you need them:

```
x = 5;
y = x/3;
z = "Fred";
```

However, illegal operations such as:

```
a = z/2;  //where z="Fred"
```

are not discovered until you execute the program. All of the operators that you can use in Java, such as ++, +=, and >>, are also legal in JavaScript.

Variables are created where you first declare them and are all global: they hold the same values even between separate functions. You can create a local variable, whose scope is limited to the current function by preceding it with the *var* declaration:

```
var x = 5;
```

Let's consider the following simple JavaScript program:

```
<html>
<body>
<Script>
for (i=0; i<10; i++)
  document.writeln(i + " " + i/3 + "<br>");
</script>
</body>
</html>
```

This simple Web document is shown in Figure 24-1 and is on your Companion CD-ROM as math1.htm.

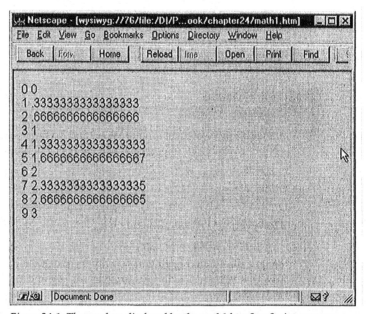

Figure 24-1: The numbers displayed by the math1.htm JavaScript program.

Note that the *for* loop has exactly the same syntax as it would in Java. It is at first tempting to equate the Java statement:

```
System.out.println(i + " " + i/3);
```

with the JavaScript statement:

```
document.writeln(i + " " + i/3 + "<br>");
```

However, the Java statement writes characters to the standard output channel, usually a DOS or terminal window, while the JavaScript statement writes HTML code to a Web page. Thus, you are not just writing text to a screen, but writing HTML code that will be displayed according to the rules of Web pages. For example, if we just wrote:

```
document.writeln(i + " " + i/3);
```

without including the <br> tag, all of the numbers would be run together on a single line. Another way to force separate lines on the screen is to enclose the text within <pre> (presentation) tags, as is done in the example code math2.htm:

```
<Script>
document.writeln("<pre>");
for (i=0; i<10; i++)
   document.writeln(i + " " + i/3 + "<br>");
document.writeln("</pre>");
</script>
```

This also forces the output to be in a Courier or typewriter-style font as shown in Figure 24-2.

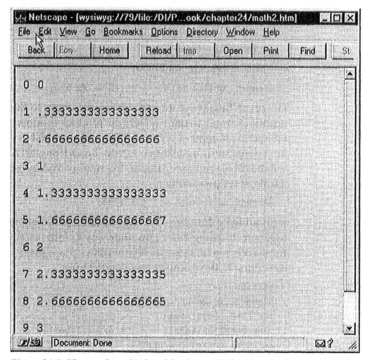

Figure 24-2: The numbers displayed by the math2.htm JavaScript program.

So to summarize, writing output to a Web page is actually writing HTML markup to a Web page, and you can affect the font size, layout, color, and style just as you would if you created a static Web page. In fact, it is this construction of dynamic Web pages that is one of JavaScript's purposes.

The JavaScript Objects on the Web Page

While JavaScript is not really an object-oriented language, it is sometimes called "object based" because a few of the parts of a Web page can be treated as simple objects. The overall object structure of the Web page consists of:

Window	The entire screen, including all frames.
Document	One entire frame.
Forms	One of the forms within the document.
Elements	The visual controls within the form.
Links	An array of the links within the document.
Anchors	An array of all the <name>= tags within the document.
Location	The current URL.
History	An object containing the browser's history list.

Each of these objects has a few methods and properties that you can use in your JavaScript programs.

The Window Object

The window object allows you to control the screen and pop up new windows. Most frequently, you use the *alert()* function, which is in fact a method of the window object. It pops up a window that says "JavaScript alert:" followed by whatever message you provide:

```
alert("You didn't enter a name");
```

The other common properties are shown in Table 24-1. You do not have to indicate the name of the window explicitly; it is always understood.

Method	Description
defaultStatus(text)	The text to appear in the status bar when not changed by an *onMouseOver* event for a particular control.
status(text)	The text that appears in the status bar.
frames()	An array of the frames that make up the window. The overall frame is the 0th element of the array.
alert(text)	Pops up an alert window.
window.open (URL, "name","features");	Opens a new window. The features, appearing as one long string in quotes, may be: toolbar=yes,no status=yes,no menubar=yes,no scrollbars=yes,no resizeable=yes,no width=pixels height=pixels
close()	Closes the current window. You should not close the main window.
confirm(text)	Displays a message box followed by yes or no. Returns *true* or *false*.
prompt(text)	Displays a message and a text entry field. Returns a string.
SetTimeout ("function", msec)	Sets a time in milliseconds after which a function is called repeatedly. This allows effects such as scrolling.

Table 24-1: Methods of the window object.

The History Object

The history object contains a reference to the browser's URL history list. You can perform the following three simple operations using the history object:

```
history.back();     //previous URL
history.next();     //forward to next URL
history.go(n);      //go to URL #n in list
```

The Document Object

The most useful method of the document object is, of course, *document.write(text)*, as we have already seen. The common use for this is to print out the last modified date at the bottom of a Web page, so that it is always correct:

```
document.write("This page last modified: ");
document.writeln(document.lastModified);
```

While the lastModified property would seem to be an ideal one to use throughout your Web pages, it is plagued with inconsistencies of implementation. For example, in Navigator 2.0 versions, it does not show up at all, unless in a separate *writeln* statement from any text as we show above. You can combine strings with this property in both Navigator 3.0 and Explorer 3.0, however.

To further compound the difficulty, the file system on the Web server also interacts with the *lastModified* method. It works correctly on UNIX systems and on Windows NT servers, but may produce bizarre dates on Macintosh servers.

The complete list of document properties is shown in Table 24-2.

Property	Description
alinkColor	The color of an active link; the color it changes to when selected.
linkColor	The color of an unvisited link.
vlinkColor	The color of an already-visited link.
bgColor	The color of the page's background.
fgColor	The foreground text color.
title	The title in the title bar. You can only set this once. Once it is displayed, it cannot be changed.
location	The current URL.
lastModified	The date the file was last modified.

Table 24-2: Properties of the document object.

Using Forms in JavaScript

You can access each of the elements in a <Form> section of a Web page in JavaScript if you give them names. If you give the form a name, you can access the state of the controls and use them to perform simple calculations. You also can respond to mouse and click events associated with each control and use them to change the form or check the validity of the data the user entered.

The only significant method for the form object is the *submit()* method, which causes it to be sent to the server.

The Button Control

The button control generates a *click* event that you can respond to by declaring an *onClick* event handler as part of the button declaration on the form:

```
<input type="button" name="Compute"
    onClick="CalcTemp(this.form)">
```

The name of the function must be in quotes, and since you will probably need to pass the name of a form to the function, we illustrate doing so in the preceding code. The expression *this.form* refers to this form in the current document *(this)*.

When the button is clicked, it calls the function *CalcTemp()*. You must declare this function in the <head> portion of the Web page so that it is sure to be loaded when the button click calls it.

A Simple Temperature Conversion Program

Let's revisit the simple temperature conversion program we introduced in Chapter 8 and see how we could write it in JavaScript. We will create a Form consisting of an input text field, an output text field, two radio buttons, and a Compute button:

```
<form name="tempcalc">
Enter temperature:<br>
<input type="text" name="Entryval" size=10><br>
Result:<br>
<input type="text" name="Results" size=10><br>
<input type="radio" name="Tempchoice">to Fahrenheit<br>
<input type="radio" name="Tempchoice">to Celsius<br>
<input type="button" value="Compute"
  onClick="convert(this.form)">
</form>
```

The radio buttons must have the same *name* properties if you wish them to work together. You can determine which of them has been checked because they constitute an array of two elements. The first button declared is referred to as *Tempchoice[0]* and the second as *Tempchoice[1]*. In either case we refer to its *status* property, which will be either *true* or *false*. The *convert* function then is:

```
<html>
<head><title>Temperature Conversion</title></head>
<script>
function convert(form)
{
//This function is called when the
```

```
//Compute button is clicked
//----------------------------------------
//read in entered value
 temp = parseFloat(form.Entryval.value)
 if (form.Tempchoice[0].status)
 //check radio buttons
  newtemp = temp*9/5+32;              //to Fahrenheit
 else
  newtemp = (temp-32)/9*5;            //to Celsius
 form.Results.value = newtemp         //display result
  }
</script>
</head>
```

This program is in the example file temper.htm and is displayed in Figure 24-3.

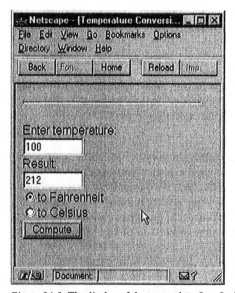

Figure 24-3: The display of the temper.htm JavaScript program.

In this simple program, we examine the status property of the check box and then set the text value of the output text box called Results. Since the convert function could be called from more than one form, we pass the form object to the function.

Properties of Form Controls in JavaScript

The major properties of the controls are listed in Table 24-3.

Control property		Meaning
Button	value	The text on the button.
checkbox	checked	*True* if checked.
password	value	Text of password-style text box.
text	value	Text of text box.
radio	checked	*True* if selected.
	length	Number of radio buttons in group.
select	length	Number of lines in list box.
	selectIndex	Index of selected line.
	selected	Indicates whether current line is selected.
	options()	Array of text lines in list box.
textarea	value	All the text in the multiline text box.

Table 24-3: Properties of controls in JavaScript.

In addition, each of the controls has a number of methods associated with it and equivalent events, as shown in Table 24-4. The methods are functions you can call to manipulate the controls. The events can be specified in the control definition, indicating what function is to be called.

Method		Event
focus()	onFocus	Set focus to this control.
blur()	onBlur	Move focus from this control.
select()	onSelect	Highlight text in text control.
	onChange	Called if user changes control.
click()	onClick	Clicks control but does not call onClick.
	onSubmit	Occurs when a Submit button is clicked. Return *true* to go on with submit, *false* to abort.

Table 24-4: Methods and events for all JavaScript controls.

Validating User Input in JavaScript

If you create a Web page with an HTML form in it, you might find it advantageous to check the validity of the data you enter before posting the form to the server. This is clearly faster than waiting for a server-side CGI script to return the same information. In the case of the dinner order form we wrote in Chapter 23, we ought to check that:

- The user entered his name.
- He selected a main course.
- He selected a type of wine.
- He selected a soup, a salad, or both.

We can accomplish this validation by either:

- Intercepting an *onSubmit* event and returning *true* or *false*.
- Changing the Submit button to an ordinary button, executing an onClick function and calling the *submit()* method for the form only if the data is valid.

We choose the second method here. The form is defined as:

```
<form method="post" action="/cgi32/java.exe?cgiserver"
name="dinner">
<!-- ----Group the order using a table---- -->
<TABLE>
<TR><TD WIDTH=295>
Name: <input type="text" width=25 name="Name"><br>
</TD>
<TD WIDTH=295>
<input type="radio" name="wine" value="redwine" onClick=0>Red
wine<br>
<input type="radio" name="wine" value="whitewine"
onClick=0>White wine<br>
</TD>
</TR>
<TR>
<TD WIDTH=295 align=center>
<select name="meats" size=5>
<option>Roast chicken
<option>Steak bearnaise
<option>Duck ala orange
<option>Dull pasta salad
</select>
</TD>
<TD WIDTH=295>
<input type="checkbox" name="soup">Soup<br>
<input type="checkbox" name="salad">Salad<br>
</TD>
</TR>
</TABLE>
<P>
<!-- Put submit centered outside table -->
<center>
<input type="button" value="Submit order" name="Submit_order"
onClick="checkForm(this.form)">
<input type="reset" name="Clear entries">
</center>
</form>
```

When the Submit Order button is clicked, the button calls the *checkForm()* method, which is shown below:

```
<script language="JAVASCRIPT">
function checkForm(form)
{
var ok_to_submit = true;          //flag to allow submit
var error="";                     //init error messages

if(form.Name.value == "")
  {
  error+="No name was entered\n";
  ok_to_submit=false;
  }
if(form.meats.selectedIndex<0)
  {
  error+="No main course selected\n";
  ok_to_submit=false;
  }
if(!(form.wine[1].checked || form.wine[0].checked))
  {
  error+="You didn't select any wine\n";
  ok_to_submit=false;
  }
if (!(form.soup.checked ||form.salad.checked))
  {
  error+="Pick a soup, salad or both";
  ok_to_submit=false;
  }
if (ok_to_submit)
  form.submit();          //submit the form
else
  alert(error);           //or display error msg

}
</script>
```

Moving On

As you can see, JavaScript can provide a quick and easy way to add logic to simple Web pages. Its primary use is for data validation before submitting a form to a CGI server, but you can also use the *document.lastModified* method to keep the message on the bottom of your Web page up-to-date. JavaScript has some other annoying uses, such as putting rotating banners in the status bar at the bottom of your Web page, but we'll leave programming them (using the *setTimeout()* method) to you: just grab any Web page with this annoying feature and look at the source. For a good introduction to the rest of the language consult Ritchey[5].

In the next chapter, we'll look at how we can establish more robust client-server communication directly in Java.

25

Using Sockets in Java

One of the most useful features of computers that utilize the TCP/IP network protocol is the *socket*. This allows any two computers to transmit a data stream back and forth using a numbered port or socket. You can send either text or binary data as long as the two computers agree on what to send and what to receive. In this chapter, we'll take up how we use sockets to set up client-server communication between Java programs on two computer systems.

TCP/IP Sockets

Sockets are part of TCP/IP communication and can have numbers between 0 and 65535. There is an extensive list of "well-known" socket numbers, such as those for sendmail, FTP, HTTP, pop3, and so forth. Some of the more common port numbers are listed in Table 25-1. You can usually assume that any socket number above 2000 is safe to use arbitrarily. If it is already in use, of course, you will get an *IO* exception when trying to open a new server on that socket.

Socket use	Port Number
telnet	23
smtp	25
ftp	20 and 21
gopher	70
finger	79
http	80
pop3	110
socks server	1080

Table 25-1: Well-known TCP/IP socket numbers.

The Socket Class

The *socket* class in Java is designed to open a client connection to a particular socket port on a particular machine:

```
public Socket(InetAddress  address, int  port);
public Socket(InetAddress  address, int  port,
                                boolean  stream);
public Socket(String  host, int  port);
public Socket(String  host, int  port, boolean stream);
// Methods
    public void close();
    public InetAddress getInetAddress();
    public InputStream getInputStream();
    public int getLocalPort();
    public OutputStream getOutputStream();
    public int getPort();
```

You create an instance of the class, specifying the machine and port number:

```
Socket mysock = new Socket(hostName, serverPort);
```

and then obtain the *InputStream* and *OutputStream* class instances from that instance of the socket:

```
datain =
  new DataInputStream(mysock.getInputStream());
dataout =
  new DataOutputStream(mysock.getOutputStream());
```

Both the socket creation and the opening of the data streams throw *IOExceptions* and must be enclosed in a *try* block. You can then read and write using those streams just as if they were files. A typical send and receive loop might simply be:

```
//create a socket on the local machine at port 6666
client cl = new client("", 6666);
while (true)
  {
  cl.sendCommandString(send);     //send the string
  String resp = cl.getResponse(); //get the response
  System.out.println(resp);       //and print it out
  }
```

where the *sendCommandString* method simply calls the DataOutputStream's *writeBytes* method:

```
public void sendCommandString(String comd)
  {
  try
    {
    dataout.writeBytes(comd+"\n");
    }
  catch (IOException e)
    {System.out.println("client error:"+e);}
  }
```

The ServerSocket Class

Our *server* class is one that spawns many instances of the *ServerSocket* class as each user attempts to connect to that port:

```
public ServerSocket(int  port);
public ServerSocket(int  port, int  buflength);
```

```
        // Methods
public Socket accept();
public void close();
public InetAddress getInetAddress();
public int getLocalPort();
```

The ServerSocket's *accept* method blocks without consuming processor time until someone opens a connection to that socket. Then, in our *server* class, we will spin off a separate thread to manage that socket connection. The code in this section is derived from that of O'Flanagan[3].

We start by initializing our *server* class as follows:

```
public class server extends Thread
{
  private ServerSocket servSock;
  Socket instSock; //a socket instance
//-----------------------------------------------
//main thread blocks on accept
//and then spins off threads
//for each socket connect
  public server(int myport)
  {
   try
    {
    servSock= new ServerSocket(myport);
    this.start();                    //run this thread
    }
   catch (IOException e)
     {System.out.println("Server error");}
  }
//-----------------------------------------
public void run()
  {
  try
    {
    while (true)         //keep making new ones as needed
      {
      instSock = servSock.accept();   //blocks here
  //create new connection
     Connection conn = new Connection(instSock);
      }
```

```
    }
  catch (IOException e)
    {System.out.println("Error while waiting");}
  }
//------------------------------------
public static void main(String args[])
{
 server csock = new server(6666); //any port you like
}
//-------------------------------------------
}
```

Then our *Connection* class simply carries out the input and output of a normal socket:

```
class Connection extends Thread
{
  DataInputStream datain;
  DataOutputStream dataout;
  StringTokenizer st;
  int token_count;
  String Response;
  Socket sock;
//-----------------------------------------
  public Connection(Socket sck)
  {
  sock = sck;
  opened_files = new Vector();
  try
    {
    datain = new DataInputStream(sock.getInputStream());
    dataout = new
      DataOutputStream(sock.getOutputStream());
    dataout.writeBytes("acknowledge\n");   //say hello
    }
    catch (IOException e)
     { System.out.println("Error creating streams");
       return;
     }
this.start();   //start this as a separate thread
  }
//-----------------------------------------
```

```java
public void run()
{
while (true)
  {
  String s = GetResponse();
  sendCommandString("acknowledge");
  }
}
//-------------------------------------------
public String GetResponse()
{
String s;
try
 {

   {
   try {
   this.sleep(200); //sleeps here until data available
   }
   catch(InterruptedException e){};
   s = datain.readLine();
   }
 }
 catch (IOException e)
   {System.out.println("response error");
    s = "";
   }
 return s;
}
//-------------------------------------------
public void sendCommandString(String comd)
//sends completely constructed command
 {
try
 {
 dataout.writeBytes(comd+"\n");
 }
catch (IOException e)
 {System.out.println("client error:"+e);}
 }
}
```

The complete programs server.java and client.java are provided on the Companion CD-ROM. To use them, start one instance of the server from a DOS prompt window:

```
java server
```

and then from additional DOS windows, start any number of clients, each with a different message string:

```
java client foo
```

```
java client HooHoo
```

and so forth. You will see all of the clients sending and receiving messages from the server in the various windows as shown in Figure 25-1.

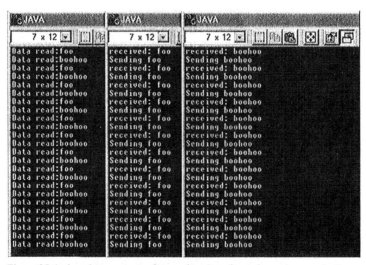

Figure 25-1: A socket server *and several* socket *client classes communicating on a single machine.*

Sockets in Applets

Note that in our example programs, we have just made the machine-name argument blank, meaning that the clients and the server are all on the same machine. Needless to say, this is not the way these features are usually used. In fact, you not only can use socket communication in applications, but in applets as well.

For security reasons, applets are restricted to communicating to the machine from which the Java code was downloaded. They cannot communicate with the local machine or with any other computer on the network. Note that this *does* mean that applets can communicate to the well-known ports of that machine and can thus emulate mail and FTP clients. However, this is not a security risk, since every other computer on the network can also communicate with these well-known ports:

```
cl = new client(getCodeBase().getHost(), 6666);
```

In our simple example program appclient.java below, we use the *client* class we have already created and connect to the socket on the host machine using the call:

```
cl = new client(getCodeBase().getHost(), 6666);
```

The complete program is shown below and is illustrated in Figure 25-2.

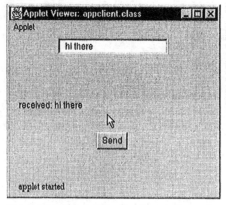

Figure 25-2: The appclient applet running and communicating with the socket server *class.*

```java
public class appclient extends Applet
{
//Simple visual applet for communicating with sockets
Label returnText;       //text is returned here
TextField sendText;     //text is sent here
Button send;            //sent when clicked
client cl;              //socket client class
//-------------------------------------------
 public void init()
 {
 setLayout(new GridLayout(3,1));
 Panel p0 = new Panel();
 Panel p2 = new Panel();
 add(p0);
 sendText = new TextField(20);
 p0.add(sendText);
 returnText = new Label("...returned text....");
 add(returnText);
 add(p2);
 send = new Button("Send");
 p2.add(send);
 //create a client instance on port 6666
//of the source machine
 cl = new client(getCodeBase().getHost(), 6666);
 //connection always returns "acknowledge"
 returnText.setText(cl.getResponse());  //acknowledge
 }
//-------------------------------------------
public boolean action(Event evt, Object arg)
 {
 if (evt.target == send)
  {
  sendClick();              //send button clicked
  return true;
  }
else
return super.action(evt, arg);
 }
//-------------------------------------------
```

```
private void sendClick()
 {
 //send the text from the text field
 cl.sendCommandString(sendText.getText());
 //display the response in the label field
returnText.setText(cl.getResponse());
 }
 }
```

Transferring Large Amounts of Data

In the examples so far, we've sent out text strings terminated with a newline character. Then the reading end of the socket connection just reads in the string using the *readLine()* method. However, if your data string is very long or if it must contain newline characters, the above methodology will surely fail. For example, some UNIX systems send data over sockets in small packets of 256 or 512 characters, and your *readLine()* method will probably be misled since the character string in the input buffer will not end with the newline character.

A more general method for handling this situation is to send a 4-byte integer indicating the number of characters that follow. Then you know that if you have only read 256 characters but 732 were sent, you must loop and wait for more to arrive. Handling binary numbers in Java can lead to errors, since the byte ordering between two different computers may be different. For example, Intel-based computers use "little-endian" numbers, in which the 4 bytes representing a 32-bit integer are laid out in memory as:

    0 1 2 3

while many UNIX processors and the Macintosh use "big-endian" representations, where the bytes are arranged in reverse order: Fortunately, this is handled automatically by the *DataInputStream* and *DataOutputStream* classes, and any byte swapping that is needed is taken care of for you invisibly.

This changes our output routine to:

```
private void SendCommandString(String comd)
{
int count = comd.length();
try
  {
  dataout.writeInt(count);
  dataout.writeBytes(comd);
  }
catch (IOException e)
  {System.out.println("write error");}
```

Our input routine is more complex as well, because we must loop until all the bytes are read:

```
public String GetResponse()
{
int count;
String s;
try
  {
    count =datain.readInt();        //get number to read
    byte b[] = new byte[count];
    int result = 0;
    while (result < count)  //count them
      {
      result  += datain.read(b, result, count - result);
      }
    s = new String(b, 0, 0, count);
  }
  catch (IOException e)
    {
    showStatus("response error");
    s = "";
    }
return s;
}
```

Parsing Long Data Streams

When large amounts of data are to be sent through socket connections, you will need to develop some simple way of separating the various arguments and their values. One simple way is to always send name-value pairs separated by a delimiter character (such as \) that will not appear in the text stream. For example, to continue with our dinner order program, we might read the data entry fields and then send a stream to the server:

```
\name\Sam Farkle\meat\roast chicken\wine\red\salad\yes\
```

where the name of the parameter is followed by its value. You can easily parse this using the *StringTokenizer* class to return each successive token.

If you feel that you'll need the backslash and can't come up with a delimiter character, you can further extend this by putting a length parameter between each argument, so that while the backslash remains the delimiter, it could also appear within the string:

```
\4\name\10\Sam Farkle\4\meat\13\roast chicken\
```

This method was developed by my colleague, Dr. John Prager of IBM Research, and is used in sending and receiving queries to various searching tools he has developed.

A Socket Dinner-ordering Program

We'll now build the last version of our dinner-ordering program, which uses a Java client connected to a Java server, communicating through a socket. Our user interface will consist of the same text field, check boxes, radio buttons, and list box of the HTML forms of the previous chapters, but this version will also have a text area control where the results or data validation error messages will appear.

The dinner menu is displayed in the applet dinnerClient.java on the Companion CD-ROM. It is illustrated in Figure 25-3 and its creation is shown below:

```java
public class dinnerClient extends Applet
{
List meat;                //list of entrees
Label yourname, order;    //Title and entry labels
TextField name;           //your name
Checkbox soup, salad;     //order soup and/or salad
CheckboxGroup wines;      //wines group
Checkbox redwine, whitewine;   //wines as radio buttons
Button placeOrder, clear;      //order and reset
TextArea Results;              //results returned here
private GridBagLayout gbl;
private GridBagConstraints gbc;
private Socket mysock;         //socket
DataInputStream datain;        //data in and out
DataOutputStream dataout;      //through socket

 public void init()
 {
  setFont(new Font("Helvetica",Font.PLAIN, 12));
  setBackground(Color.lightGray);
  gbl = new GridBagLayout();
  gbc = new GridBagConstraints();
  setLayout(gbl);
  gbc.ipadx = 5; gbc.ipady = 3;  //make buttons higher
  gbc.insets.left =4;  gbc.insets.right =4;
  gbc.insets.bottom =4;  gbc.insets.top =4;
  gbc.anchor= GridBagConstraints.WEST; //left aligned

  order = new Label("Order Your Dinner Here");
  order.setFont(new Font("Helvetica",Font.PLAIN, 18));
  addComponent(order, 0,0,2,1);
```

```
yourname=new Label("Your name"); //name text box
addOne(yourname, 0,1);
name = new TextField(24);
addOne(name, 1,1);

meat = new List(5, false);     //meat list box
addComponent(meat, 0,2,1,5);
meat.addItem("Roast chicken");
meat.addItem("Steak bearnaise");
meat.addItem("Coq au vin");
meat.addItem("Reddened blackfish");
meat.addItem("Somnolent pasta salad");

wines=new CheckboxGroup();     //wine radio buttons
redwine=new Checkbox("Red wine", wines, false);
whitewine=new Checkbox("White wine", wines, false);
addOne(redwine,1,2);
addOne(whitewine,1,3);

soup = new Checkbox("Soup");  //soup and salad checks
salad = new Checkbox("Salad");
addOne(soup,1,5);
addOne(salad, 1, 6);

Panel p0 = new Panel();     //submit and clear buttons
addComponent(p0, 0,7,2,1);
placeOrder=new Button("Place order");
clear = new Button("Clear");
p0.add(placeOrder);
p0.add(clear);

Results = new TextArea(4, 40); //answer text area
addComponent(Results, 0, 8, 2, 4);
Results.hide();
}
```

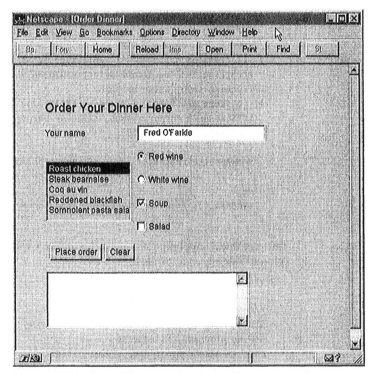

Figure 25-3: The dinnerClient applet for ordering dinner using socket connections to the server.

The critical routine in this program checks the validity of the data and either opens a socket to the server or displays an error message in the text area control:

```
private void clickedOrder()
  {
  //check validity of order and send it to the server
  String errString = "";
  String username= name.getText();
  if (username.length()<= 0)    //check for name
    errString += "You didn't enter your name\n";
```

```
if (meat.getSelectedIndex() < 0)        //main course
  errString += "You did not select a main course\n";
//require red or white wine
if (! (redwine.getState() || whitewine.getState()))
  errString += "You didn't select a wine\n";
 //require soup, salad or both
if (! (soup.getState() || salad.getState()))
  errString += "order a soup, salad or both";
if (errString.length() >0)
  {
  showResult(errString);     //display error messages
  }
else
  sendMenu(); //or send to server if no errors
}
```

The *sendMenu()* method then opens the socket, constructs the command string, and sends it:

```
private void sendMenu()
  {
  //compile command string and send it off
  String comd = "";
  String winename, maincourse;
  comd += makeCommand("name", name.getText());
  if (redwine.getState())
    winename="red";
  else
    winename="white";
  comd += makeCommand("wine", winename);
  comd += makeCommand("meat", meat.getSelectedItem());
  if (salad.getState())
    comd += makeCommand("salad", "yes");
```

```
if (soup.getState())
  comd += makeCommand("soup", "yes");
sendCommand(comd, "", 6666);  //send to server
showResponse();          //display reply
try{
  datain.close();        //close connection
  dataout.close();
  mysock.close();
  }
catch(IOException e){};
}
```

in conjunction with the *sendCommand* method:

```
private void sendCommand(String s, String hostname, int port)
  {
  //open socket and send request
  try
   {
  mysock = new Socket(hostname, port);
  datain  = new
    DataInputStream(mysock.getInputStream());
  dataout = new
    DataOutputStream(mysock.getOutputStream());
  int count = s.length();
  dataout.writeInt(count);
  dataout.writeBytes(s);
  }
  catch (IOException e)
     {System.out.println("socket creation error");}
  }
```

The result of ordering our meal is shown in Figure 25-4, where a text area is made visible and the response from the server is displayed.

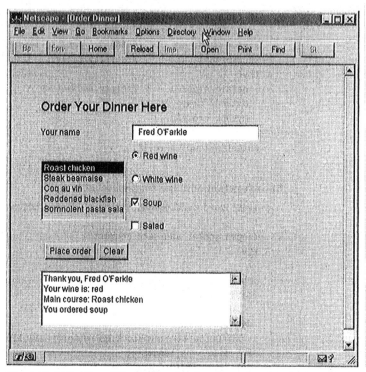

Figure 25-4: The dinnerClient applet, showing the results of placing an order.

Note that this is a one-shot communication system. We open the socket, send the request, get a response, and then close the port. We could, of course, keep the port open and continue to send commands as needed. In the case where the server can execute several possible commands, the first element of the command string becomes the command and that command routine then parses the rest of the string as it requires.

The Server for Ordering Dinner

The crux of the dinnerServer.java application is that once it receives a command, it parses it and sends an acknowledgment back:

```java
public void run()
    {
    int count = 0;
      String s = getResponse();
      System.out.println("Data read:"+s);
      String menu =calcMenu(s);
      System.out.println("sending:"+menu);
      sendCommand(menu);
      try
      {
      datain.close();
      dataout.close();
      sock.close();
      }
      catch(IOException e)
        {System.out.println("close error");}
    }
//------------------------------------------
private String calcMenu(String s)
{
StringTokenizer tok = new StringTokenizer(s, "\\");
String response = "";
while (tok.hasMoreTokens())
  {
  String type = tok.nextToken();
  String value = tok.nextToken();
  if (type.equals("name"))
    {
    response += "Thank you, "+value +"\n";
    }
  if (type.equals("wine"))
    {
    response += "Your wine is: "+ value + "\n";
    }
```

```
        if (type.equals("meat"))
          {
          response += "Main course: "+value+ "\n";
          }
        if (type.equals("soup"))
          {
          response += "You ordered soup\n";
          }
        if (type.equals("salad"))
          {
          response += "You also ordered salad\n";
          }
      }
    return response;
    }
    //-------------------------------------------
      private void sendCommand(String s)
      {
      try
        {
      int count = s.length();
      dataout.writeInt(count);
      dataout.writeBytes("\\"+s+"\\");
        }
      catch (IOException e)
         {System.out.println("socket creation error");}

      }
```

We have not indicated where the dinner orders are stored or sent, but we presume that they are sent by e-mail to the chef.

Executing a Native Program on the Server

Java provides you with an extremely simple way to launch local programs from your server program. In fact, wrapping existing C programs in the Java client-server methodology provides you with a powerful way of making a simple applet-based user interface to a C program that may have only an unfriendly line command interface.

All you have to do in the Java server application is to obtain a copy of the run-time environment and use its *exec* method to launch the program:

```
Process p = null;
Runtime rt = Runtime.getRuntime();
try
  {
  p = rt.exec("prog1 -c foobar");
  }
catch (IOException e){};
```

If the program you launch sends output to the console (standard out), you can read it in from that process's input stream:

```
InputStream dataresp = p.getInputStream();
int avail =0;        //bytes available
try
   {
  avail = dataresp.available();
   }
catch (IOException e){};

byte b[] e new byte[avail];
int count = dataresp.read(b);
String s1 = new String (b, 0, 0, count);
```

This leaves you with a String containing the output of the C program you launched.

Another Solution: the Fat Client

For some kinds of operations, downloading a compact table of data and manipulating that data locally makes a great deal more sense than sending continual CGI requests to a Web server when you merely want to browse or inspect data. Since the data are downloaded completely, to the client machine, this is known as a "fat" client. When all of the data are on a server and fetched in small chunks, we refer to that as a "thin" client.

An example of this is a program I wrote for the Connecticut Swimming organization for their Web site, to allow meet directors to look up who the certified swimming officials were by team or by level of certification. The original data structure for each official is contained in a Visual Basic program used by the official's chairman to maintain these lists and produce mailing labels. It is illustrated below:

```
Type kidrec
  frname As String * 10     'child's first name
  bday As Single            'birthday
  team As String * 5 'team initials
End Type

Type ofrec
  frname As String * 25     'first name
  lname As String * 25      'last name
  address As String * 25    'street address
  city As String * 20
  state As String * 2
  zip As String * 5
  phone As String * 15
  cert As String * 10       'level of certification
  exdate As Single          'expiration date
  clinic As String * 12     'official clinic attended
  clinicdate As Single      'date of clinic
  comment As String * 50    'any useful comment
  active As String * 1      'whether active
  cardexpire As Single

  kid(1 To 3) As kidrec     'array of 3 kids per official
End Type
```

A 259-byte structure like this is stored for each official, with the children's names filled into the kidrec structures within. The levels of certification are Referee, Administrator, Starter, and Stroke, and meet managers typically want to know:

◈ What officials are available who have children on the teams that will be attending my meet?

◈ Who are the officials certified at a given level that I could call for assistance?

To solve this problem, we took the raw data file, which for Connecticut is only about 80K, and put it on the Web server for their home page. Then we wrote a Java program to download the entire file into memory and make queries against it. The user interface for this program is shown in Figure 25-5, and the program is offsearch.java on your Companion CD-ROM.

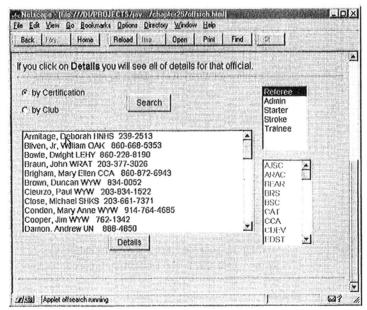

Figure 25-5: The user interface for querying the swimming officials database for Connecticut.

The key to analyzing this data file quickly is to download the data file in 259-byte chunks and store each in an instance of the OfObject without decoding it further. Then, we return information from this binary byte array using a series of simple accessory functions that fetch and convert data as needed:

```
class OfObject
{
  byte[] ofbytes;
```

```java
    public OfObject(byte b[])
    {
    ofbytes= b;                    //store data in objects
    }
//-------------------------------------------
public String getFrname()
{
 return new String(ofbytes, 0, 0, 25).trim();
}
//-------------------------------------------
public String getLname()
{
 return new String(ofbytes, 0, 25, 25).trim();
}
//-------------------------------------------
public String getCert()
{
 String thiscert =
  new String(ofbytes,0, 117, 10).trim();
 return thiscert;
}
//-------------------------------------------
public boolean isCert(String cert)
{
String thiscert = getCert().toUpperCase();
return (thiscert.startsWith(cert.toUpperCase()));
}
//-------------------------------------------
public boolean isActive()
{
String active = new String(ofbytes, 0 ,197,1);
return (! active.equals("N"));
}
//-------------------------------------------
public String getAddress()
{
return new String(ofbytes, 0 ,50,25);
}
//-------------------------------------------
public String getTown()
{
```

```java
return new String(ofbytes, 0 ,75,20);
}
//----------------------------------------
public String getKid(int i)
{
return new String(ofbytes, 0 ,202+(i)*19,10);
}
//----------------------------------------
public String getKidClub(int i)
{
return new String(ofbytes, 0 ,202+(i)*19+14,5);
}
//----------------------------------------
public boolean hasClub(String club)
{
boolean found =false;
for (int i =0; i<3; i++)
  {
  if (club.equals(getKidClub(i)))
    found = true;
  }
return found;
}
//----------------------------------------
public String getPhone()
{
return new String(ofbytes, 0, 102, 15).trim();
}
}
```

The routine for downloading and initializing the data is:

```java
URL ofurl;
InputStream f = null;
Vector boffarray;
ClubList clubs;
final int  OFFSIZE=259;
OfObject ofob;

//Now read in the data
ofurl = new URL(docbase, "ctoff1.rec");
```

```
f = ofurl.openStream();
boffarray = new Vector(300);
BufferedInputStream bi = new BufferedInputStream(f);

try
 {
 do
  {
  byte b[] = new byte[OFFSIZE];
  int sz = tot= off = 0;
  do
   {                      //read from web site
   sz = bi.read(b, off, OFFSIZE-tot);
   tot = tot + sz;
   off += sz;
   }
  while (tot < OFFSIZE);
  ofob = new OfObject(b);
  boffarray.addElement(ofob);        //add object to vector
  }
 while (bi.available() >0);
 }
catch (IOException e)
 {showStatus("error reading in officials file ");}
```

You can see this program at work at the site:

```
http://www.1ornet.com/~ctsi/officials.htm
```

The files for this program are on your Companion CD-ROM as offsearch.java and ViewDetails.java, along with a slightly modi-fied version of the binary data file, ctoff1.rec.

Moving On

In this chapter, we've taken the last step in client-server communi-cations using Java—we've built both the client and the server using Java and connected them using sockets. We will take up our final major topic in the following chapter—how you can carry out math operations in Java.

26

Math Classes & Matrices

In this chapter we'll take up the *Math* class. No, not the one you had in high school, but the class that contains most of the math functions you must have been wondering about all through this book. Then we'll use some of these methods to build a useful math object: the *matrix* class, to illustrate yet another way that the object-oriented approach can be useful.

The Math Class

All of the standard mathematical functions you'd expect in a computer language have been encapsulated in the *Math* class. This class contains final static methods that you can call directly using the format:

```
x = Math.abs(x);    //take the absolute value of x
```

The class also contains the constants *pi* and *e*.

The complete set of these math methods is shown below:

```
// Fields
    public final static double E;
    public final static double PI;
```

```
// Methods
    public static double abs(double  a);
    public static float abs(float  a);
    public static int abs(int  a);
    public static long abs(long  a);
    public static double acos(double  a);
    public static double asin(double  a);
    public static double atan(double  a);
    public static double atan2(double  a, double  b);
    public static double ceil(double  a);
    public static double cos(double  a);
    public static double exp(double  a);
    public static double floor(double  a);
    public static double log(double  a);
    public static double max(double  a, double  b);
    public static float max(float  a, float  b);
    public static int max(int  a, int  b);
    public static long max(long  a, long  b);
    public static double min(double  a, double  b);
    public static float min(float  a, float  b);
    public static int min(int  a, int  b);
    public static long min(long  a, long  b);
    public static double pow(double  a, double  b);
    public static double random();
    public static double rint(double  a);
    public static long round(double  a);
    public static int round(float  a);
    public static double sin(double  a);
    public static double sqrt(double  a);
    public static double tan(double  a);
```

These transcendental functions have the same meaning and application as in any other scientific programming language, such as FORTRAN or Pascal, and thus round out the capabilities of Java as a fully capable language. Now we'll use a couple of these functions in building some classes to handle matrices in the sections that follow.

Using Matrices

A *matrix* is a two-dimensional array of numbers that is widely used in various fields of science and mathematics. Many matrices are square (2 X 2, 3 X 3, etc.), but they need not be. You can add, subtract, and multiply matrices, as well as invert and diagonalize them. Thus, a matrix is an ideal example of the kind of abstraction we encounter in object-oriented programming: where the object itself is the best judge of how to carry out an operation on itself.

Let's consider a general 3 X 3 matrix:

$$\begin{bmatrix} a_{11} & a_{12} & a_{13} \\ a_{21} & a_{22} & a_{23} \\ a_{31} & a_{32} & a_{33} \end{bmatrix}$$

This matrix is a square array of numbers having subscripts from 1 to 3 in both directions. In matrix algebra, we often represent a matrix by a single capital letter: A. If we have two such matrices:

$$A = \begin{bmatrix} a_{11} & a_{12} \\ a_{21} & a_{22} \end{bmatrix} \quad B = \begin{bmatrix} b_{11} & b_{12} \\ b_{21} & b_{22} \end{bmatrix}$$

we can write matrix addition as:

$$C = A + B$$

The C matrix then contains the cell-by-cell sum of the two arrays:

$$C = \begin{bmatrix} a_{11} + b_{11} & a_{12} + b_{12} \\ a_{21} + b_{21} & a_{22} + b_{22} \end{bmatrix}$$

Subtraction is carried out in an analogous fashion.

Matrix multiplication can occur only when the number of columns in the first matrix is equal to the number of rows in the second. Then the product $A \times B$ can be obtained by multiplying each element in each of the rows of the first matrix by each element in the corresponding column of the second matrix and summing these products for a given row and column.

If A consists of m rows and B consists of n columns, then we construct the matrix C by multiplying each row of A into each column of B. The element C_{ij} is the product of the ith row of A and the jth column of B:

$$c_{ij} = \sum_{k=1}^{p} a_{ik} b_{kj}$$

Thus, the order of multiplication is important: the operation is not commutative.

Building a Matrix Class

A *matrix* class should be a class that can hold an instance of the rectangular array and perform simple operations with other instances of the class. For example, we should be able to write:

```
Matrix c = A.add(b);
```

to add matrix B to matrix A. So we ought to be able to write *add*, *subtract*, and *multiply* methods at the very least. Further, we should be able to create an empty *matrix* class or use an existing rectangular array to create an instance of the *matrix* class. We therefore need the following two constructors:

```
public Matrix (int xsize, int ysize)
  {
  xdim = xsize;                    //save size
  ydim = ysize;
  x = new float[xdim][ydim];       //create matrix
  xindex = yindex = 0;
  }
//------------------------------------------
public Matrix(float mat[][])
  {
  x = mat;                         //reference to array
  xdim = mat.length;               //compute sizes
  ydim = mat[0].length;            //and store them
  }
```

Matrix Addition

A matrix *addition* method is very simple. It adds the current matrix to one passed as an argument and returns a new matrix of the sums:

```
public Matrix add(Matrix y)
  {
  //create new matrix
  float z[][] = new float[xdim][ydim];
  for (int i=0; i< xdim; i++)
    {
    for (int j=0; j<ydim; j++)
      z[i][j]= x[i][j] + y.getVal(i, j);
    }
  return new Matrix(z);    //return matrix
  }
```

Accessor Functions

Of course, we need a way to get and put data in the *matrix* class. We'll have the usual *get* and *put* methods by index:

```
public float getVal(int i, int j)
  {
  xindex=i;
  yindex=j;
  return x[i][j];
  }
//--------------------------------------
public void putVal(float a, int i, int j)
  {
  xindex=i;
  yindex=j;
  x[i][j] = a;
  }
```

And we'll have a way to move data to the matrix and increment to the next position automatically:

```
public boolean putNext(float a)
{
//stores next value in matrix
boolean ret = false;
xindex++;
if (xindex >= xdim)
   {
   xindex =0;
   yindex++;
   }
if (yindex < ydim)
   {
   x[xindex][yindex] = a;
   ret = true;         //success flag
   }
return ret;            //true if stored OK
}
```

Of course, we also need to be able to ask for the size of the matrix:

```
public int getXsize()
{
return xdim;
}
//----------------------------------------
public int getYsize()
{
return ydim;
}
```

Matrix Multiplication

Matrix multiplication is slightly more involved arithmetically, but it works pretty much the same way as addition does. Since matrix multiplication is valid only if the number of rows of the first matrix equals the number of columns in the second matrix, the multiply routine tests for this before carrying out the computation. It returns a new matrix if multiplication is successful and a *null* if not:

```
public Matrix multiply(Matrix y)
{
int col1, col2, col3;
int row1, row2, row3;
float mSum;
row1 = ydim;
col1 = xdim;
row2 = y.getYsize();
col2 = y.getXsize();
//x matrix must have number of columns
//equal to the number of rows in y matrix
if (col1 == row2)
  {
  //the number  of columns in the product matrix z
  //must be equal to the number of rows in x
  //and the number rows = number of cols in y
  col3 = row1;
  row3 = col2;
  Matrix z = new Matrix(col3, row3);
  for (int i = 0; i < row2; i++)
    {
    for (int j = 0; j < col2; j++)
      {
      mSum = 0;
      for (int k =0; k <col1; k++)
        mSum += x[i][k] * y.getVal(k, j);
      z.putVal(mSum, i, j);
      }//next j
    }  //next i
  return z;
  }
else
  return null;
}
```

Inverting Matrices

While dividing matrices is not a meaningful operation, matrix inversion is very useful. If we define the unit matrix I as a matrix having ones in the diagonal and zeros everywhere else:

$$I = \begin{bmatrix} 1 & 0 & 0 & 0 \\ 0 & 1 & 0 & 0 \\ 0 & 0 & 1 & 0 \\ 0 & 0 & 0 & 1 \end{bmatrix}$$

then we can define the *inverse* of a matrix A^{-1} as that matrix that, when multiplied by the original matrix A, produces the unity matrix I:

$$A \times A^{-1} = I$$

We can use matrix inversion as a convenient way to solve simultaneous equations. Suppose we have a series of simultaneous equations such as:

$$a_1 x_1 + b_1 x_2 + c_1 x_3 = k_1$$
$$a_2 x_1 + b_2 x_2 + c_2 x_3 = k_2$$
$$a_3 x_1 + b_3 x_2 + c_3 x_3 = k_3$$

We can write this in matrix form as:

$$\begin{bmatrix} a_1 & b_1 & c_1 \\ a_2 & b_2 & c_2 \\ a_3 & b_3 & c_3 \end{bmatrix} \begin{bmatrix} x_1 \\ x_2 \\ x_3 \end{bmatrix} = \begin{bmatrix} k_1 \\ k_2 \\ k_3 \end{bmatrix}$$

or just as:

$$MX = K$$

where M is the matrix of coefficients, X is the column matrix of variables, and K is the column matrix of constants. Rearranging this simple equation, we have:

$$M^{-1}K = X$$

so if we can determine the *inverse* of the M matrix, we can solve for the x's.

Solving a Set of Simultaneous Equations

Let's consider the three equations:

$$5x_1 + 3x_2 - 4x_3 = -10$$
$$3x_1 + 7x_2 + x_3 = 23$$
$$3x_1 - 3x_2 + 2x_3 = 20$$

We can rewrite these as a matrix algebra statement:

$$\begin{bmatrix} 5 & 3 & -4 \\ 3 & 7 & 1 \\ 3 & -3 & 2 \end{bmatrix} \begin{bmatrix} x_1 \\ x_2 \\ x_3 \end{bmatrix} = \begin{bmatrix} -10 \\ 23 \\ 20 \end{bmatrix}$$

Thus, if we can invert this matrix, and multiply it by the constant column matrix, we can solve for the values of x.

The matrix *invert* method follows one given by Johnson [s] and by Cooper [1] and is given on the Companion CD-ROM in the program matrix.java. It returns the inverted matrix in place rather than in a new matrix. It operates in place on the matrix itself, so the matrix itself contains the inverted answer, replacing the initial matrix data.

If we put these matrix data into this routine, invert it, and multiply by the column vector –10, 23, 20, we find that:

$$x_1 = 3$$
$$x_2 = 1$$
$$x_3 = 7$$

as expected.

The Much Maligned Date Class

While the *Date* class is not strictly a *Math* class, since it is part of the java.util package, we need to discuss it here in terms of how you use it computationally in programs. The *Date* class is an internal representation of year, month, day, hour, minute, and second. However, it only represents dates since January 1, 1970. Some also have objected to the fact that the months are numbered from 0 through 11, rather than from 1 to 12. The *Date* constructors are as follows:

```
public Date();
public Date(int  year, int  month, int  date);
public Date(int  year, int  month, int  date,
                      int  hrs, int  min);
public Date(int  year, int  month, int  date,
                      int  hrs, int  min, int  sec);
public Date(long  date);
public Date(String  s);
```

Then you can manipulate Date objects using these methods:

```
public boolean after(Date  when);
public boolean before(Date  when);
public boolean equals(Object  obj);
public int getDate();
public int getDay();
public int getHours();
public int getMinutes();
<Computer public int getMonth();
public int getSeconds();
public long getTime();
public int getTimezoneOffset();
public int getYear();
public int hashCode();
public static long parse(String  s);
public void setDate(int  date);
public void setHours(int  hours);
public void setMinutes(int  minutes);
public void setMonth(int  month);
```

```
public void setSeconds(int  seconds);
public void setTime(long  time);
public void setYear(int  year);
public String toGMTString();
public String toLocaleString();
public String toString();
public static long UTC(int  year, int  month,
    int  date, int  hrs, int  min, int  sec);
```

You can use the *Date* class for timing Java programs by creating an instance of the *Date* class at the start of a loop and another instance at the end of a loop, and then using the *getSeconds()* method to subtract the two of them and determine the elapsed time:

```
Date start = new Date();   //get current time
longloop();                //call long computation
Date stop = new Date();
System.out.println(stop.getSeconds -start.getSeconds
        + " seconds elapsed");
```

Wrapping Up

In this chapter, we've studied the *Math* class and looked at how to construct a *Matrix* class and use it to add, multiply, and invert matrices. We've also touched on the *Date* class. Now that you've seen the scope of mathematical operations that you can carry out in Java, you are really a completely educated Java programmer.

Throughout this book, we have seen that Java is a powerful object-oriented language and that the mental gearshift you need to begin writing in a fully object-oriented style is a very small shift indeed. We've seen that despite the apparent sparseness of methods in the Java window toolkit, we can write some powerful visual applets and applications and give them a fairly professional look.

We've also seen that Java allows you to write multithreaded applets and applications so easily that it can become second nature to spin off threads whenever an activity may be time consuming.

And finally, we've seen that Java is network ready. With the URL classes and socket connections, you can write sophisticated client-server applications in a high-level language without any of the complexity that other language models impose on you.

At this point, you are ready to strike out on your own and develop substantial Java applications and applets. Good luck, and keep your Java classes pouring.

APPENDIX A

About the Companion CD-ROM

Navigating the CD-ROM

This CD-ROM contains valuable software and example files that correspond to exercises described in the book.

Using the Example Files

All of the programs discussed in each chapter of the text are included in both source and compiled form in the chapternn subdirectory of the CD-ROM, where "nn" is the chapter number. For example, in the \chapter4 directory, you will find the source file Rect1.java, as well as its compiled form, Rect1.class.

You can examine the source file with any text editor, such as EDIT, Notepad, or WordPad. You can compile these programs after having installed the Java SDK by typing

```
javac Rect1.java
```

and you can execute the compiled program by typing

```
java Rect1
```

If you have installed a copy of Symantec's Café or Visual Café, you can use its much faster compiler, named sj instead of javac.

Some chapters include applets as well as applications. You compile these in the same way, but must execute applets using either the appletviewer program or by reading them into your Web browser. For example, in the \chapter6 directory, you can run the program Rect2.class by typing

```
appletviewer Rect2.html
```

which will read in and load the Rect.class file.

Installing the Shareware

Each of the shareware programs resides in its own directory. To install a program, first copy its files to the hard drive, then activate the setup or install file for that program by double-clicking it. Please remember that shareware programs must be registered and paid for if used beyond the trial period, as stated in each program's readme or installation instructions.

Software Descriptions Program	Description
Java Developer's Kit 1.0.2	The JDK helps you to develop applets that conform to the final applet API; create applets that run in all Java-enabled browsers; develop Java applications and experiment with the debugger API (and a prototype command-line debugger). This version of the JDK is for Windows 95. To see Sun Microsystem's JDK documentation go to http://java.sun.com/products/JDK/1.0.2/ftp_docs.html on the World Wide Web and double-click on the following hyperlink: ftp://ftp.javasoft.com/docs/JDK-1_0_2-apidocs.zip.

Software Descriptions Program	Description
WinZip 6.1	For Windows 95 or NT. Features the WinZip Wizard for easy unzipping. Includes tight integration with the Windows 95 shell: drag and drop TO or FROM the Explorer or ZIP and UNZIP without leaving the Explorer. This is an evaluation version of WinZip 6.1, and purchase of this book and the Companion CD-ROM does not constitute fulfillment of the user's obligation to the program's author. *1996*Win100 Award Winner, *Windows Magazine* *1995*Finalist, *PC Computing* MVB Awards *1994*Best Utility, Shareware Industry Awards "The best all-purpose compression utility Windows 95 and NT," *Windows Sources*, 3/96
Alibaba WWW Server	This 30-day demo version for Windows 95 is a multithreaded high performance WWW server; implemented as NT system service; with HTTP 1.0 protocol and SSL security. Alibaba also features CGI (DOS-CGI, WINCGI 1.3, 32-bit CGI, DLL interface, and ISAPI); GET, POST, and HEAD commands; definable mimetypes and Aliases. For more information about Alibaba, or to order the full version, go to http://www.csm-usa.com.

Table A-1: Programs on the Companion CD-ROM.

Technical Support

Technical support is available for installation-related problems only. The technical support office is open from 8:00 A.M. to 6:00 P.M. Monday through Friday and can be reached via the following methods:

Phone: (919) 544-9404 extension 81

Faxback Answer System: (919) 544-9404 extension 85

E-mail: help@vmedia.com

FAX: (919) 544-9472

World Wide Web: http://www.vmedia.com/support

America Online: keyword **Ventana**

Limits of Liability & Disclaimer of Warranty

The author and publisher of this book have used their best efforts in preparing the CD-ROM and the programs contained in it. These efforts include the development, research, and testing of the theories and programs to determine their effectiveness. The authors and publisher make no warranty of any kind expressed or implied, with regard to these programs or the documentation contained in this book.

The authors and publisher shall not be liable in the event of incidental or consequential damages in connection with, or arising out of, the furnishing, performance, or use of the programs, associated instructions, and/or claims of productivity gains.

Some of the software on this CD-ROM is shareware; there may be additional charges (owed to the software authors/makers) incurred for their registration and continued use. See individual program's README or VREADME.TXT files for more information.

APPENDIX B

References

1. Cooper, James, *Object Oriented Programming in Visual Basic*, Pinnacle Publishing, Kent, WA, 1996.

2. Cowlishaw, Michael, *The NetRexx Language*, Prentice-Hall, Englewood Cliffs, NJ 1996.

3. Flanagan, David, *Java in a Nutshell*, O'Reilly & Associates, Inc., Sebastopol, CA, 1996.

4. Gosling, J., Yellin, F. et. al., *The Java Application Programming Interface*, Vols. 1-2, Addison-Wesley, Reading, MA, 1996.

5. Johnson, K. J., *Numerical Methods in Chemistry*, Marcel Dekker, New York, 1980.

6. Lam, Richard B., *Netscape Programmer's Guide*, SIGS Books, New York, 1997.

7. Niemeyer, P., and Peck, J., *Exploring Java*, O'Reilly & Associates, Inc., Sebastopol, CA, 1996.

8. Oliver, Dick, *Netscape 2 Unleashed*, Sams.net, Indianapolis, IN 1996.

9. Ritchey, Tim, *Programming JavaScript for Netscape 2.0*, New Riders, Indianapolis, IN 1996.

APPENDIX C

Printing in Java

The Java 1.0 specification does not make any provision for printing, in either applets or applications. You will find some solutions to this problem below. Java 1.1 does provide an interface for printing; we will outline that as well.

Printing in Java 1.0

There are several well-known "tricks" for printing from applications in Java 1.0:

- ❦ Send characters directly to the LPT1: port as a file.
- ❦ Create a PostScript file and write it to an LPT port attached to a PostScript printer.
- ❦ Create an HTML file, then tell Netscape Navigator to load it and print it.

Sending Characters to the Printer Port

This method simply sends text to the printer. It will work for PCL printers or dot matrix printers, but not for PostScript printers. The following string prints the text "fooie" on a printer attached to port LPT1 (of course this only works on Windows systems):

```
public class testtext
{
  public static void main (String argv[])
  {
  OutFile f = new OutFile("lpt1:");
  f.println("fooie");
  f.close();
  }
}
```

Sending PostScript Files to the Printer

If you have a PostScript printer, you can create or send a file directly to the port. The following PostScript file box.ps contains the instructions to draw a box on the page:

```
%!PS-Adobe-1.0
%%BoundingBox: 0 0 612 792
newpath
400 400 moveto
0 72 rlineto
72 0 rlineto
0 -72 rlineto
closepath
4 setlinewidth
stroke
showpage
```

and the following simple program will send it to a PostScript printer attached to LPT1:

```
public class testps
{
//reads lines from a file and sends then
//to a PostScript printer on lpt1
public static void main (String argv[])
  {
  OutFile f = new OutFile("lpt1:");
  InputFile fin = new InputFile("box.ps");
  String s = "";
  do
    {
    s = fin.readLine();    //read a line
    if (s != null)
      {
      f.println(s); //and print it
      }
    }
  while (s !=null);
  f.close();
  }
}
```

Sending Information to Netscape Navigator

You can also write a little DDE program in Visual Basic which can be launched from Java. The program openurl.exe on your example disk is a command line program which takes a filename as an argument and loads it into Navigator. This communication is done by DDE and was provided for use by Dr. Dick Lam of IBM Research.

Once you have loaded an HTML file into Navigator, you can use a simple VB *SendKeys* method to send Alt/F, P, Enter, to cause it to print the current page. You again can launch this from a Java program. The VB program is:

```
Private Sub Printit_Click()
On Local Error GoTo aperr
  AppActivate "Netscape -" 'turn on Navigator
```

```
    SendKeys "%FP{Enter}", True     'send Alt/F P Enter
appexit:
    Exit Sub
aperr:
    MsgBox (Str$(Err) + "Netscape not running")
    Resume appexit
End Sub
```

Printing in Java 1.1

Java 1.1 introduces a new class called *PrintJob* and a new interface to the *PrintJob* class called *PrintGraphics*. This interface returns a Graphics object bound to a printer rather than the display.

When you create an instance of the *PrintJob* class, the underlying system takes care of any needed dialogs asking which printer and any printer properties:

```
PrintJob pj = getPrinJob(Frame f, String jobtitle,
        Properties pr);
```

You can then obtain page information using:

```
Dimension sz = pj.getPageDimension();
int res = pj.getPageResolution();
```

You get the Graphics object from the *PrintJob* class using:

```
Graphics pgr = pj.getGraphics();
```

and once you have this object you can use any graphics method for printing to a page. Each call you make to *getGraphics()* returns the Graphics handle to a new page; each call you make to the *pgr.dispose()* method terminates that page.

Using NetRexx to Learn Java

The Rexx language, originally designed by Mike Cowlishaw of IBM Research, was originally intended as a simple, interpreted batch and interactive language for mainframe computer operating systems. Subsequently, it was made part of OS/2. Rexx is a fully general language, with logical and looping constructions, as well as input and output to the console and to files. In both mainframe systems and OS/2, it is frequently used to allow users to write fairly elaborate programs which take input data and eventually call system programs and resources to carry out complex functions.

NetRexx

NetRexx is a new Rexx-derived language with more object-oriented features that maintains the overall simplicity of use. It is an ideal language for Rexx mainframe programmers to use to migrate to Java, however, because NetRexx is actually compiled to Java. As an example, this is a simple "Hello World" program in NetRexx:

```
/* Print out Hello World*/
say 'Hello World'
```

The NetRexxC compiler, which itself is written in Java, compiles this program to the standard Java program:

```
public class HelloWorld
{
 static public void main(String argv[])
 {
 System.out.println("Hello World");
 }
}
```

and then invokes the javac compiler to produce the familiar class files.

NetRexx also provides a way for you to deal with graphics and with applets. The following is a simple Hello World applet:

```
/*Simple Hello World Applet*/
class HelloApplet extends Applet
  method init
    resize(200, 40)

method paint(g=Graphics)
  g.drawString("Hello World", 50, 30)
```

This is translated in a similar fashion.

In summary, if you are an experienced Rexx programmer, this can be a very simple way for you to move towards Java with minimal pain. You can obtain a copy of NetRexx from

```
http://www2.hursley.ibm.com/netrexx/netrexx.htm
```

Features of Java 1.1

Java 1.1 will introduce a host of powerful new classes and features: some will be in the initial release and some in later releases. Some of the changes are simply new classes, but some are fundamental improvements in the overall Java system.

The Java 1.1 Event Model

In the current 1.0 event model, all events are sent to nearly all control elements which can then process or ignore them. This leads to either having long, confusing *handleEvents()* if-else chains or making each control a new subclass.

While the 1.0 event model will be retained in Java 1.1 for compatibility, the 1.1 event model called the *delegation* model will be the preferred approach. Each event is propagated from a source object to a listener object. This means that useless events will no longer be sent to all controls. You register your interest in an event by using an *add*Event*Listener* method for each control, where "Event" is one of the usual events: mouse, keyboard, focus, etc.

Then you simply write that event listener routine, and that event will be sent to your listener when it occurs on that control.

Java Windowing Class

Java 1.1 will provide support for a number of new awt classes that you can use for improving the look and feel of your applications.

- **Desktop Colors** - Most operating systems allow you to define the default colors for application windows. This class allows you to access these colors so you can make your applications compatible.

- **Mouseless Operations** - This class allows you to define keystrokes that replace mouse clicks on buttons, check boxes, and menu items. It also allows you to define a tab order for controls.

- **Popup Menus** - This implements menus that pop up anywhere on the screen instead of just dropping down from the menu bar.

- **ScrollPanes** - As you might expect, this is an implementation of a scrollable area that you can draw on.

Java Data Transfer

Data transfer in the Java world consists of moving data to and from a clipboard and (eventually) using drag and drop. Drag and drop is not supposed to be part of the initial delivery of Java 1.1, but has been specified and will be delivered eventually. In both cases, the objective is to send arbitrary data formats between applications, even if they are not both Java applications. It includes the concept of "data flavors," which specify the format of the data that can be interchanged. These flavors will be specified as standard MIME types, like "application/text."

Remote Method Invocation

This RMI specification describes a uniform way to execute processes on remote machines as well as on your home machine. This amounts to registering a server which can serve remote methods and defining stubs on your local machine for these remote methods.

Included in RMI is Object Serialization, the ability to send objects from one machine to another without having to understand the data and object structure format and transmission methods.

Java Beans

Java Beans is a specification for writing software components. These components may be visual objects such as new types of controls which would be used in conjunction with a Builder tool (a GUI builder) to construct graphical user interfaces. They also might be applications which could themselves be embedded into other applications.

In the case of visual components, the builder queries the component for its properties, such as color, size, and other options, so they can be displayed and customized by the user. These components will have properties which can be set, events that you can listen for, and persistence so that you can store the customized state of the control.

In addition, Java Beans support *introspection*, a term clearly invented in California, which allows the enclosing program object to analyze how the component works.

Java Beans support design-time and run-time behavior, so that at design time you may need to load a lot of customization code, but at run time, only the final customized control information is loaded.

As the Beans model is implemented, many of the controls you originally saw as Visual Basic VBXs and OCXs will undoubted be implemented as Java Beans.

Index